CW00566429

Children's Literature and Social Change

*Some Case Studies from
Barbara Hofland to Philip Pullman*

Dennis Butts

The Lutterworth Press

The Lutterworth Press
P.O. Box 60
Cambridge
CB1 2NT

www.lutterworth.com
publishing@lutterworth.com

ISBN: 978 0 7188 9208 1

British Library Cataloguing in Publication Data
A catalogue record is available from the British Library

First published in 2010

Contents

Introduction

> It may be that mainstream literary historians assume that books written for children are independent of the forces that influence literary change.[1]

This book covers a period of over two hundred years of British history, a time which saw great changes in society, from the late-eighteenth century when the country was still largely an agricultural nation, through the upheavals of the Industrial Revolution, the great parliamentary reform acts, the coming of the railways and powered flight, devastating wars from Waterloo to the present day, and the emergence of a global economy.

During this period children's literature changed from the crudely-printed pocket-sized books illustrated with copper-plate engravings of John Harris, to the lavishly produced and seriously reviewed works of today, a period in which children's author Philip Pullman has won the Booker Prize, a highly regarded award for adult fiction, as well as seen his works published in an expensive Collector's Edition and become the subject of major film and theatrical productions.

Literature is the result of various cultural, economic and social forces of the age in which it was produced, and these forces have a connection with the texts of their time which is more than 'background' or 'context'. It is not simply that children's books carry references and allusions to their society – such as railways, the Indian Mutiny or urban life in the 1930s – rather, the very form and structure of these books, and their authors' responses, are affected by these social forces, and, directly or indirectly, influence society in return.

The American scholar Mitzi Myers puts it this way:

> extraliterary cultural formations shape literary discourse and ... literary practices are acts that make things happen – by shaping the psychic and moral consciousness of young readers but also by performing many more diverse

kinds of cultural work, from satisfying authorial fantasies and legitimating or subverting dominant class and
gender ideologies, from mediating social inequalities to
propagandizing new knowledge and discoveries to ad-
dressing live issues like slavery and the condition of the
working class.[2]

This book does not attempt to be a comprehensive, year-by-year
history of children's literature; rather it investigates the way children's books are affected by and respond to their society. It looks at
how, particularly in times of social change – such as the Industrial
Revolution in the early-nineteenth century, and the collapse of empire
and rise of the Welfare State in the twentieth century – cultural,
economic and social forces have influenced children's literature. It
explores a number of individual cases in detail, each selected for their
particularly interesting social significance.

The subjects chosen for study are not only interesting in themselves, but they illustrate some of the ways in which authors and their
books relate and interact with different aspects of social change. Some
of the early authors, such as Barbara Hofland and Charles Kingsley,
seem to reflect the dominant values of their age. Barbara Hofland's
simple tales of domestic life under times of stress reveal a good deal
about popular attitudes towards industrial change, Christianity and
utilitarianism in the early nineteenth century. Charles Kingsley's robust adventure stories reflect the rise of a more muscular Christianity,
and its connections with imperialism and racism in the middle of
the century. Other writers, however, reveal more complex responses
to society. G.A. Henty's historical tales from the 1870s onwards
appeared during the years of the British Empire's rapid expansion,
and his works seem to endorse its values explicitly. But the narrative
structure of his stories occasionally reveal fissures and gaps which
illustrate some of the tensions and contradictions in the very values
of the society he wished to support. The structure of Robert Louis
Stevenson's *Kidnapped* (1886) reveals something similar about the
state of the United Kingdom at this time, for his use of the narrative
polarities of David Balfour and Alan Breck Stewart seem to comment
on Anglo-Scotch relations towards the end of the century.

The works of Edith Nesbit and Amy Le Feuvre reveal changing
reactions towards upheavals in society. The stories of Le Feuvre – produced over a long literary career stretching from the 1890s to the 1920s
– went through a transformation, as she more or less accepted the
social changes which led her from an unquestioning evangelicalism in

her early years to an incipient feminism in her later. Nesbit's stories, on the other hand, developed from the earlier amusing and optimistic family tales to much darker work as she became more critical of social inequality in the late Edwardian age.

But literary responses to society can be revealed not only by analysing the works of individual authors, but also by considering the literature produced over a period of time and examining the values of a particular genre. A study of children's books of the 1840s, for example, shows the most astonishing revolution in taste, and reveals its connection with contemporary social and political reforms. An examination of the popular form of flying stories in the first half of the twentieth century, written by over thirty different writers, such as P.F.C. Westerman and Captain W.E. Johns, suggests the genre tended to reflect the prevailing ideologies of the age in a fairly uncritical and passive way. A review of children's literature produced in the 1930s, however, suggests that whilst many writers showed a desire for quietism and escapism, Geoffrey Trease and a small minority wanted to challenge that mood.

The last two chapters examine the relationship between children's literature and society in more recent years. The cheerful anarchy of British children's stories of the 1970s reflects the long tradition of such books in England, but may also be related to the so-called 'permissive society' of that period, while the bleaker fiction produced in the 1990s may have been affected by the consequences of political change in those years. The final chapter on Philip Pullman reinforces this point from a wider perspective. His historical tales of the 1980s and 1990s are compared with the Victorian works of G.A. Henty to explore the effects of social and political changes, particularly those connected with war and imperialism, over the period of one hundred years.

One broader recurring feature of children's literature that seems to be related to social change is also important: the apparent interchange which occurs between periods when children's books are predominantly serious and didactic, and periods in which the literature is more light-hearted and entertaining. The publisher and critic Frank Eyre defined this process as the 'cyclical pattern in British children's books throughout the centuries, consisting of a continual alteration between the most determinedly moral stories calculated to improve and uplift young readers, and books designed for enjoyment'.[3]

Eyre calculated that these trends, whether towards moral stories or books written for enjoyment, tended to last about fifty years, before another swing of the pendulum brought in the alternating fashion, although changes in taste may fluctuate more rapidly than he suggested in 1971. He also felt that with each swing of the pendulum, the movement towards didacticism became less pronounced, so that books produced in each successive didactic period became easier to read, and less obviously designed to have a purpose or moral.

These fluctuations in taste can be traced throughout the history of children's books in England, and seem related to political and social changes in general. For British society is democratic; it elects its own government, and a characteristic of this system in Britain is that it tends to choose alternating political parties as the mood of the country changes over periods of time. Thus it can be argued that Mrs Hofland's moral tales of the 1820s reflect the didactic climate of her age, but a massive swing of the pendulum brought in a new period of imaginative and exhilarating fantasy and fun in the 1840s. Kingsley and Henty showed a return to didactic values from the 1860s, until the more relaxed works of Stevenson and Nesbit began to appear. One has to be wary of becoming too schematic in interpreting Eyre's thesis, because the tales of Amy Le Feuvre and the genre of the flying story seem to suggest a return to more instructive forms, although in the 1930s one can see that freer, livelier books were also being written. The works produced in the 1990s, however, do seem to reveal aspects of a reversion to didacticism for reasons which are discussed in chapter eleven.

Another major factor in the relationship between what is happening in children's books and society relates to the conditions of readership and publishing. Few would question the importance of various educational initiatives, such as the beginning of the Sunday Schools Movement from the 1780s, which helped to introduce and spread the habit of reading. The Church of England and the Nonconformist Churches expanded elementary education still further from the beginning of the nineteenth century, and in 1834 the government made its first financial grant for the education of the poorer classes, so that the Newcastle Commission of 1861 could reveal that two and a half million children were attending school. Even so, that amounted to only one in seven of the population, and it needed Forster's Education Act of 1870 to provide free elementary education for all, and another Act in 1902 to regularise secondary education, by which time five million children were in schools. Only in 1944 was free secondary education ensured for all children. This was slow progress, to be sure, but it produced remarkable results regarding literacy and reading. It has been calculated that in 1714 only 45% of men and 25% of women were literate, but by 1841 the numbers had risen to 67% of men and 51% of women, and by 1900 97% of both men and women. Education was providing a public able and eager to read books, and a steadily growing market for publishers to meet that demand.[4]

John Newbery (1713-1767) was probably the first bookseller and publisher to realise what was happening in the eighteenth century. Although selling patent medicines and other goods, he published between twenty and thirty juvenile books for a rising middle class prosperous and ambitious enough to want books for their children. He began with *A Pretty Little Pocket Book* selling for sixpence (or eight pence with a ball or pincushion) in 1744, and his success encouraged rivals and imitators such as John Marshall and William Darton also to publish children's books. The advertising and marketing of books specifically designed for boys and girls became increasingly important. Newbery had realised that a publisher must not stop at producing only one or two books of a particular kind, but needed to provide a steady stream of works, as John Harris (1756-1846), his most famous successor did, supplying not only story books and picture books, but works on factual subjects as well, establishing a breadth of product that led to the Harris imprint becoming well-known.

Technological changes in the early-nineteenth century, such as the introduction of steam-printing and papermaking machinery, brought great improvements, so that by 1837 an edition of 5,000 copies could be printed in the time it previously took to produce 500 copies. This all helped to reduce costs. Book illustrations, once coloured by hand, were also gradually replaced by lithography and other mechanical methods which proved to be cheaper. Thus between 1825 and 1850 the average price of a book was halved.

Publishers such as Blackie, Longman and Macmillan became more powerful in the children's market in the nineteenth century, and the 1840s marked a clear transition from an age of enterprise and opportunism to one where industrial mass-production of books enabled economies of scale so that more books could be printed at less cost. Publisher's profits varied, of course, depending upon prices and sales, but authors benefited when their methods of being paid changed from their receiving a lump sum or a share of any profit, to a system based on a royalty calculated on the price and sales of a book.

The Education Act of 1870 helped to create an even larger market for children's books – literature and school textbooks – of which firms such as Blackie took full advantage. As literacy increased and technology continued to improve production in the twentieth century, so publishers moved increasingly towards the standardisation of their works, and strived to find best-sellers. This has led to spectacular sales and profits. In 2005, for example, it was announced that the 'Harry Potter' books written by J.K. Rowling had sold over 300 million copies world-wide, and that she herself had amassed more than £280 million from the sales of her books. The danger of such success is, of course, that both the format and the contents of children's books may be subject to pressures to conform to a formula that has proved successful elsewhere.[5]

In light of these important developments, the relationship between the authors and their publishers is raised when particularly appropriate. For example, when examining Barbara Hofland's long career, one is bound to ask whether she would have written so much, and sometimes so clumsily, if her primary publishers, John Harris and Longman, had treated her more generously. Blackie's methods of mass-production and standardisation may be seen as directly related to and perhaps the cause of G.A. Henty's formulaic and repetitive narratives. Amy Le Feuvre's long connection with her evangelical publishers, the Religious Tract Society, receives attention, as well as the activities of the publishing house of John Hamilton, who produced the flying stories of Captain W.E. Johns among many others. The importance of the print industry must never be forgotten in trying to examine the relationship between children's books and social change.

To sum up, this book attempts to show the relationship between children's literature and society by considering a number of individual examples. An era's events, ideologies and *zeitgeist* deeply influence what is written, and are more important, more pervasively penetrating, than a simple framing device for a story. When society and its ideologies change, so does its literature. But literature is not a passive construction which simply reflects society. It can react against, protest, subvert or seek to change what appears to be dominant. And if society or its leading ideology is divided or contradictory, its literature reveals those divisions and contradictions too. As D.H. Lawrence once famously said, 'Never trust the artist; trust the tale'.[6]

* * * * *

Although substantially revised, some of this book draws in varying proportions on work published earlier, and I am grateful to those who have generously granted me permission to use some of my original publications, particularly the Ashgate Press, *Popular Children's Literature in Britain*, edited by Julia Briggs, Dennis Butts and M.O. Grenby, Aldershot, 2008 ('Finding and Sustaining a Popular Appeal: the Case of Barbara Hofland' and 'Exploiting a Formula: the Adventure Stories of G.A. Henty'); the John Hopkins University Press for the article 'How Children's Literature Changed: What Happened In The 1840s' (this article first appeared in *The Lion and the Unicorn*, Vol. 21, No. 2, April 1997, pp.153-162); Manchester University Press for 'Imperialists of the Air: Flying Stories 1900-1950', which appeared in *Imperialism and Juvenile Literature*, edited by Geoffrey Richards, Manchester, 1989; for the permission of the Oxford University Press for introductions to the World's Classics editions of *Allan Quatermain* (1995) and *King Solomon's Mines* (1989) by Rider Haggard, and *The Railway Children* (1991) by E. Nesbit; and for 'Didacticism and Anarchy in Recent Children's Books from America and England' from Gerard J. Senick (author), Melissa Reiff Hug (editor), *Children's Literature Review* © 1998 Gale, a part of Cengage Learning, Inc. Reproduced by permission: www.cengage.com/permissions.

Chapter One

Barbara Hofland: The Moral Tale and the Industrial Revolution

> Religion promotes industry, industry gains respect, respect gains recommendation, recommendation gains business, business gains wealth, and thus religion itself leads to prosperity.
>
> (*The Evangelical Magazine*, 1804)[1]

Barbara Hofland is not a major writer. Born in 1770, and thus the contemporary of such novelists as Jane Austen and Walter Scott, she wrote modest little tales for children and teenagers which achieved some popularity in their day. But it is often these largely unregarded minor authors or works (the flying stories of the 1930s are another example discussed later), who – perhaps because of their lack of individuality and genius – reflect the dominant values, popular attitudes and ideas of their age. Writers such as Rider Haggard, Edith Nesbit and Geoffrey Trease may confront society in challenging ways, but Mrs Hofland's tales are worth reading for the way in which they articulate widely held views of their time.

The years between 1820 and 1850 were years of turmoil, as Britain emerged from the Napoleonic wars into a world of industrial expansion and social and political turbulence. The Industrial Revolution, as well as producing economic prosperity for some, also brought distress and hardship, not only to such rapidly expanding towns as Birmingham and Manchester, but also to agricultural regions in the south and west, and led to the violence of the agricultural 'Swing' riots and the great Chartist demonstrations. For many, the first half of the nineteenth century has indeed been justly referred to as 'The Bleak Age'.

Yet this turbulent period was also one of technological progress. The three decades between 1820 and 1850 were an era of railways and steamships, and of important developments in manufacturing and mining. A new industrial society was establishing itself, and the achievements of Faraday and Brunel, Stephenson and Hudson have to be seen alongside those of the politicians Earl Grey, Lord Melbourne and Robert Peel. The Great Exhibition of 1851 stands out as a fitting symbol of the success of their efforts. Although the land-owning aristocracy had survived the French Revolution, and an expanding urban class worked the factories and mills of the Industrial Revolution, the main thrust behind this movement towards improvement and progress was the ideology of the rising middle classes. Influenced initially by the Evangelical movement at the beginning of the century, they ardently embraced the Protestant work ethic, and transformed it into a gospel of work by the end of the period. The keystones of this class were modesty and moderation, prudence and self-help, respectability and thrift. If its philosophical underpinning lay in the materialistic utilitarianism of Jeremy Bentham, its Bible came to be Samuel Smiles's *Self Help* of 1859.

The middle classes built their lives upon a combination of Puritan morality and economic aspirations. Weekdays were dominated by purposeful work and Sundays by attendance at church or chapel. Although family life had relaxed slightly from the severities prac- tised at the height of the Evangelical revival, and continued to relax throughout the period, the father was still very much the head of the family, with the role of the mother essentially supervisory. The average family's four or five children would have been brought up on rigid gender-based lines, with the boys expected to follow their fathers into the world of business, and daughters raised to become ladylike in preparation for marriage.

The tradition of the moral tale, with its emphasis upon moral and religious didacticism, which had emerged in the late eighteenth century through such figures as Thomas Day (1748-1789), Maria Edgeworth (1767-1849) and Hannah More (1745-1833) continued to flourish with such writers as Mrs Sherwood (1775-1851) and her sister Mrs Cameron (1781-1858). Barbara Hofland (1770-1844) certainly shared a good deal in common with these writers and admired Maria Edgeworth in particular. She was, however, a more devout believer than such secular writers as Edgeworth and Day, and less doctrinaire in her religious beliefs than Hannah More or Mrs Sherwood. More significantly, her works also reflected the way the character of moral tales began to change as the industrial revolution gained pace and the climate of opinion developed.

As society changed, some writers began gradually to articulate their religious and moral teaching within a much denser social context than earlier writers had attempted. Although the daughter and wife of a clergyman, Alice Catherine Mant (1788-1869) was distinctively more secular than evangelical in *The Cottage in the Chalk-Pit* (1822), her account of a family's struggles after their father becomes destitute. The anonymous *Life and Adventures of Lady Anne* (c.1826) combines praise of the young heroine's conduct under testing circumstances with a vivid picture of the wretched treatment of orphans at the time, and anticipates Dickens's *Oliver Twist* (1838), not least in its fantastic denouement and its depiction of a wide range of society, including clergymen, the school-mistress, gardeners, shopkeepers and pedlars. Mrs Tonna (1790-1846), who wrote under the name of 'Charlotte Elizabeth', was an evangelical writer whose works sometimes dealt with industrial conditions, and, in *Perseverance; or, Walter and his Little School* (1826), with the issue of slavery.

Barbara Hofland always displays a strong social awareness in her simple moral tales, visible from the publication of her first story *The History of an Officer's Widow* in 1809. For this predilection the vicissitudes of her long, arduous and ultimately heroic life are almost certainly responsible. Born in Sheffield, the daughter of an iron-monger who died when she was only three, she seems to have been brought up by a maiden aunt. As well as publishing poetry in the local press, she ran a milliner's shop for a time until her marriage to Thomas Hoole, a local businessman, in 1796. His early death in 1798, leaving her with an infant son to support, was neither the first nor last in a long line of tragedies. To make matters worse, Hoole's business collapsed shortly after his death, and money left to his son was also lost when Hoole's trustees became insolvent. Resourcefully, the widow collected together her verse which had been printed in the Sheffield *Iris* newspaper, and successfully published her collected *Poems*, which sold over 2,000 copies in 1805. With the money raised she bought and ran a school in Harrogate for a time, but had financial problems when some parents often failed to pay the fees. A second marriage, this time to the handsome landscape painter Thomas Hofland, took her to London. Hofland's erratic artistic successes and uncertain health encouraged his wife to redouble her literary efforts, and children's books, adult novels, and school textbooks poured forth as she attempted to keep her family afloat. (The main reason for Mrs Hofland's amazing industry must be attributed to the meagre pay-ments of her publishers; John Harris, for example, only gave her £10 for her most popular work *The Son of a Genius* in 1812, and although Longman's usually offered a lump sum of £25 plus a share of the profits for later books such as *Integrity* (1823), these usually only amounted to a few pounds annually, such as £2-4-1 in 1830.)[2]

In 1816 Hofland fathered an illegitimate son, Thomas Richard Hofland, whom his wife took in, nursed, and treated as her own for the rest of her life. Despite this setback, husband and wife next worked together on an important assignment for the Marquis of Blandford, heir to the Duke of Marlborough. The Marquis had bought the mansion of Whiteknights near Reading, and commissioned the Hoflands to produce a book which would describe his showplace, with illustrations by Hofland and a text written by Barbara. For nearly three years they collaborated on the project, but by the time the handsome volume was completed in 1819, the Marquis was virtually bankrupt, and the Hoflands did not receive a penny for their labours. Hofland's career proceeded erratically, the failure of an exhibition in 1821 being followed by modest successes later, and he became subject to frequent outbursts of temper and even abused his wife. Although Barbara had adopted Hofland's illegitimate son Thomas, the death of Frederic, her son by her first marriage, in 1833 was another heavy blow, but she continued to write prolifically despite her own failing health. After a painting expedition to Italy, Hofland died in 1843. His widow published her last children's book *Emily's Reward* in 1844, and died later that year.

Not surprisingly, her tales often depict a moving picture of family life; ordinary people, frequently children or adolescents, struggle in adverse circumstances (such as bankruptcy or the death of parents) to maintain their integrity and Christian values, and at the same time exercise all kinds of economic ingenuity to support themselves. Brought up in the manufacturing city of Sheffield where, because of the often-domestic nature of the iron industry it really was possible for a man to work himself up from apprentice to master – and for his children to squander his gains just as quickly – Mrs Hofland knew at first hand the truth of the old saw about moving from clogs to clogs in three generations.

Ellen, The Teacher (1814) and *The Blind Farmer and his Children* (1816) are early examples of Mrs Hofland's characteristic combination of Christian values and business affairs; later works such as *Decision* (1824), where the young heroine becomes an iron-merchant, and *Elizabeth and her Three Beggar Boys* (1833) have similar preoccupations.

An examination of *The Son of a Genius: A Tale for the Use of Youth* (1812) reveals these characteristics in more detail. The most popular of all Mrs Hofland's stories, it reached its fourteenth edition

by 1841, and remained in print long after that. This degree of popularity is undoubtedly owing at least in part to the theme of the book,
for in introducing this tale of the vicissitudes of a poor artist's wife
and family, Mrs Hofland declared that her major aim was to show
that 'the most brilliant talents, enlarged conceptions, and refined sens-
ibilities ... may be rendered useless, and even prejudicial, unless they
are directed by prudence, humility, and discretion; and above all, that
strict integrity, founded on religious principles, that "fear of God,
which is the beginning (and the end) of wisdom".'[3]

The narrative is thus firmly structured from the beginning to articulate a particular set of Christian and moral attitudes, and does so
through the story of the unhappy life and struggles of Lewis, the artist of
genius, his long-suffering wife Agnes, and their son Ludovico (named
after his father's favourite artist). A clergyman's daughter living in
the Lake District until Lewis meets her on a sketching tour, Agnes
only enjoys a short period of happy marriage before she realises that
her husband's temperament, alternately enthusiastic and depressed,
makes it difficult for him to support her and her baby son. Moves to
Manchester, York and Leeds all promise well for a time, but in each
case Lewis, despite his undoubted talents, finds it difficult to settle to
regular employment, and eventually he is thrown into prison for debt.

By now Ludovico and his mother have been forced to try to earn
something to support the family – his mother takes up glove-making
and Ludovico sells drawings in Leeds Market. They pay off Lewis's
debts, but when he is released from gaol and manages to sell a picture
in London, he promptly moves there, just as impetuously as he had
tried other ventures. In London, however, he finds it difficult to find
customers and has no patrons. Despite the efforts of his family, he
gradually sinks into depression, begins drinking, falls seriously ill,
and finally dies lamenting his wasted life. The story of a man of
genius is, in other words, the tragedy of a man of unfulfilled talents.
And it of this kind of story that Mary Mitford was presumably thinking when she told Mrs Hofland, 'You are the mistress of our tears, as
Miss Austen is of our smiles, and,' she goes on, 'I think you have the
advantage.'[4]

This is generously said, and indeed it is too generous. Although
Mrs Hofland was able to imagine the complexity of a man who is not
really bad, but because of instability of temperament actually does
harm to those he loves, she was not able to realise such a personality
in sufficiently credible or concrete terms. In chapter six, for example,
Lewis drifts from teaching and decides to concentrate on producing a
single large picture, but when that fails to sell he renounces painting

for ever, and throws himself into designing machinery. When, however, he learns that his large picture has sold after all, he throws off design and returns to painting. One's unease is not about the existence of such instability but the way such revelations are sketchily compressed into a single chapter and presented largely from the out-side by way of Mrs Hofland's narratorial assertions. Lewis is there to prove a thesis, of course, but the proof would be more convincing if Mrs Hofland tested it out with more realistic material.

The book is not without dramatic details or incidents. Indeed the story proceeds by a mixture of short scenes in which dialogue is quite prominent, but alongside much reported or summarised action. The episodes in Leeds Market where young Ludovico tries to sell his own drawings, and in London where he has to deal with his father's dealers and potential patrons, including the painful scene when the undertaker's men come to take his father's body away, are rendered with considerable skill and economy. One has to say that, if part of the book's energy comes from the flawed figure of Lewis, far more comes from the morally successful characters of Mrs Lewis and her son Ludovico, who is, of course, the book's true hero. It is they who are hurt by Lewis's unstable temperament, and have to endure his follies and excesses, and it is Ludovico in particular who has to demonstrate – for he never actually has to learn – the virtues of self-control and prudence his father lacked. Their successes balance and more than balance the sense of Lewis's failure, but it is Mrs Hofland's way of registering their success which is particularly interesting.

The number of references to money in the tale is quite extraordinary, and helps to signal its marked difference from earlier moral tales. When Agnes marries Lewis we are told that her father 'had not a shilling in the world to give his daughter',[5] and though Lewis was left 'about two thousand pounds' on his father's death,[6] by the time they move to Manchester he 'had not more than fifty pounds left in the world'.[7] When affairs deteriorate in Leeds, we learn that Mrs Lewis is 'surrounded by creditors she could not satisfy'.[8] A few pages later we are told that Ludovico, 'after lamenting many hours … over the dead body of his beloved brother, witnessed the still severer pang which his mother felt, when emptying his little purse of the few hard-earned shillings which remained, she put them in the hands of his father, and besought him to take advantage of the night and hasten out of the country, ere the law should seize him.'[9] In this desperate situation Ludovico tries to support his mother and baby-sister by selling drawings and earns 'a crown piece, and two shillings',[10] then fifteen shillings[11] and later 'half-a-guinea',[12] while a pedlar gives him 'six and twenty shillings' for pictures he has sold.[13] On his release from prison, Mr Lewis earns money as a teacher,[14] and sells two views of the Lakes for 'two guineas'.[15]

When affairs continue to deteriorate in London, furthermore, we learn that Ludovico is only offered six guineas for his father's pictures which are worth more than twice that,[16] and he actually succeeds in selling one for twenty guineas.[17] Finally, after his father's death, when Ludovico is offered an apprenticeship by a kindly philanthropist who is impressed by his industry and honesty, he learns that the apprenticeship is worth three hundred and fifty pounds,[18] and this, with the money from his father's long-forgotten invention and his poetry, means that Ludovico, his mother and sister all finish up happy and prosperous.[19]

It is clear from even this selective summary of references to money in *The Son of a Genius* that Mrs Hofland sees and wishes her readers to see some kind of relationship between what she regards as the upholding of Christian virtues, trust in God, patience, charity, realism, self-control, and their reward not simply in spiritual blessings, but in immediate terms on this earth. This belief is suggested not merely by the overall pattern of her books, but by quite specific references within them. In chapter four of *The Son of a Genius*, for example, while Lewis is in prison for debt, Ludovico begins selling his own drawings in Leeds Market, where he meets an old woman trying to eke out an existence selling paper bags. Despite his own desperate plight, Ludovico feels sorry for her and buys one, actually giving her three pence instead of the two pence she normally charges. As he does so, Ludovico remembers St. Peter's words: 'silver and gold have I none, but such as I have give I unto thee'. On the next market day, Ludovico, having learned how to make paper bags himself in the meanwhile, gives the woman nine bags for her to sell. But his own sales are disturbed by a violent argument between two corn-merchants over a missing receipt, and his pictures are knocked down and spoiled. When he gets them home, however, he discovers not only a bank-note worth five guineas sticking to his muddy pictures but also the missing receipt; and he is handsomely rewarded for restoring them to the corn-merchant, as well as successfully selling a lot more of his own pictures. For Ludovico has shown Christian feeling, ingenuity and honesty, and Mrs Hofland is anxious for her readers not to neglect any of these qualities.

Indeed she makes them clear throughout the book, as, for example, when Mrs Lewis, warning Ludovico not to rely on his father's behaviour and rely only on his talents, says:

My dear child, God has given to you and to *all* men *tal-ents*; by the prudent and persevering, who not only *use* but *improve* them, everything really desirable may always be attained; but without industry, and the proper application of that industry, no natural gift can possibly avail them: therefore, though it is only just and right that you should indeed *thank* God for enabling you to be of use to your parents, and praise *Him*, who is indeed the giver of every good and perfect gift; seeking with humility, and diligence, for his blessing on your endeavours, and his direction in all your pursuits; yet remember it is foolish and presumptuous, to expect success, even in a good cause otherwise than as he has appointed, and it is his *will* that we attain all real advantages, both for this world, and that which is to come, by earnestly *endeavouring* to obtain them by vigilance.[20]

And this same philosophy, this same belief, in the interconnections between religious belief, industry and success, is expressed again at the end of the book, not this time by Mrs Lewis to Ludovico, but by Mrs Hofland directly to her young readers:

And you who do in any measure participate the sorrows of Ludovico, who lament either the misfortune or misconduct of those parents, who are still hallowed in your eyes, and dear to your hearts; take courage from his example, and learn from his history, that in the severest trials, comfort and support may be derived from faith and prayer, poverty relieved by industry and patience, and comfort expected from unforseen sources, since our Heavenly Father never fails to send help to his children in the hour of need.[21]

The particular interest of Mrs Hofland's tales lies very often in this way she shows us people, frequently children or adolescents, struggling in adverse circumstances both to maintain integrity and Christian virtue, and at the same time exercising all kinds of industry and business acumen in order to support themselves and their families. And it is a part of her belief that this combination of qualities is related in some way, and, though tested out in many trying circumstances, is nearly always rewarded.

Thus, while most of her books are based upon the exploration or, more often, the assertion of certain moral qualities, Christian goodness, honesty, self-knowledge rather than vanity, and family loyalty, an important thread of economic activity, often of the sharpest kind, almost always runs through them too. The three novels about widowhood, *The Clergyman's Widow* (1812), *The Merchant's Widow* (1814) and *The Officer's Widow*, all show women wrestling with financial problems after their husbands' deaths.[22] *The Blind Farmer* depicts the economic struggles of a farmer's family after he is evicted from his farm, and *Elizabeth and her Three Beggar Boys* is about a working class housewife who adopts three boys and brings them up, despite her own poverty. *The Daughter of a Genius* (1823) has many similarities to *The Son of a Genius*, while *Alicia and Her Aunt* (1822), *The Affectionate Brothers* (1816), *Ellen the Teacher* and *William and his Uncle Ben* (1826) all deal with young people whose fathers either die or leave them to fend for themselves. In the remarkable story *Decision* (1824) the father handles his business affairs so badly that it is left to his daughter Maria to sort out the family finances by setting up as an iron-merchant herself. *Self-Denial* (1827) deals in part with the extravagance of the heroine's fiancé, while *The Young Crusoe* (1829) is about work and survival in its most basic terms.

Mrs Hofland's belief in the necessity of certain values and her optimism about their material reward was not completely new. It appears in some of Hannah More's *Cheap Repository Tracts* of 1795-1798, and Gillian Avery, among others, has pointed to the simple materialism of many children's books from 1770 onwards. 'Be punctual and diligent, obedient and truthful, do not lie or thieve or blow up your sister', she says, parodying some of these stories. 'Beware of mad dogs and gaming, and you will live to be a successful sugar planter and to give your rivals a handsome funeral. This in essence seems to be the uncomplicated and cheerful message of the old-style late Georgian book'.[23] What is new about Mrs Hofland's work in the first decades of the nineteenth century is the much greater realism of detail and complexity with which she handles this kind of material in a more achieved and sophisticated fiction, and which she relates to a whole system of Christian values in a more industrialised urban society than the rural background of many earlier moral tales. There is more about budgetary management than mad dogs in her books, and the pressures of debt and bankruptcy are never far away – matters with which Mrs Hofland was more than familiar through first-hand experience.

Max Weber connected the rise of Capitalism with the Protestant Ethic, of course, and sought to show how, as a result of the Reformation, Protestants (especially Calvinists) stressed the importance of work on this earth for the greater glory of God. During the seventeenth century, he argued, the idea of work as a religious duty became widely accepted, and profit-making was part of this. 'If that God, whose hand the Puritan sees in all the occurrences of life, shows one of his elect a chance of profit,' said the seventeenth-century divine Richard Baxter (1615-1691), 'He must do it with a purpose. Hence the faithful Christian must follow the call by taking advantage of the opportunity.'[24]

Even if we think Weber over-emphasised the impact of Calvin, underestimated the influence of mercantilism in the Netherlands, or was simply not aware of the traditional praise of honest labour recommended in England at least as long ago as the medieval *Piers Plowman*, there seems little doubt that by the eighteenth century many people were recommending work as a religious or ethical duty, the predictable economic consequences of which were then taken by some people as evidence of divine approval. Although challenging Weber in several respects, R.H. Tawney, for example, related his general thesis to the developments of Puritanism in eighteenth century England, where working and making money were increasingly regarded as signs of virtue. There grew up, he says, a new religious and economic philosophy, and

> a creed which transformed the acquisition of wealth from a drudgery or a temptation into a moral duty was the milk of lions. It was not that religion was expelled from practical life, but that religion itself gave it a foundation of granite. In that keen atmosphere of economic enterprise, the ethics of the Puritans have some resemblance to those associated later with the name of Smiles. The good Christian was not wholly dissimilar from the economic man.[25]

Mrs Hofland was not a Puritan, but a moderate and liberal member of the Church of England. She was, however, sympathetic to that unconscious system of beliefs which between the sixteenth and nineteenth centuries saw a relationship between religious faith, the need to practice certain rules of conduct, and their economic consequences, and then tended to cite those economic consequences as evidence of that religious belief and practice. Because of this, it is tempting to argue that there is a contradiction in Mrs Hofland's tales between her interest in work and money, and her profession of Christianity, as if she were only interested in financial matters but felt the need to pay lip service to a more respectable moral creed. But to do so would be a mistake. Mrs Hofland's values are Christian, of a broadly ethical rather than a strictly theological character, with an emphasis on faith in God, patience, honesty, compassion and industry, virtues which she believed, perhaps a little naively, tended to lead to economic survival and even prosperity. She does not make the mistake of identifying wealthy people automatically with recipients of grace, nor does she ever advocate actions which are in conflict with Christianity. There is no trace of Pecksniff's hypocrisy in her work, nor is there that tension between money-making and the confession of sin which characterises Defoe's *Moll Flanders* (1722). Her heroes and heroines are good, honest, compassionate beings, whose virtue is rewarded in this world as well as the next, like characters in the novels of Fielding, Jane Austen and Dickens.

At the beginning of the nineteenth century this belief was widespread, and had not yet hardened into the kind of theological justification of self-help and *laissez-faire* associated with Samuel Smiles and his contemporaries. We find Mrs Hofland's philosophy expressed, for example, in the lives of good men such as Henry Thornton (1760-1815), described by E.M. Forster as 'pious, benevolent, industrious, serious, wealthy, shrewd',[26] and we find it even in the august pages of *The Evangelical Magazine* itself:

> Religion promotes industry, industry gains respect, respect gains recommendation, recommendation gains business, business gains wealth, and thus religion itself leads to prosperity.[27]

But Mrs Hofland does just a little more than articulate some of the Protestant Ethic of the time, and although her way of doing so was perhaps unconscious and is often embarrassingly clumsy, it can sometimes be very moving. In Ian Watt's study of *Robinson Crusoe*, he shows how Robinson Crusoe can be regarded as an illustration of Economic Man, and he relates Defoe to the Puritan tradition in the way he sees Crusoe constantly searching his soul and analysing his motives.[28] Barbara Hardy develops this idea and argues that Crusoe undergoes various experiences such as defiance of his father, shipwreck and a self-examination amounting to a religious conversion before he is rescued. 'It is a religious conversion,' she says, 'which explains Robinson Crusoe's highly implausible endurance of solitary confinement, and which underlies his enterprise and prosperity.'[29] Thus Robinson Crusoe does well on the island because Providence is rewarding him for his religious conversion and good deeds.

There is a similarly Providential element about some of the coincidences, which are often a clumsy feature of Mrs Hofland's tales, but can occasionally achieve a moving effect by being linked to earlier events in their stories, in ways rather like those referred to by

Ian Watt and Barbara Hardy. When Ludovico tries to refuse the corn-merchant's reward in *The Son of a Genius*, his mother re-assures him with the words

> Take it, my love, by *all* means, since Mr Higgins has the goodness to give it to you, and consider it not only as his gift, but that of a gracious Providence who has given you another friend in the hour of need, remembering also, that although this appears an accidental good, yet it came to you in the prosecution of a regular system of industry, which is ever beneficial.[30]

There are coincidences and coincidences, in other words, and some are based upon divine recognition of worth and justice. In *Ellen the Teacher*, quite late in the story Ellen's brother, Tom, rescues an old lady from a coach accident, and she turns out to be their grandmother who had treated their mother so harshly in the first chapter. Now she is overcome with remorse for her cruelty and makes up for it with generous financial settlements.

Similarly, in *The Blind Farmer* Sir Harry Eustace gives money to the titular character so that he may have an expensive eye-operation, not knowing that it is the same farmer whom he had foolishly evicted at the start of the tale. Later on in the story he helps the farmer's son in his career as an artist, again unaware of the moral connection between them. Mrs Hofland and her readers, however, know perfectly well the significance of his actions. If Mrs Hofland does at times seem to stretch the long arm of coincidence too far, using the device a little crudely or sentimentally, there is still something clumsily moving about her belief that Providence does look after ill-treated children or battered adults who have lived good lives. 'Even matters of chance seem most marvellous,' says Aristotle, 'if there is an appearance of design as it were in them',[31] and many of Mrs Hofland's apparent co-incidences fit into her moral pattern.

Chapter Two

How Children's Literature Changed in the 1840s

> Were we required to characterise this age of our by any
> single epithet, we should be tempted to call it, not an Hero-
> ical, Devotional, Philosophical, or Moral Age, but above
> all others, the Mechanical Age.
>
> (Thomas Carlyle, 'Signs of the Times', 1829)[1]

Although the 1860s, with the first appearance of *The Water-Babies*
(1863) and *Alice's Adventures in Wonderland* (1865), are usually
regarded as heralding the Golden Age of children's literature, what
occurred in the 1840s, though less discussed, actually represents
a much greater watershed. With the first appearance of books by
such writers as Hans Andersen (1805-1875) and Captain Marryat
(1792-1848), this earlier decade was far more significant in the history of children's books than anything that followed later in the
nineteenth century.

The main thrust behind Britain's extraordinary industrial progress
between 1820 and 1850 was the ideology of the rising middle classes,
who, influenced by the Evangelical movement at the beginning of
the century, ardently embraced the Protestant work ethic. They built
their lives upon a combination of Puritan morality and economic ambition, believing in the virtues of self-help and an authoritarian view
of society in general and the family in particular.

Their books for children reflected these values. As we have seen,
although the tradition of the moral tale, often evangelical in tone,
continued in the work of such writers as Mrs. Sherwood, the moral
tale was changing in character and becoming less explicitly theological. The once-popular moral tales of Mrs. Barbara Hofland, in
their pictures of ordinary lower middle-class lives, often deal quite

explicitly with the details of bankruptcy and business affairs. Her story *Decision* of 1824 boldly portrays a young heroine working as an iron-merchant because her father has squandered the family fortune.

The increasing secularisation of the moral tale is paralleled by changes in the contents of many of the juvenile periodicals. Although the spirit of Mrs Sherwood continued to walk through the pages of *The Children's Friend* which began in 1824, *The Child's Companion*, which was started by the Religious Tract Society in the same year, published articles on geography and history as well as religion, while *The Children's Weekly Visitor* of 1832 contained essays on the British rule of India as well as poetry about a snowdrop. Indeed by the 1840s even *The Children's Friend* was publishing anecdotes about foreign travel and essays about crocodiles and volcanoes. As this adoption of a wide range of topics makes evident, the secularisation (and commercialisation?) of society that swept through Britain in the 1820s and 1830s quickly came to be reflected in children's literature.

Edgar Taylor complained about some aspects of this process in the preface to his translation of *German Popular Stories* by the brothers Grimm as early as 1823. Criticising adult neglect of fairy tales, Taylor wrote that 'Philosophy is now made the companion of the nursery: we have lisping chemists and leading-string mathematicians; this is the age of reason, not of imagination; and the loveliest dreams of fairy innocence are considered as vain and frivolous.'[2] Secularism and rationalism were becoming the dominant values.

This trend is particularly noticeable in the success of the sales of 'Peter Parley'. The original Parley, Samuel Goodrich (1793-1860) was an American writer and publisher, who had set himself up in opposition to the traditional fairy tales which he regarded as extravagant and immoral fantasies of the imagination. Starting with *Tales of Peter Parley about America* (1827) and *The Tales of Peter Parley about Europe* (1828) Goodrich concentrated upon producing simple educational works with an emphasis on history and geography. He enjoyed enormous success in America, and, influenced particularly by Hannah More (1745-1833), enjoyed incredible popularity in Britain, too. F.J. Harvey Darton identified no fewer than six different authors who issued books under Goodrich's pseudonym, such as *Peter Parley's Visit to London*, during the Coronation of Queen Victoria in 1838.[3] *Peter Parley's Magazine*, which ran from 1839-1863, and *Peter Parley's Annual* (1840-1892) also contained many articles about history, travel and science which asserted the importance of factual information for young readers. Although these magazines display considerable variety in their mixture of anecdotes and stories, essays about 'Uncle John's visit to the Polytechnic Institute, Regent Street' and on Conchology (*Peter Parley's Annual*, 1842) reflect the widespread influence of utilitarianism on an age which had established the Society for the Diffusion of Useful Knowledge in 1827 and the British Society for the Advancement of Science in 1831. Thomas Carlyle (1795-1881) had identified these trends in 1829 in his essay 'Signs of the Times', where he wrote:

> Were we required to characterise this age of ours by any single epithet, we should be tempted to call it, not an Heroical, Devotional, Philosophical, or Moral Age, but, above all, the Mechanical Age. It is the Age of Machinery, in every inward or outward sense of that word. Nothing is now done directly, or by hand; all is by rule and calculated contrivance.[4]

Even more ominously Carlyle went on to suggest that the mechanisation which was characteristic of an industrial society would affect human behaviour:

> These things, which we state lightly enough here, are of deeper import, and indicate a mighty change in our whole mode of existence. For the same habit regulates not our modes of action alone, but our modes of thought and feeling. Men are grown mechanical in head and heart, as well as in hand.[5]

The protests of Catherine Sinclair (1800-1864) who complained bitterly about this obsession with stuffing children's heads with information in her entertaining tale *Holiday House* shows how far the tendency had gone by 1839. 'Plodding industry is in the present day at a very high premium', she says, in her Preface, continuing, 'in those school-rooms where there has been a society for the suppression of amusement, the mental energies have suffered as wealth as the health'.[6] There is little doubt about the dominance of utilitarianism in this period, and, with the exception of Catherine Sinclair's high-spirited tale of the mischievous pranks of the Graham children and their tolerant Uncle David, there is very little that could have prepared readers for the startling developments which were to follow in the 1840s.

But then in fewer than ten tumultuous and decisive years everything changed. Harriet Martineau's imaginative romance about Norwegian pirates, *Feats on the Fiord* (1841) and Captain Marryat's historical tale about the British civil war, *The Children of the New*

Forest (1847), established the adventure story. Harriet Mozley's *The Fairy Bower* of 1841 and Elizabeth Sewell's *Amy Herbert* of 1844 showed how moral tales could be transformed into realistic and psychologically profound family stories.

Despite the predominance of moral tales in the first half of the nineteenth century, folk and fairy tales had continued to be published. The first English translation of the brothers Grimm folk tales had appeared in 1823, followed by T.W. Croker's *Fairy Legends and Traditions of the South of Ireland* in 1825-1828. The revival of chapbook literature had also carried on the tradition of romances, nursery rhymes and fairy tales, such as the Shropshire publisher Houlston's edition of *The History of Sir Richard Whittington and his Cat* in 1825. But this process accelerated in the 1840s when Sir Henry Cole (1808-1882) produced his collection of such tales as 'Jack the Giant-Killer' under the collective title of *The Home Treasury* from 1842; W.J. Thoms published many of the old ballads and stories for children in a series entitled *Gammer Gurton's Story Books* from 1845 onwards, and in 1849 J.O. Halliwell produced his *Popular Rhymes and Nursery Tales*. Most strikingly in 1846 there appeared the first translation into English of Hans Andersen's *Wonderful Stories for Children* by Mary Howitt (1799-1888). In F.J. Harvey Darton's words 'The fairy tale had at last come into its own'.[7]

At the same time the quality of book production and illustration also changed dramatically. The square, dumpy volumes of the 1830s were replaced by a great outpouring of children's books of all sizes, often with attractive colours and fine illustrations. Cole in particular considered the visual quality of children's books most important, and employed such artists as William Mulready and John Linnell to illustrate them. After the first few titles of *The Home Treasury* were coloured by hand, the colour plates were printed, and were among the first children's books to have colour-printed illustrations. Well printed and with ornate decorations, '*The Home Treasury*', it has been said 'had the most distinguished design treatment ever given to children's books up to this time'.[8]

When we remember that these same years also saw the publication of such delightful fantasies as F.E. Paget's 'modern' fairy story, *The Hope of the Katzekopfs* (1844) and R.H. Horne's touching and inventive *Memoirs of a London Doll* (1846) – not forgetting Edward Lear's immortal *Book of Nonsense* (also 1846) – we can see that a literary revolution had taken place. The question is how and why.

It is not too difficult to offer a kind of Marxist explanation for these developments. Georg Lukács, in his *Studies in European Realism*,[9] argues, for example, that after the failure of the European revolutions of 1848, most middle-class writers became alienated from society. They turned away from the practice of committed democratic realism to produce either escapist experimental literature, like Baudelaire (1821-1867) or Mallarmé (1842-1898), or to concentrate upon a quasi-documentary realism like Zola (1840-1902) and George Gissing (1857-1903). (The pessimism of Charles Dickens's later novels, such as *Little Dorrit* of 1857, might be cited as further evidence.) Now, although the parallels are not precise, one can argue that what happened in British children's literature in this period reflects these same changes. The fantasies of Hans Andersen, Henry Cole (1808-1882) and Edward Lear (1812-1888) might be said to demonstrate the desire to escape from almost intolerable contemporary burdens, as do the works of their successors Charles Kingsley (1819-1875) and 'Lewis Carroll' (Charles Lutwidge Dodgson, 1832-1898). (Tom escapes from the *laissez-faire* evils of chimney-sweeping into a fantastic dream-world.) The moral tales of Mozley (1803-1852) and Sewell (1815-1906), on the other hand, turn in upon themselves, and portray the psychological problems of their characters worrying about the niceties of behaviour, rather than engaging with such issues as a wealthy person's responsibilities towards the poor. Although it would be an exaggeration to call it Gissingesque, R.H. Horne's *Memoirs of a London Doll*, in describing how the doll-heroine is passed from one owner to another, ranging in class from a Countess to a poor street-musician, might be interpreted as a quasi-documentary account of London's social strata in mid-Victorian times.

Such an explanation for what happened to children's literature in Britain in the 1840s is not entirely convincing, however. Not only does it seem too deterministic, and misread the ways decent and humane writers like Andersen and Horne (1803-1884) were protesting about social conditions – Horne actually worked for a time on a government investigation into child labour – but it would be historically inaccurate. Not only were most of the crucial texts published *before* 1848, before the failure of the revolutions, in other words, but there also existed a few works published earlier, such as Sara Coleridge's extraordinary prose-romance *Phantasmion* (1837), Sinclair's *Holiday House* (1839), and Captain Marryat's *Masterman Ready; or, The Wreck of the Pacific* (1841-1842), which had already pointed the way to the later changes.

Covering similar ground in her study of American children's books over this period, Anne Scott MacLeod emphasises the importance of social change in reshaping American children's fiction between 1820 and 1850. In her essay 'From Rational to Romantic; The Children of Children's Literature in the Nineteenth Century', she shows how the dominance of Maria Edgeworth-like moral tales about rational young children was overthrown by writers who were so appalled by the plight of the children of the urban poor that they began to depict such children as innocent and helpless in order to emphasise the wrongs of the social system which failed to help them. These changes, she argues, introduced into American fiction of the 1850s by such writers as Sara Parton (1811-1872), eventually led to the full-blooded appearance of the romantic child in *Little Lord Fauntleroy* by Mrs. Frances Hodgson Burnett (1849-1924) in 1886. Thus Romanticism came to replace Rationalism in American children's literature.[10]

Although Anne Scott Macleod's account of developments in America is luminous and persuasive, British history is different, and it is so in at least two major ways. First, developments in children's literature seem to have been more complicated in Britain than America between the years 1820 and 1850. Although the didactic moral tale continued to survive in Britain, it gradually changed its character, asserting its teaching within a much denser social context and taking more account of money and economics than Anne Scott MacLeod's account of America suggests. The works of Barbara Hofland, which were discussed earlier, are a clear example of this tendency, as we have seen. The very title of Harriet Martineau's series of tracts, *Illustrations of Political Economy* (1832-1834) is a clear indication of how far British society had moved from the days of Hannah More's religious *Cheap Repository Tracts* of 1795. Similarly, the influence of Peter Parley's publications, with their insistence upon facts and information, cannot be underestimated in this period. But the political developments were different too. The period between the end of the Napoleonic wars and the Great Exhibition of 1851 has to be seen as one of constant struggle, as the British people and its rulers sought to deal with the problems of the industrial revolution. The rapidly growing towns and the appalling conditions in them, the stresses of the factory-system, the decline in agriculture, the inadequacies of public education all produced tensions and agitation manifested by such recurring public outbursts as the rural 'Swing Riots' of the 1820s, the mass-meetings to urge parliamentary reform in the 1830s, the growth of the Chartist movement, and the great protests calling for the repeal of the Corns Laws in the 1840s. The fatalities sustained at 'Peterloo', the transportation of the 'Tolpuddle Martyrs' in 1834, and the Newport Uprising of 1839 which left at least a dozen Chartists dead as well as fifty wounded, are all evidence of the Bleak Age and the picture of a society on the edge of catastrophe.

But political reform was also on the move. Fuelled by public unrest, and informed by a series of government reports, such as the Sadler's Committee Report on Factory Children's Labour in 1831 and the (Manchester) Statistical Society's Reports on Education (1834-1837), changes were gradually introduced, too gradually in some cases, but, under the influence of such men as the philanthropist Lord Shaftesbury (1801-1885), steady and insistent for all that. Following the Great Reform Act of 1832, and the Abolition of Slavery a year later, came a number of other reforms. The Factory Act of 1833 limited the numbers of hours children could be employed in textile mills, for example, and the first steps in the state provision of education were established by government grants of public money for this purpose in 1839. (National literacy rates were, in fact, already rising before the state spent a farthing on education)[11] Crucially, the Corn Laws were repealed in 1846. And this apparently arcane legislation, by which Peel, the Conservative Prime Minister, against the interests of his party, reduced the duties on corn imported into Britain in order to help alleviate the effects of the famine in Ireland, was the most dramatic evidence that more humane ways were being sought of trying to deal with society in the face of awesome and complex problems. Attitudes towards weakness and suffering began to change, and there grew up ideals of public service in which, in Raymond Williams's words, 'the effort towards civilisation is actually promoted by a genuine altruism and the making of positive institutions'.[12]

In this reconstruction of social attitudes, the literature of the time was, of course, of vital importance, and it is difficult to imagine that the social changes would have taken place without the inspiration of such writers as Wordsworth (1770-1850) and Dickens (1812-1870). Concern about the employment of children in factories and mines had been a subject of public debate at least since the Report on Children in Manufactories of 1816, but it is found most eloquently perhaps in Elizabeth Barrett's indignant poem 'The Cry of the Children' in 1844:

> But the young, young children, O my brothers,
> They are weeping bitterly!
> They are weeping in the playtime of the others,
> In the country of the free.[13]

Criticism of schools was widespread, too. The achievements of Dr Arnold of Rugby School and the Registrar-General's annual reports on working-class illiteracy both encouraged debates about the contents and methods of education, but it was novels, such as Dickens's

Nicholas Nickleby (1839) and Charlotte Brontë's *Jane Eyre* (1847) which really awakened the public conscience.

What seems to have happened in the 1840s, then, is that the culture of the period – or what Raymond Williams called 'the structure of feeling'[14] – shifted, and that this operated through all the elements in society, including literature, politics, economics and children's books. The dominant middle-class ideology, based upon the enthusiastic embracing of *laissez-faire* capitalism, and a hierarchical view of society, especially promoting the roles of authoritarian parents and submissive children, began to change. Confronted by the horrors of the industrial revolution and the violent protests which they aroused, the virtues of utilitarianism came to seem inadequate. The consequences of the Bleak Age led to Chartism and threatened revolution. Sensitive and humane writers, such as Charles Dickens and Mrs Gaskell (1810-1865), saw this clearly, and *Barnaby Rudge: A Tale of the Riots of 'Eighty* (1841), and *Mary Barton: a Tale of Manchester Life* (1848) express this vision. Engels' *The Condition of the Working Class in England* (1845) showed how near the catastrophe was, while Benjamin Disraeli (1804-1881), a future Tory Prime Minister, graphically described the major cause of the conflict in the famous dialogue about Britain's two nations in his novel of 1845 called *Sybil*:

> 'Two nations: between whom there is no intercourse and no sympathy; who are as ignorant of each other's habits, thoughts, and feelings, as if they were dwellers in different zones, or inhabitants of different planets; who are formed by a different breeding, are fed by a different food, are ordered by different manners, and are not governed by the same laws.'
> 'You speak of—' said Egremont, hesitatingly.
> 'THE RICH AND THE POOR.'[15]

The changing sensibility recognised the need for some kind of political accommodation, and the shift in public consciousness which had sought to ameliorate the harshest features of the industrial revolution through the repeal of the Corn Laws and other social legislation, particularly that dealing with the treatment of children in mines and factories, and in providing some kind of education, is reflected in the more restricted world of the newly emerging children's literature. Nowhere is this desire for an accommodation seen more clearly than in Captain Marryat's historical novel *The Children of the New Forest* of 1847. Marryat's story of the four young Beverley children's adventures after their father dies fighting for the Royalist cause during the civil war contains far less moralising not only than earlier Evangelical novels or moral tales, but even less than Marryat's own previous works, such as *Masterman Ready*, where daily prayers are regularly said. In order to save their lives, Jacob Armitage, an old family servant and forester, takes the children, disguised as his grandchildren, to live in his own modest cottage in the New Forest, where he teaches them how to hunt and keep house. But after the death of their elderly mentor, the children are portrayed as having to fend for themselves entirely on their own in the Forest, quite free from the constraints of adult supervision in a way which is new in English children's books. The young children have to learn to stand on their own feet, practising farming and financial trading, as well as avoiding being threatened by robbers or by suspicious Parliamentary troopers. Although the Beverley sisters are presented as the rather passive stereotyped females of their day, good at cooking and sewing, Humphrey, the younger brother, proves adept at farming and animal husbandry. But in the figure of the eldest boy, Edward, who is only thirteen when the story opens, and is fiery, arrogant, brave, persevering, and yet sympathetic, the nineteenth-century's first authentic teenage hero makes his appearance. Angered by the death of his father and humiliated by the loss of his estate, he shows his skill at hunting and bravery in rescuing the young heroine Patience from a dangerous fire, and in the course of the novel learns to control his reckless nature and achieve maturity.

More than that, however, through its account of the struggles between the Parliamentary and the Royalist forces in seventeenth century England, Marryat's novel articulates the tensions between the two nations that threatened to engulf Britain in the 1840s.

An unsuccessful Reform candidate for Parliament who had also served briefly during the 1839 Rebellion in Canada, Marryat is clearly sympathetic to the royalist cause in *The Children of the New Forest,* but he is in fact deeply critical of the extremists on either side. While denouncing the regicides, he is unafraid to criticise the king's absolutism. Gradually Edward learns from the moderate Parliamentarian Heatherstone. 'He said that the king wished to be absolute, and wrest the liberties from his subjects, and that they were justified in opposing him', Edward tells his brother, continuing 'The king was obstinate, the people resolute, until virulent warfare inflamed both parties, and neither would listen to reason'.[16] Wounded several times in his distinguished naval career, Marryat knew at first hand what war really meant. Thus his novel expresses a movement away from antagonism between the two opposing sides in the civil war towards reconciliation, and this is suggested not only by Edward's gradual appreciation of the integrity of Intendant Heatherstone, the moderate Parliamentarian, but by Edward's growing love for Heatherstone's daughter Patience. Thus their marriage at the end of the novel carries a powerful symbolism as Marryat suggests a resolution of those destructive forces which threatened to tear Britain apart in the 1840s, as they had in the seventeenth century.

The changes in children's books in the 1840s, in other words, reflect the changing values of a new Age. The emerging children's literature, with its growing tolerance of children's playful behaviour, its recognition of the importance of feelings as opposed to reliance upon reason and repression, and its relaxation of didacticism because it was less certain of dogmas, all reflect what was happening in the world beyond children's books. It is surely remarkable that, whereas fairy tales had to fight for recognition in the 1820s, no fewer than four different translations of Hans Andersen's stories for children should have been published in the year of 1846 alone.[17]

The loving, almost extravagant, care which Henry Cole bestowed upon his production of *The Home Treasury*, the gaiety and warmth of Horne's fantasies, the vigour and growing independence of Marryat's adventure tales, the exhuberance of Edward Lear and poetry of Hans Andersen, all show that attitudes to children and to childhood were being transformed. When we seek explanations for changes in children's literature, it is necessary to look for more than purely literary or political explanations, but attempt a consideration of a culture which includes both but also more than them alone. It is no coincidence that the 1840s were years of economic change and political demonstration, but also the years of *Dombey and Son* and *Jane Eyre*, of William Wordsworth and Hans Christian Andersen and Edward Lear.

Chapter Three

Muscular Christianity and the Adventure Story

Finally, my brethren, be strong in the Lord, and in the power of his might. Put on the whole armour of God, that ye may be able to stand against the wiles of the devil. For we wrestle not against flesh and blood, but against principalities, against powers, against the rulers of the darkness of this world, against spiritual wickedness in high places. Wherefore take unto you the whole armour of God, that ye may be able to withstand in the evil day, and having done all, to stand.

(St. Paul's *Epistle to the Ephesians*, chapter 6, vv.10-13)

The Lord Jesus Christ is not only the *Prince of Peace*; he is the *Prince of War* too.

(Charles Kingsley, *Brave Words for Brave Soldiers and Sailors*, 1855)[1]

The history of the British boys' adventure story is pretty well known now. Its origins in romances and ballads, the novels of Daniel Defoe (1660-1731) and Sir Walter Scott (1771-1832), and its development through the works of such writers as Captain Marryat, R.M. Ballantyne (1825-1894), G.A. Henty (1832-1902) and Rider Haggard (1856-1925) into the twentieth century with W.E. Johns, (1893-1968) and the historical tales of Geoffrey Trease (1909-1998) and Rosemary Sutcliff (1920-1992) have been discussed by many scholars and critics such as Margery Fisher, Martin Green and Joseph Bristow.[2] This chapter, by contrast, focuses on the religious, specifically Christian element, in the development of the genre, particularly in the middle of the nineteenth century, to suggest how it arose, to describe some of its characteristics, and then to trace how it gradually changed.

Christianity had, of course, often played a part in the earliest stories of adventure. *Robinson Crusoe* of 1719 is a kind of romance about divine providence, as the hero sees his shipwreck as a punishment for disobeying his father and going to sea, and the story is shot through with Christian meaning. For the first time in his life, Crusoe kneels down to pray and then begins to read the Bible daily after he is thrown on to the desert island, we remember. *Robinson Crusoe's* most famous juvenile successor, *The Swiss Family Robinson* of 1816 is about a pastor and his family shipwrecked on a desert island and is also full of religious pieties. The evangelical writers of the early nineteenth century, such as Hannah More and Mrs Sherwood, produced their realistic domestic tales mainly in order to promote Christian values, although adventure stories such as Mrs Hofland's *The Young Crusoe* and Captain Marryat's *The Children of the New Forest* tended to be more secular in their attitudes at this time.

During the 1830s even the evangelical literature began to change its character, as was discussed in earlier chapters. Such magazines as the *Children's Weekly Visitor*, which began in 1832, though containing a weekly Bible lesson, are much more secular than earlier periodicals. Indeed the enormously popular books by the American writer 'Peter Parley' (Samuel Goodrich, and the various British imitators who borrowed his pseudonym), contained an enormous quantity of history, travel, natural history and other subjects which showed a much greater emphasis upon facts. Even such stories as Parley's 'Tale of Youthful Courage' (1844), the adventures of two boys captured by Red Indians, begins by comparing the Hudson River with the Thames, the Loire, the Tagus and the Andes. Utilitarianism was beginning to dominate an age which saw the establishment of the Society for the Diffusion of Useful Knowledge in 1827 and the British Society for the Advancement of Science in 1831, as already noted.

From the 1850s, however, a new kind of boys' story began to appear in which robust, middle-class young men pursued their adventures heroically but with a strong sense of Christian faith, a manner which at least partly inspired the term 'muscular Christianity'. The origins of the phrase are somewhat obscure. The *O.E.D.* says that the term was first applied from about 1857 to the ideal of character exhibited in the writings of Charles Kingsley (1819-1875), and quotes from *The Edinburgh Review* of January 1858. This says of Charles Kingsley that the principal characteristics of the writer whose works earned this burlesque though expressive description, are his deep sense of the sacredness of all the ordinary rela-tions and the common duties of life, and the vigour with which he contends … for the great importance and value of animal spirits, physical strength, and hearty enjoyment of all the pursuits and accomplishments which are con-nected with them.[3]

Charles Kingsley's *Westward Ho!* of 1855 is the most famous, and in many ways the best, example of the genre. This strange, powerful, prejudiced, and sometimes tedious tale – it is nearly a quarter of a million words long – is set in the sixteenth century during the English War with Spain. The story focuses upon the life and adventures of Amyas Leigh, a young boy from Bideford, and, in Elspeth Huxley's opinion, 'the quintessential muscular Christian'.[4] We first meet him as a schoolboy longing to go to sea, and follow him through his jour-neys with Sir Francis Drake and later his bitter service in Ireland. But when he, like many of his companions, falls in love with the local beauty Rose Salterne, they form a Brotherhood of the Rose to protect her. When she is subsequently abducted by the Spanish nobleman Don Guzman, Amyas and his companions launch a rescue mission and sail to the West Indies. Amyas' ship is damaged on the way, and so they abandon it and march inland to capture a great Spanish galleon, rescuing the beautiful Indian maid Ayancora in the process. However, Amyas then discovers that Rose and his brother Frank have become victims of the Inquisition, causing him to become bitterly anti-Spanish and obsessed with taking his revenge on the evil Don Guzman. When the Armada attacks, Amyas pursues Don Guzman to his death, until a great storm strikes and Amyas is blinded. Only then does he come to realise how he has sinned in his obsessive desire for blood-vengeance, and begins to repent. Now appropriately contrite, he returns home safely to Devon to marry Ayancora, completing the traditional romance pattern.

This is a good example of Kingsley's 'muscular Christianity', for Amyas and his stout companions cheerfully fight the Spanish as their Christian duty. The nature of Kingsley's moral discrimination is made quite clear, for while Amyas's violence in pursuit of personal revenge is sinful, Kingsley has no doubt that it is morally absolutely right to fight the Spanish in a just cause. The book is thus rife with count-less battles and sea-fights. The horrors of the Spanish Inquisition are vividly described, as are the British massacres in Ireland. Despite this predilection of the book as a whole towards violent action, however, most of Amyas's deeds, such as his attack on a Spanish gold-train and rescue of some poor Indian captives, are characterised as brave and courageous, not least as they were inspired by the words of the great Elizabethan seaman and cavalier hero, Sir Humphrey Gilbert:

> We are going in God's cause; we go for the honour of God's gospel, for the deliverance of poor infidels led captive by the devil; for the relief of any distressed countrymen unemployed within this narrow isle; and to God we commit our cause. We fight against the devil himself; and stronger is He that is within us than he that is against us.[5]

British children's literature had contained examples both of Christian feeling and exciting adventures earlier, of course, but the intensity of their combination in works that began to appear in the 1850s requires some kind of tentative explanation.

During the 1840s, as was argued in the previous chapter, children's literature's dominant utilitarian character began to change – an increasing capacity for warmth, laughter and imaginative enjoyment began to appear in the works of Edward Lear and Hans Andersen, while a more serious brand of adventure story, full of a sense of responsibility, was being produced by writers such as Captain Marryat and Harriet Martineau (1802-1876).

During the 1850s two events in particular seem to have deeply affected public attitudes. The Crimean War of 1854-1856 with its harsh physical conditions and heroic disasters such as the Charge of the Light Brigade aroused intense feelings of patriotism. Kingsley himself was deeply involved, writing to his friend F.D. Maurice (1805-1872) in October 1854 about one of the bloodiest battles:

> It seemed so dreadful to hear of those Alma Heights being taken and not to be there; but God knows best, and I suppose I am not fit for such brave work.... But I can fight with my pen still.... Not in controversy, but in writing books which will make others fight.[6]

Kingsley's passionate involvement led him to produce a pamphlet called *Brave Words to Brave Soldiers and Sailors* in the winter of 1854-1855 in which he tried to inspire fighting as a Christian duty: 'The Lord Jesus Christ,' he said, 'is not only the *Prince of Peace*; he is the *Prince of War* too. He is the Lord of Hosts, the God of Armies, and whosoever fights in a just war, against tyrants and aggressors, he is fighting on Christ's side, and Christ is fighting on his side; Christ is his captain and his leader, and he can be in no better serve. Be sure of it; for the Bible tells you so.'

We see something of this same praise for Christian valour and heroic fighting when Hereward, the last of the old English, takes up his sword against King William and the Norman invaders in Kingsley's later story *Hereward the Wake* of 1866. Hereward slaughters and beheads fifteen Normans in order to rescue his mother at the Battle of Bourne. And subsequently Wilton of Ely makes Hereward a knight, and urges him 'to take back his sword in the name of God and of St. Peter and St. Paul, and use it, like a true knight, for a terror and punishment to evildoers, and a defence for women and orphans, and the poor and oppressed, and the monks the servants of God.'[7]

Just as traumatic as the Crimean War were the events of the Indian Mutiny which followed. Lasting from 1857-1859, it was marked by dreadful atrocities committed on both sides, as well as brave deeds. Sir Henry Havelock (1795-1857), for example, marched with a small force 126 miles in ten days in the heat of the Indian summer, winning four battles on the way, before recapturing Cawnpore from an army nearly four times its size. As well as a brilliant soldier, Havelock was also a devout Christian who used to pray for two hours each morning before marching at 6 a.m. 'Thanks to Almighty God who gave me the victory,' he wrote to his wife after an early success, 'I now march to retake Cawnpore.' Later in the year Havelock also successfully achieved the Relief of Lucknow. Not surprisingly, he became a legendary hero – with a statue built in his honour on the west side of Trafalgar Square. Through models such as Havelock, the notion of the Christian soldier began to gain currency from the 1850s. James 'Quaker' Wallace, another hero of the Mutiny, chanted the Scottish version of the 116th psalm as he charged into action, while the image of Bible-reading, mystical Brevet-Major Gordon (1833-1885) became famous for his brave exploits in the Far East in the early 1860s long before his death at Khartoum in 1885.[8]

The achievements of such men as Dr Thomas Arnold (1795-1842), the famous Headmaster of Rugby School (1828-1842), had also opened up a debate about the purpose of education earlier in the nineteenth century. Arnold attacked the bullying and drunkenness which then existed in many schools, and made Christian values and the College chapel central to school life. While emphasising the importance of learning and spiritual values, however, Arnold also encouraged games and sports for exercise and relaxation. His influence was enormous – from the 1850s disciples such as C.J. Vaughan (1816-1897), Headmaster at Harrow from 1845-1859, and Edward

Thring (1821-1887), Headmaster at Uppingham from 1853-1887, both of them friends of Kingsley's, began to develop a philosophy of education which combined Christianity with a vigorous and competitive athleticism. Rowing, football, cricket, even boxing all became more and more important, not only in order to improve physical health but to instil discipline and moral values. A.C. Wilson, Second Master at Lancing from 1851-1869, said 'The great value of a school is that it is, or ought to be, a place of moral discipline, and this discipline is taught as much in the playground or cricket field as in the classroom.'[9]

Tom Brown's Schooldays of 1856, by Charles Kingsley's great friend Thomas Hughes (1822-1896), not only established the popularity of the school story but is perhaps one of the best known examples of this 'muscular Christianity'. In the first part of the book we are introduced to the Brown family living in Uffington, where Squire Brown's eldest son Tom grows up with the village boys before going to Rugby School in the 1830s. Here he is befriended by East who introduces him to the ways of the school and Tom even plays in the extremely strenuous annual Rugby match on his first day. At a great concert after the match, he hears the Head Boy, Old Brooke, praise the new Head Master, Dr Arnold, and then gradually becomes used to school life. He gets lost in a cross-country run, survives being bullied by and scorched by Flashman, and is caught by a gamekeeper illegally fishing. At the end of term Tom is nearly expelled and receives a stern warning from the Head Master.

When Tom returns for the new session, he is put into a study with a rather delicate new boy, Arthur, instead of his old friend East. Although Tom rather resents this at first, he gradually falls under the influence of Arthur's Christian behaviour, beginning to say his prayers and to read the Bible regularly, but also in his turn introducing Arthur to such activities as bird's-nesting and cricket. When fever sweeps the school and Arthur falls seriously ill, Tom realises how much he has come to value his friendship, and, when Arthur recovers, Tom gives up using cribs for schoolwork. Perhaps as a result of Arthur's influence, even the boisterous East receives Christian confirmation. Gradually all three boys change, and Tom especially becomes a more self-disciplined character. The story ends with the great cricket-match between the school and the M.C.C., in which both Tom and Arthur play. In a kind of Epilogue, years later, when Tom hears of Dr Arnold's death, he returns to the school chapel to pay tribute to the great Headmaster who helped him to grow up.

The book is clearly serious. It is about a character's development, tracing Tom's growth from his earliest years in the village to his emergence as a responsible Christian adult. It has a warm and vigorous narrative, full of memorable incidents such as Flashman's bullying, Arthur's fever, and Tom's great fight with Slogger Williams. It is full of relationships, with East, with Arthur, with the great Doctor, with Diggs, the clumsy fifth-former who helps Tom, and with Martin, the mad scientist. But it is also about fighting, of which Hughes, the author, is a firm advocate. This is the preface to Tom's fight with Slogger Williams, when Tom steps in to protect Arthur after an argument with Slogger about school-work:

> After all, what would life be without fighting, I should like to know? From the cradle to the grave, fighting, rightly understood, is the business, the real, highest, honestest business of every son of man. Everyone who is worth his salt has his enemies, who must be beaten, be they evil thoughts, and habits in himself, or spiritual wickednesses in high places, or Russians or Border-ruffians, or Bill, Tom, or Harry, who will not let him live his life in quiet till he has thrashed them.
>
> It is no good for Quakers, or any other body of men, to uplift their voices against fighting. Human nature is too strong for them, and they don't follow their own precepts. Every soul of them is doing his own piece of fighting, somehow and somewhere. The world might be a better world without fighting for anything I know, but it wouldn't be our world; and therefore I am dead against crying peace when there is no peace, and isn't meant to be. I'm as sorry as any man to see folk fighting the wrong people and the wrong things, but I'd a deal sooner see them doing that, than that they should have no fight in them.[10]

So a corpus of children's literature emphasising the importance of combining Christian faith with vigorous, heroic activity, inspired by Charles Kingsley and Thomas Hughes, developed (F.W. Farrar's school-story *Eric, or Little by Little*, of 1858, though immensely popular, does not quite fit into this genre because although undoubtedly evangelical, it is hardly 'muscular'). R.M. Ballantyne, a devout member of the Scottish Free Church, produced a whole series of adventure stories with boy-heroes who combine a strong, brave and energetic character, with a simple faith in God. *The Coral Island: A Tale of the Pacific Ocean* of 1858 is the best known example. *The Coral Island* is clearly a *Robinsonnade*, narrating the adventures of three boys, Ralph, Jack, and Peterkin, who are shipwrecked on a desert island in the tropics. They build an encampment, explore the island, live off the proceeds of hunting – not to mention the abundance of ripe fruit – and rescue some natives from attack by cannibals. Later, a party of pirates capture Ralph, but he manages to outwit them and return to the island with their schooner. In the last part of the story, the three companions escape from the island, but are themselves captured by cannibals until a missionary arrives who successfully converts the cannibals to Christianity, and so frees the boys to return home.

There is plenty of vigorous action in the story. The boys defy sharks, survive storms and drive off an initial threat from cannibals, whose chief Jack manages to kill with a wooden club after a ferocious fight. Confronted by a dying pirate, however, Ralph regrets his own neglect of true religion, and helps to comfort the dying man with the words 'Believe on the Lord Jesus Christ, and thou shalt be saved'.[11] The treatment of the missionaries, though laughably unconvincing, is also quite sincere, for though Ballantyne's story abounds in adventure and romance, it never fails to assert the importance of Christianity.

Ballantyne's desert-island adventure, with its picture of British boys exploring the tropics and civilising the natives, contains within it elements of imperialism, of course. And the transition from evangelical and 'muscular' Christianity towards something more like a belief in colonialism and the British Empire is also seen in the books of W.H.G. Kingston (1814-1880).

Kingston is most famous for his tales of adventure at sea, and an early story seems to anticipate Kingsley's more full-blooded 'muscular Christianity' for it contains a strong religious element. *Peter the Whaler; His Early Life and Adventures in the Arctic Regions* of 1851 shows the fifteen year-old hero rebelling against his clergyman father and being sent to sea in order to escape being punished for poaching. Then, after exciting adventures whaling in the Arctic and fighting off pirates, Peter returns home to tell his father 'I have come back infinitely richer. I have learned to fear God, to worship Him in His works, and to trust to His infinite mercy.'[12] But, although Kingston retained his Christian faith, his later works, still full of thrilling adventures in faraway places, seem to place a much greater emphasis on imperialism and the *Pax Britannica*. In his periodical *Kingston's Magazine for Boys*, published from March 1859, Kingston's 'Editorial' specifically addresses itself to boys who will one day be 'battling with the realities of life under the suns of India, in the backwoods of Canada or the States, on the grassy downs of Australia, over the wide ocean, among the isles of the Pacific, or on the distant plains of Columbia'.[13] Kingston's most popular books, 'The Three Midshipmen Series', consisting of *The Three Midshipmen*

(1862), *The Three Lieutenants* (1875), *The Three Commanders* (1876) and *The Three Admirals* (1877) closely resemble some of Marryat's high-spirited nautical novels such as *Midshipman Easy* of 1836, and concentrate on the virtues of the heroic British naval officer in a variety of adventures, including sea-battles. Although poverty and poor health seem to have driven Kingston back to more quasi-religious writing towards the end of his life, there is little doubt about the secular and nationalist values of his most popular novels in mid-career.[14]

Secularisation was indeed spreading rapidly from the 1860s, particularly in the public schools through the accelerating growth in those institutions of athletics and competitive games. As Harrow, Lancing, Marlborough, and Uppingham increasingly emphasised the importance of physical education, so many other schools followed their example. More resources were spent on pitches, and on new gymnasia and staff. Registers and statistical records were assiduously kept. The whole elaborate and hierarchical apparatus of house matches, colours, and competitive games between schools was established, and the significance of particular events grew exponentially. Attendance at Lords for the annual cricket match between Eton and Harrow reached twenty-four thousand in the 1870s, for example.[15]

But the ideal of *mens sana in corpore sano* was gradually being replaced by a belief in the value of competitive sport for other reasons. As J.G. Cotton Minchin said, 'If asked what our muscular Christianity has done, we point to the British Empire. Our Empire would never have been built up by a nation of idealists and logicians. Physical vigour is as necessary for maintenance of our Empire as mental vigour.'[16] Thus there was a gradual change from the 'spiritual' manliness of the 1850s and 1860s, suggested by Kingsley and Hughes, to the ludic ideology of the 1870s and 1880s, associated with a greater emphasis on physical development in the name of secular patriotism and imperialism. It is a far cry from Dr Arnold's views on education. 'Muscular Christianity' is being replaced by muscularity and patriotism.

This process is particularly evident in the development of the two main genres of boys' fiction from the 1870s – the adventure story and the school story.

Kingston, the author of so many thrilling sea-stories, was succeeded in 1880 as the editor of the significantly named *Union Jack: Tales for British Boys*, a penny weekly devoted to adventure stories, by G.A. Henty, who became the most prolific exponent of the genre in the last decades of the century. A widely experienced war-correspondent who had begun his career in the Crimean War, Henty began writing for children when poor health made further strenuous travelling impossible. Soon he was producing four books a year, ranging from historical works such as *With Clive in India; or, The Beginnings of Empire* in 1884 to stories about contemporary events, such as *With Buller in Natal; or, A Born Leader* of 1901. By the time of his death in 1902 Henty had produced nearly eighty books for his main publisher Blackie alone, as well as numerous essays, short stories, campaign histories and adult novels for other publishers. He is by this prolific output supposed to have taught history to generations of schoolboys.[17]

The hero of Henty's stories is usually a teenage boy, the son of a clergyman or farmer perhaps, who leaves home at the beginning of the tale as the result of a domestic crisis, in order to seek his fortune elsewhere. Often accompanied by a faithful companion, the young hero undergoes various difficulties, shipwrecks, attacks by hostile natives, skirmishes, unjust captivity, and treachery, until the narrative rises to a great climax which is often a fierce battle against powerful opponents, before the hero triumphs and returns home safely.

Religious didacticism has completely disappeared from these stories, but Henty took his moral responsibilities seriously, trying to guide his young readers – 'My Dear Lads', as he often calls them in his prefaces – towards such virtues as honesty, loyalty and resourcefulness, but especially pluck. All Henty's books articulate a confident belief that the British possession of such qualities is unequalled, and that the British Empire is an unrivalled instrument for justice and civilised values.

Here first, to give an example of how important athleticism combined with moral decency had become, is the description of sixteen-year-old Charlie Marryat, the hero of *With Clive in India*:

> He was slight in build, but his schoolfellows knew that
> Charlie Marryat's muscles were as firm and as hard as those
> of any boy in the school. In all sports requiring activity and
> endurance rather than weight and strength he was always
> conspicuous. Not one in the school could compete with him
> in long-distance running, and when he was one of the hares
> there was but little chance for the hounds. He was a capital
> swimmer and one of the best boxers in the school. He had
> a reputation for being a leader in every mischievous prank;
> but he was honourable and manly, would scorn to shelter
> himself under the semblance of a lie, and was a prime
> favourite with his masters as well as his schoolfellows.[18]

There is not much mention of Christianity here, nor in the works of Henty's contemporaries and successors, such as Sir Henry, Rider

Haggard, 'Herbert Strang' (pseudonym of George Herbert Ely [1866-1958] and James L'Estrange [1867-1947]) or Captain F.S. Brereton (1872-1957), who wrote adventure stories such as *With Rifle and Bayonet* (1901)

The dilution of Christian values can most clearly be seen in the production of the weekly magazine the *Boys' Own Paper* which began in January 1879. Though occasionally containing brief paragraphs on religion, this magazine, which was actually created by the Religious Tract Society to try and counter the appeal of the violent but popular 'penny dreadfuls', accepted the need to concentrate on publishing attractive but secular adventure and school stories in order to reach the widest possible number of juvenile readers, as indeed it did, reaching figures, it has been calculated, of around a quarter of a million by the 1880s.[19]

Significantly, the first number of the *BOP* opened with the story of 'My First Football Match' by 'An Old Boy' later identified as Talbot Baines Reed (1852-1893). After the success of *Tom Brown's Schooldays*, other school stories had followed, such as *Schoolboy Honour* by the Rev. H.C. Adams (1817-1899) in 1861, and *Stories of Whitminster* by 'Ascott Hope', actually Robert Hope Moncrieff (1846-1927), in 1873. But it was Talbot Baines Reed's serials for the *BOP*, later published in book form, such as *The Fifth Form at St. Dominic's* (1882) and *The Cock House at Fellsgarth* (1893), which became the greatest influence on the genre of the school story since Thomas Hughes, and laid down the lines for future development. Less didactic than earlier writers, Reed exploited the ingredients of the school story, such as rivalry over games, with skill and zest. *The Fifth Form at St. Dominic's*, with its exciting cricket and Rugby matches, was extremely popular. Frequently reprinted, it sold 750,000 copies in penny edition in 1907. (By contrast, Lewis Carroll's *Alice in Wonderland* had sold 150,000 copies by 1898.[20]) The success is deserved, for Reed makes a lively use of the conventions established by Hughes, but developed them with a significant change of tone. Christian values are faintly present, but there is much less explicit didacticism than in Hughes's book, and there is far more humour and good-natured tolerance. Reed develops a story of some complexity by describing the first year of young Stephen Greenfield's career at St. Dominic's, but contrasting his naïve and amusing experiences with the more challenging issues facing his fifth-form brother Oliver. Reed intertwines the two plots with great skill, linking them through the character of a corrupt sixth-former, and fluently moving from a serious account of Oliver's attempt to win the important Nightingale

Prize and to cope with accusations of cheating, to comical descriptions of Stephen's squabbles with his fellow-juniors. Reed's picture
of school-life contains touching glimpses of schoolboy honour, and
is much more realistic, amusing and secular than the insistently religious didacticism of earlier stories.

By the end of the nineteenth century, in other words, those values
loosely associated with the phrase 'muscular Christianity' had almost
disappeared. The ideal of the Christian Soldier Hero was being replaced by a different figure, a youth or man of honour certainly, and
certainly athletic, but more devoted to secular values such as patriotism and imperialism and loyalty than to Christianity.

The famous poem of 1898 about 'Clifton Chapel' by Sir Henry
Newbolt (1862-1938) ends not with thoughts of God but praise for
the public schoolboy who dies for his country:

> '*Qui procul hinc,*' the legend's writ, –
> The frontier grave is far away –
> '*Qui ante diem periit:*
> *Sed miles, sed pro patria.*' [21]

And in the same year his poem 'Vitai Lampada' memorably expresses
the way Christian values have been replaced by others:

> There's a breathless hush in the Close tonight –
> Ten to make and the match to win –
> A bumping pitch and a blinding light,
> An hour to play and the last man in.
> And it's not for the sake of a ribboned coat,
> Or the selfish hope of a season's fame,
> But the captain's hand on his shoulder smote
> 'Play up! play up! and play the game!'

> The sand of the desert is sodden red, –
> Red with the wrack of the square that broke; –
> The Gatling's jammed and the Colonel dead,
> And the regiment blind with dust and smoke.
> The river of death has brimmed his banks,
> And England's far, and Honour a name,
> But the voice of a schoolboy rallies the ranks:
> 'Play up! play up! and play the game!'

> This is the word that year by year,
> While in her place the School is set,
> Every one of her sons must hear,
> And none that hears it dare forget.

This they all with a joyful mind
Bear through life like a torch in flame,
And falling fling to the host behind –
'Play up! play up! and play the game!'[22]

As a final footnote to this discussion of 'muscular Christianity' and its influence on children's books in the nineteenth century, one cannot help observing that attendance of spectators at Lord's for Eton versus Harrow cricket matches which had reached the figure of 24,626 in 1871, had declined to 2,466 by 1972.[23] But that, as they say, is another story.

Chapter Four

Conflicting Loyalties: Ideology and Form in the Tales of G.A. Henty

Henty ... taught more lasting history to boys than all the schoolmasters of his generation.

(G. Manville Fenn)[1]

The great Education Acts of 1870 (England and Wales) and 1872 (Scotland) made elementary education compulsory for all children, and created an urgent need for school books. The firm of Blackie and Son (originally based in Scotland, but also operating from London by about 1860) was eager to meet this new demand and began educational publishing about 1879. Many Victorian schools and Sunday schools also began to award prizes to their pupils about this time, and, to quote Peter Newbolt, 'From educational publishing to "rewards" was a natural line of progression which it only took Blackie three years to follow.'[2] So Blackie began publishing 'Reward books', as well as educational books. One of their leading writers, Thomas Archer, introduced Henty, a friend and fellow club member, to the firm, and in 1882 Blackie's first catalogue of publications for the young included two of Henty's books for boys, *Facing Death* (1882) and *Under Drake's Flag* (1883).

George Alfred Henty was an experienced journalist and writer, as already noted. When the Crimean War broke out, he left Cambridge and joined the Hospital Commissariat of the army, reaching Balaclava in the spring of 1855 with his brother Fred. Working to organise provisions amid the chaos of the Crimean campaign, Henty visited the battlefield of Inkerman and also witnessed the siege of Sevastopol. During this time some of his letters home describing the war were seen by the editor of the *Morning Advertiser*, who invited him to contribute regularly to the paper, thus beginning Henty's career as a writer. His stint as Crimean war correspondent was to be relatively short-lived, however – in June 1855 Frederick died at Scutari during an outbreak of cholera, and Henty himself was invalided home after a severe illness shortly afterwards.

On his recovery Henty was sent abroad again to help to organise the hospitals of the Italian Legion, also serving in Belfast and Portsmouth before leaving the army. For the next few years he tried mining engineering in Wales and Sardinia before becoming in 1865 the special correspondent of the *Standard* newspaper, covering the Austro-Italian war in 1866. Henty followed this project by accompanying Lord Napier's expedition against King Theodore of Abyssinia in 1867-1868.

During these years Henty's career as a writer was taking off. In 1867 he published an adult novel *A Search for a Secret*, and in 1868 had several articles published in such magazines as the *Cornhill* and Dickens's *All the Year Round*. His despatches from Abyssinia also appeared as *The March to Magdala* (1868). Most important of all, during 1868 Henty seems to have written his first book for children, *Out on the Pampas*, the tale of a family settling in Argentina. Although the book was not published by Griffith and Farran until November 1870, there is little doubt that this is Henty's first book for juveniles, originally intended for his own children, Charles, Hubert, Maud and Ethel, whose names are shared by the main characters.[3] The book was no best-seller and soon Henty was busy reporting on the Franco-Prussian War. He was actually in Paris during the time of the Commune and was deeply affected by the whole conflict, using some of his experiences to write his second children's book *The Young Franc-Tireurs* (1872). There was a gap of eight years before Henty wrote for children again, for he revisited Russia, and then, in 1873, sailed with Sir Garnet Wolseley on the Ashanti Campaign, which again produced a book of despatches, *The March to Coomassie* (1874).

Revolution in Spain sent Henty off to report the struggles of the monarchy there, and a year later he reported on the tour of India made by the Prince of Wales. Shortly after, in 1876, the Turco-Serbian War broke out, and once more Henty's duties as a war correspondent claimed him. By the time the armistice was announced Henty was thoroughly worn out. Although he struggled on, his health broke down and he never worked as an active war correspondent again; he settled down to his last career as a professional storyteller.

Henty was writing in the heyday of British imperialism. In 1815 the British Empire had hardly existed. Although the West Indies supplied Britain with sugar, Australia was regarded as little more than a convict station, and on the African continent, European colonists were to be found only at Cape Colony, and even they were mainly Dutch. Canada was largely unexplored, and New Zealand was inhabited only by its indigenous population. India was the one major possession overseas Britain cared about, although at the time three quarters of what was to become the Raj was ruled by native princes and the rest by the East India Company. However, new forces were at work, and during Henty's lifetime Britain vastly extended its overseas territories, forming the New Zealand Colonisation Company, consolidating its control of India, and acquiring the whole of Burma and large areas of Africa, including Uganda, Nigeria and Zanzibar. The area over which Queen Victoria ruled in 1897, usually painted in red in British maps of the world, was four times greater than at her accession in 1837. Improvements in communications by railways, steamships and the electric telegraph, together with the availability of cheaper newspapers, made the British public more aware of affairs overseas. Newspaper reports from Special Correspondents, such as W.H. Russell of the *Times* and Henty himself, helped to sharpen the public consciousness of such events as the Charge of the Light Brigade, the Indian Mutiny, the Zulu Wars, and the Relief of Mafeking during the second Boer War.

The explorations of Captain Cook and Mungo Park in the late eighteenth and early nineteenth centuries, the dramatic encounter of Livingstone with Stanley in Africa in 1871, and the travels of such men as Sir Richard Burton all intensified the interest in adventures in exotic places. When the domestic economic situation seemed to offer only the grim alternatives of either unemployment or dreary factory work, many began to look overseas. As well as searching for opportunities of trading with British colonies, hundreds of thousands of Britons emigrated to America, Australia, Canada and South Africa, often because there was more scope for enterprise and even the possibility of adventure. By way of this dispersal of so many of its citizens, links between Britain and its great Empire overseas were gradually extended and strengthened.

Thus Henty's literary career coincided with the high tide of imperialism. Although there was significant debate on the question of empire, most Britons, under the leadership of imperialist politicians such as Benjamin Disraeli, Lord Salisbury and Lord Rosebery, generally supported the maintenance and expansion of British territorial possessions overseas, and endorsed the notion that the British Empire was an unrivalled instrument for peace and justice. In particular, many Victorian children, especially boys, partook of this interest in the Empire. Many expected to find work in the far reaches of the growing empire when they left school, be it in commerce, the armed forces or as public servants. For their part, many girls, according to the conventions of the age, were expected to become the loyal companions or helpmates of their husbands. The United Services College at Westward Ho! in Devon was actually founded to help prepare boys to serve in such countries as India, and it is no coincidence that Rudyard Kipling (1865-1936), who wrote so much about the British Empire, was a pupil there. In such a climate, it is no surprise that boys and girls clamoured for adventure stories, full of thrilling deeds in faraway places (generally under British control), in which the heroes and (less often) the heroines were young people like themselves.

G.A. Henty fitted enthusiastically into the literary tradition which endorsed these views – his works embodied the spirit of the age. As Kathryn Castle has said, 'Henty ... exemplified the ethos of the new imperialism, and glorified its military successes', and, to quote Mawuena Logan, Henty's works were popular because they 'reflect the attitudes, anxieties and aspirations of the Victorian people'.[4] Earlier writers, such as Captain Marryat, R.M. Ballantyne and W.H.G. Kingston had already produced children's books exploiting the appeal of adventure, but none of them matched Henty's passionate imperialism.

What kind of stories did Henty write for his youthful late-Victorian readers? We know from various accounts which he gave of his literary methods that when Henty began work on a story, he borrowed ten books from the London Library and read up on the appropriate historical background. He then worked in his study with two or three books around him and plenty of atlases. It was said he did not plan his stories in advance, but began work at half-past nine in the morning lying on his sofa and smoking, while dictating to his secretary. At one time Henty even used his secretary to provide synopses of the historical battles for his books. He usually worked in the mornings till one o'clock, and then in the evenings from half-past seven until ten. In this way Henty reckoned to produce 6,500 words in a fair day's work, and, though he often devoted six months of the year to his great hobby of yachting, could produce three books a year. The shortest time in which he wrote a book was the twenty-four days it took him to produce *With Buller in Natal* (1901), a story of 140,000 words.[5]

Not surprisingly, writing at such speed led to a heavy reliance on a formula-type approach, with the same elements recurring in volume after volume, whether the stories were of the distant past or of comparatively recent events. To begin with, the moral purpose of Henty's writing never changed. When in 1883 he lamented the closing of the weekly magazine, *The Union Jack*, which he had edited, he reminded his readers of the lessons he had tried to teach on every page, that 'lads should be true, honourable, manly and brave under all circumstances'.[6] Although Henty was never as Evangelical as earlier children's writers, he was almost as didactic as far as his ambition to teach moral behaviour was concerned.

Henty also wanted to teach history. In an article published in the *Boy's Own Paper* after his death, according to Guy Arnold, Henty said:

> The idea of writing historical books first occurred to me in consequence of the success which attended the production of *The Young Franc-Tireurs* which I wrote on the conclusion of the Franco-German War. I next wrote *The Young Buglers*, a story of the Peninsular War, and the result determined me to stick to historical stories, and if I lived long enough, to treat all the wars of England. My object has always been to write good history. Of course, to make it go down with boys it has to be mixed with a very large amount of personal adventure, but I have never permitted myself to deviate in the very slightest degree from historical facts, except where the boy hero is, so to speak, on the loose.[7]

Henty's stories are saturated with his belief in the British Empire, and these explicit values often form the basis of the *Prefaces* addressed to 'My Dear Lads' which are found at the beginning of many of his tales. Although Henty is not uncritical of aspects of British policy or of personal misbehaviour, his pride in the acquisition and administration of the British Empire clearly shines through. In his *Preface* to *St. George for England: A Tale of Cressy and Poitiers* (1885), for example, we read:

> My Dear Lads,
> You may be told perhaps that there is no good to be obtained from tales of fighting and bloodshed – that there is no moral to be drawn from such histories. Believe it not. War has its lessons as well as Peace. You will learn from tales like this that determination and enthusiasm can accomplish marvels, that true courage is generally accompanied by magnanimity and gentleness, and that if not itself the

very highest of virtues, it is the parent of almost all the
others, since but few of them can be practised without it.
The courage of our forefathers has created the greatest empire in the world around a small and in itself insignificant
island; if this empire is ever lost, it will be by the cowardice
of their descendants.[8]

The heroes of Henty's books are usually potentially 'manly' boys of
fourteen or so, of no great intellectual or social distinction, perhaps the
son of a clergyman or doctor, but endowed with a good deal of pluck.
Charlie Marryat, the hero *With Clive in India*, was described in chapter
three, and Yorke Harberton, the hero of *With Roberts to Pretoria: A
Tale of the South African War* (1902), is another example:

Yorke Harberton was ... nearly sixteen, and was a typical
public-school boy – straight and clean-limbed, free from
all awkwardness, bright in expression, and possessed of a
large amount of self-possession, or, as he himself would
have called it, "cheek"; was a little particular about the set
of his Eton jacket and trousers and the appearance of his
boots; as hard as nails and almost tireless; a good spec-
imen of the class by which Britain has been built up, her
colonies formed, and her battlefields won – a class in point
of energy, fearlessness, the spirit of adventure, and a read-
iness to face and overcome all difficulties, unmatched in
the world.[9]

These boy-heroes are not perfect, Henty says, and indeed quite often
get into trouble for offences like fighting a bully or neglecting school
rules, but they are intrinsically loyal and true, especially to their
mothers. They may forget an important cricket match, but they never
forget their friends, and their self-confidence may degenerate into
'cheek' but never into cowardice.

The other characters in Henty's works are less important but just
as stereotyped. Women generally appear as patient mothers, girls as
gentle sisters, and the pretty girl next door often survives to marry
the hero at the end of the story. But Henty was not crudely sexist,
and brave heroines play a prominent part in some stories, such as
The Plague Ship of 1889 and *A Soldier's Daughter* of 1906. The
hero's parents are usually shadowy figures typically dismissed from
the story quite soon after the beginning. Headmasters are sternly just,
but with a friendly twinkle in their eye to show their sympathy for
the hero's minor offences. Villains are often foreigners characterised
by two main features, physical cruelty and treachery, and generally

get their just deserts. Loyal and faithful servants, on the other hand, are generously rewarded, and sometimes accompany the hero on his return to England.

The story usually opens with some crucial incident in the hero's early boyhood which disturbs the expected tenor of his career. Ralph Conway's father's death is announced in the first chapter of *One of the 28th: A Tale of Waterloo* (1890), for example, leaving him with a widowed mother to protect, while Cuthbert Hartington's father dies and his estate is bankrupted at the beginning of *Two Sieges* (1916). Consequently, the hero is forced to make his own way from early on, and by the end of the novel has managed this, often by great feats of courage and enterprise, acquiring prize money, profits or rapid military promotion – and sometimes all three.

The hero's exploits typically involve battles and war, although it would be wrong to think of Henty only as a military writer. He could and did write about social disturbances, such as the Luddite Riots in *Through the Fray* (1886), and even the tales of war include much else, such as struggles against natural disasters or mysteries about missing wills and so on. There are even attempts at humour and romance. Henty's basic formula, however, usually led him to place his young hero in a historical situation of some importance and then interweave his adventures with those of known public events in the ways suggested by the novels of Sir Walter Scott. Thus Ned Hearn sails with Francis Drake on the Spanish Main in *Under Drake's Flag*, and Beric, the hero of Henty's Roman-era novel *Beric the Briton* (1893) actually becomes the Emperor Nero's librarian.

After a crisis near the beginning of the book, probably connected with the loss of a fortune or death of a parent, the young hero, who has already shown some taste of his mettle by defeating the school bully or catching a thief, sets off on a series of adventures in each of which he triumphs, before a great culminating crisis, which again is successfully surmounted and followed by a prosperous homecoming. Often, about half way through the narrative the hero is captured and thrown into prison. Thus the eponymous hero of *Jack Archer* (1883) is incarcerated by the Russians during the Crimean War, and Vincent in *With Lee in Virginia* (1890) is jailed by Union soldiers. Inevitably the hero quickly manages to escape, perhaps helped by his faithful servant, and eludes his pursuers. Frequently, at another point in the story a minor character will tell the story of his own adventurous life, partly as a contrast to the hero's activities, and partly, too, as a way of delaying the hero's own approaching crisis. There is often, although not always, a happy wedding to follow the hero's homecoming.

Henty did vary the pattern of these formulaic elements, some-times modifying the treatment of an episode, but the structure of his narrative is usually very consistent indeed. These story-patterns reproduce the same kind of structure – dealing with hero, quest, ad-ventures and homecoming – as are found in many traditional stories, from epics such as the *Odyssey* to modern folk-tales. The regular use of this familiar narrative structure offers readers many advantages, of course. Youthful readers, struggling with long and difficult books, having already read one of Henty's stories, can soon realise that they are on familiar ground. The reader is thus reassured psychologically, but may also achieve aesthetic pleasure as he or she learns to ap-preciate the skilful way in which the writer uses the formula.

With Kitchener in the Soudan: A Story of Atbara and Omdurman (1903) is a fairly typical example of the way Henty exploits his familiar formula and yet manages to freshen it up with imaginative variations. Fifteen-year-old Gregory is the only son of Mrs Hilliard, and they are living in Cairo anxiously longing for news of Gregory's father who disappeared on an expedition to the Soudan years earlier. When his mother dies, young Gregory – who is athletic and has already won a prize for fencing – leaves home to search for his miss-ing father. Because he has lived in Egypt for many years Gregory is able to utilise his knowledge of Arabic and other languages to make himself useful to the army, and joins General Kitchener's campaign to re-conquer the Soudan. He acquires a faithful native companion, Zaki, and, as the two proceed southwards, they have a number of adventures. Taken prisoner by the Dervishes, Gregory is released after the British victory at Atbara, and joins the final advance to the historical battle of Omdurman, when the army enter Khartoum. Gregory finally meets a native who remembers seeing some white prisoners captured years earlier, and with his help Gregory succeeds in retrieving his missing father's papers. At last Gregory discovers what happened to his father, and learns that he himself is now a Marquis.

Here we can see how Henty uses the adventure-story structure of the hero, the quest, the crisis, and the triumphant homecoming, in ways which are familiar and yet interestingly varied. The way the hero loses his parents follows the familiar literary conventions, but the story does have a slightly unusual opening with an extended account of the father's early career. The acquisition of a native com-panion is familiar, but the hero's special 'magical' gift, in this case his knowledge of Arabic, and the descriptions of the problems of Egypt and the Soudan are also slightly unusual features. The account of his journey from Cairo to Khartoum is a fresh and novel experience, but the successful military exploits, within the context of British imperialism, return the reader to familiar ground. Even the triumphant ending reveals a gentle surprise when Gregory discovers that he has inherited a title.

Henty's use and reliance on his narrative formula was enormously helped by his principal publisher, John Alexander Blackie. The firm of Blackie was large and diversified, and controlled the whole processes of printing, binding and publishing. This enabled it to develop a system of mass-production, whereby its books could be produced with considerable uniformity of print, page-size and even length. This standardisation meant that the binding-cases for all books could be planned in advance and so help to achieve great economy. Blackie published books in two price ranges, at five shillings or six shillings each. Those at five shillings had 352 pages, and those costing a shilling more contained 384 pages. Henty seems to have accepted these demands quite comfortably, for of the sixty-nine full-length books he wrote for Blackie, thirty-six were exactly 384 pages, and twenty-three reached precisely 352 pages. Six of his other ten books made totals of between 380 and 392 pages. Indeed, such practical matters may have been more help than hindrance – Henty was already an experienced journalist when he began to work for Blackie, used to writing for order; knowing an agreed length was expected probably encouraged him to produce his stories to a regular formula. It is clear that Henty got on well with his publisher, for after an initial contract with them in 1887, they renewed it with better terms in 1891.[10]

Henty's stories always work most smoothly as narratives when he is secure in his ideology, and his African novel *By Sheer Pluck; A Tale of the Ashanti War* (1884) for example, does so because it is, in Mawuena Logan's words 'a prime example of a colonialist point of view'.[11] But Henty's formula does not always work so well. It sometimes creaks a little, when, for instance, the stories reflect ideological tensions either within Henty himself or within British society in general.

Henty's treatment of the American War of Independence in *True to the Old Flag: American War of Independence* (1883) is an example of the way in which his adventure stories sometimes reflect the powerful divisions in Victorian society and the author. The story opens with the young British-American hero Harold Wilson growing up in Boston with his loyalist family. When war breaks out, Harold and his friends journey north to Canada to warn of an impending American attack. The warning is ignored and Washington triumphs at Trenton Ferry. There then follows a lengthy and curious interlude in which, after helping General Burgoyne capture Ticonderoga, Harold hears of the British defeat at Saratoga, but, realising there will be no further fighting until the following Spring, he decides to return to Canada again, and rescues a young girl who has been captured by the Iroquois. Fighting his way through blizzards and across frozen lakes, Harold has many adventures, but finally manages to outwit the Native Americans and returns safely to Detroit. (This has taken the reader to chapter 18 of the book's twenty-one chapters.) Harold now rejoins the British army in the South and helps in the defence of Savannah. He spends the rest of the war scouting for the British until Cornwallis's surrender at York Town. Harold then decides to leave Republican America and he settles down on a farm on the St. Lawrence in loyalist Canada.

It is obvious from even this brief summary of the plot of *True to the Old Flag* that something is not right with the novel. Henty has chosen to write a tale about the American War of Independence, but failed to treat the war with any kind of justice. References to George Washington, a fairly central figure one might have thought, are extremely thin in the book, and there is no mention at all of the heroic episode of Valley Forge. Defeats and victories are sometimes led up to with considerable preparation, but the ensuing battles are then often dealt with very briefly – only a single paragraph in the case of Trenton Ferry.

Most odd of all is the way Harold, the young hero, is simply detached from the major events of the war, while he goes off North enjoying adventures among the Iroquois reminiscent of Fenimore Cooper's *Leatherstocking* tales. In a book of twenty-one chapters, no fewer than ten are concerned with fighting the Indians, and even in the eleven chapters dealing with the War of Independence Harold is only marginally involved as a scout or an observer.

Thus, whereas in most of his historical novels Henty normally integrates the *personal* adventures of his fictitious young hero with the *historical* events of the story he is covering, here Henty portrays Harold's adventures as often quite independent of the great historical events with which he pretends to deal. Harold misses the battles of Lexington and Concord, attends Bunker's Hill only as a spectator, and then misses the battles of Philadelphia, Saratoga, Camden and York Town almost completely.

There is thus a sharp dislocation in the book between Harold's *personal* adventures, which are mainly accounts of triumphs and successes over the Indians, and the major *historical* events of the War, which are mainly accounts of British failures and disasters against the American colonists.

Henty was a passionate supporter of British imperialism, as we have seen, and his attitude towards the American War of Independence is naturally coloured by this doctrine. He thought that the British were right and that the Americans rebels were wrong. Although he admits that the British government did some foolish things, he was simply incapable of seeing that, as the fateful events of 1774-1775 unfolded, many Americans, brought up on the same ideas of *Magna Carta* and the 'Glorious Revolution' as he had been, felt that they were being deprived of rights to which they were entitled *as British citizens*.

Though an imperialist, Henty was like a Palmerstonian Whig, who wanted freedom for everyone abroad but not at home – for places like Greece and Italy which were ruled by foreigners, but not for British colonists. He would have approved of Patrick Henry's great cry – 'Give me liberty, or give me death!' – in almost every circumstance except the historical one in America.

Thus his account of the War is both partial and grudging. The British fought bravely in a just cause, but were incompetently led and overwhelmed by superior numbers. Henty simply finds it impossible to believe that the American colonists fought well because (like Burke and Chatham and Tom Paine) they believed in the justice of their cause, and because, with forces composed initially of farmers and shopkeepers, they were led against a professional army by men of character and genius like George Washington.

But British imperialism, even in Victorian Britain, was not greeted with the universal enthusiasm which is sometimes supposed. Burke and Chatham had expressed doubts about the British treatment of the American colonies in the eighteenth century, and a line stretching from Cobbett via John Stuart Mill and Godwin Smith to W.S. Blunt and Bernard Shaw continued throughout the nineteenth century. 'How is it possible for us to justify our conduct upon any principle of morality?' asked Cobbett about the British treatment of India in 1808; and in 1896 Shaw said of the Englishman:

> He is never at a loss for an effective moral attitude. As the great champion of freedom and natural independence, he conquers and annexes half the world and calls it Colonisation.... There is nothing so bad or so good that you will not find an Englishman doing it; but you will never find an Englishman in the wrong. He does everything on prin-

ciple. He fights you on patriotic principles; he robs you on business principles; he bullies you on manly principles; he supports his king on loyal principles and cuts off his king's head on republican principles. His watchword is always Duty; and he never forgets that the nation which lets its duty get on the opposite side to its interest is lost.[12]

When Lord Cornwall is surrendered after the battle of York Town, and the British regiments, after laying down their arms, marched back to camp, their military bands played a series of melancholy tunes including one which everyone recognised as 'The World Turned Upside Down'. Henty knew that if the American cause were just, the result of the American War of Independence threatened the whole basis of British imperialism from Canada to India, and from Australia to South Africa. Understanding the dissonance of Henty's position helps to explain the fractured structure of *True to the Old Flag*. It is as if Henty's intellectual honesty and objectivity as a historian obliged him to record those dull chapters of military and imperial disaster in America, while his emotional and patriotic sympathy compelled him to seek consolation in those often historically irrelevant chapters recounting Harold's triumphs over the native Indians in Canada.

Structural deviations in Henty's novel about the American Civil War reveal similar ideological difficulties. The main plot of *With Lee in Virginia: A Story of the American Civil War* (1890) is one of his most interesting, for in telling the tale of his young hero, Vincent Wingfield, the story of a plantation-owner who becomes a scout in Lee's southern army, Henty not only gives his readers the usual mixture of dash and danger, heroic exploits, escapes and successes, but also handles Vincent's moral development with a skill not always found in his other books.

To begin with, although Vincent is always likeable, he is often impetuous and thoughtless. (He is only aged fifteen.) Although he tries to protect the slave, Dan, from a beating, his mother points out that such interference, however well-meant, only undermines the overseer's authority in the job he was hired to do. When Vincent anticipates the time he will be old enough to give orders legitimately, his sisters sharply point out that he will need to change a good deal because at present he only seems to be interested in horse-riding.

Although we are meant to admire Vincent's generous impulses, we are also meant to feel that he lacks judgement. But when he joins Lee's Confederate army, he begins to learn to balance his lively spirits with more prudence. His sisters comment on the change that is taking place in him. The patience and courtesy with which he treats Lucy Kingston, who nurses him when he is wounded, marks another stage in his development. When he learns that another slave has been kidnapped, he no longer takes the law into his own hands, but consults a lawyer, and takes out a legal warrant for the criminal's arrest. Then, as the Civil War nears its close with the defeat of the South, Vincent, in a crowning act of his new responsibility, persuades his mother not only to free their slaves immediately, but also to give them land and wages, so that the dangers of sudden and anarchical freedom will be avoided. Vincent marries the young woman who nursed him, and becomes master of his estate, of course: due reward for his bravery in the war but also for his gradual growth to maturity and for his moral qualities. Vincent is one of Henty's most sustained attempts at the depiction of moral development, and the attempt is not without some success.

But, as well as using the military events of the American Civil War as part of the historical context for Vincent's adventures, Henty also uses plantation life and slavery in the South to depict its social context. And here, although Henty praises the magnanimity of Grant and Sherman in places, as well as criticising the cruelty of some slave-owners, Henty's ideological position is that of a liberal-minded supporter of the South. Indeed, in the American-Scribner edition of the story, in a preface 'To My Many Readers Beyond the Atlantic', he confesses that 'I have written this story from the Confederate point of view.'[13] This means that, while not uncritical of the worst aspects of slavery, Henty basically defends slavery as a tolerable social system. 'The slave with a fairly kind master is to the full as happy as the ordinary English labourer', Vincent's father says,[14] and that this is not simply the dramatically appropriate opinion of a plantation-owner is confirmed a few pages later by the author's own comment: 'taken all in all the negroes on a well-ordered estate, under kind masters, were probably a happier class of people than the labourers upon any estate in Europe'.[15]

Henty is not completely starry-eyed about the situation. He denounces physical cruelty to slaves, and dislikes the practice of separating families through the sales of mothers, fathers, and their children to different owners. He shrewdly saw that it was often the small farmers with fewer than twenty slaves who did more harm than the wealthier and more patrician owners of large plantations.

Henty's views are inadequate, even if we see that he was not a simple-minded racist. His view of slaves is that of the sentimental stereotype. The negroes are 'very like children and indulgence would spoil them', says Mr Wingfield,[16] and we are told that they are 'naturally indolent and shiftless'.[17] With good masters, their condition is better than Europeans, we are told repeatedly, not least because 'the climate was a lovely one'.[18] (Over 100 degrees in the shade!) Henty simply disregards many of the realities of the situation. The widespread cruelty, sexual exploitation of female slaves, and the entire economic basis for slavery are all virtually ignored or minimised. Why, if they were so happy, to paraphrase Augustin Taveau, a planter from South Carolina, did even the loyal family slaves desert their masters at the moment of their greatest need? Why did slavery collapse in the way it did, if the slaves liked it so much?[19]

But if we read *With Lee in Virginia* and find it, in Marxist terms, only an articulation of the dominant slave-owning ideology, we do Henty and his class a disservice. For Henty is so interesting a subject for study because he is in many ways representative of the Victorian *bourgeoisie*, with all its virtues as well as its faults, with its genuine compassion as well as its materialism. Victorian Britain was in fact deeply divided over the issue of slavery and the war between the States.

'The ruling classes, especially the millowners and cotton merchants, regarded the secession of the southern states as another movement of national self-determination, and cherished strong sympathies for the southern aristocratic communities', says the historian David Thomson. He adds, however, that 'The working classes in general, led by the Radicals, saw that slavery was an issue involved in the Civil War, and that the future of constitutional government and national unity lay with the forces of Lincoln and the North'.[20]

Describing the divisions in British society even more succinctly, E. Halévy says, 'So far as generalisations can be made, upper-class opinion and opinion in Southern England favoured, without necessarily approving the Southern cause. Radical, middle and working-class opinion was strong for the North.'[21]

An analysis of the narrative structure of *With Lee in Virginia* shows how Henty's story reflects these divisions over the issue of slavery in Britain. For the account of Vincent's career and moral development is accompanied and almost paralleled by a sub-plot about slave-characters in ways which surely reflect British unease about slavery in America. Indeed, this sub-plotting is done with such skill and emphasis as to threaten to undermine Henty's whole *apologia* for the South. There is, in fact, a tension between the main plot, which contains Henty's defence of slavery, with the subplot which asks challenging questions about it.

From the very first chapter Vincent's adventures involve him directly with slaves, such as when he intervened to help Dan escape a beating. From then on, it is possible to construct a story revealing the courage, ingenuity, and sufferings of slaves which runs throughout the novel, and which contradicts Henty's stereotyping of them as childlike, lazy and well-treated. Indeed, this sub-plotting is so strong as to play a substantial part in sixteen of the book's twenty chapters.

After Dan's beating in the first chapter, the next three chapters deal with Tony, another slave, who is so ill-treated by his overseer Jackson that Vincent helps him escape to Canada. Tony's wife Dinah is then sold by Jackson in order to punish Tony, but she becomes a loyal servant to the Wingfields, and nurses Vincent when he is hit by shrapnel. The slave Dan re-appears to help Vincent escape from prison in chapter 10, and accompanies him on his long journey south. It is the ex-slave Tony, now a sergeant in the Union army, who helps Vincent escape again when he is caught spying, and likely to be executed. There is, of course, considerable symbolism present in the parallel between Vincent helping the slave escape in chapter 3, and the slave helping Vincent to escape in chapter 19.

Thus, through these stories of the slaves Dan and Tony, and the sufferings of Tony's wife Dinah (sold and separated from her husband in chapter 2 and then kidnapped in chapter 14), Henty reveals a somewhat different picture of slavery from the views he expresses elsewhere, and does something to redress the simplistic nature of his more explicitly stated attitudes. In a story which is full of journeys, you could say that the journeys of the main plot deal with the battles of the Civil War, while the journeys of the sub-plot deal with slavery and imprisonment – both Vincent's own escape from prison and his attempts to free the slaves. Thus the structure of the book oscillates between battle-journeys in support of slavery and secession, and slave-journeys in support of abolition and the Union. There is clear conflict between the story's professed ideology and its narrative form.

It was by its stamina and robust energy that Victorian society was able to contain so many contradictory impulses within itself, and in examining the works of G.A. Henty we see the same, sometimes contradictory, energy. Henty used the popular form of the boys' adventure story to articulate some of the most powerful ideologies of Victorian England, but the displacements and tensions found in the fractured structures of some of his stories reveal the contradictions and divisions which lay behind some of those ideologies.

Chapter Five

Rider Haggard and the Pattern of Defeat

We did not notice the melancholy end of every adventure….
(Graham Green, 'Rider Haggard's Secret')[1]

The work of Charles Kingsley and G.A. Henty largely celebrated the values of the society in which they lived, although the fractured narrative structure of some of Henty's stories reveal a number of the contradictions of the age. Rider Haggard, on the other hand, so typical a staunch supporter of the status quo in many ways, went on to question and to challenge its values, particularly in his later works.

In 1885 Henry Rider Haggard was an ex-colonial administrator and unsuccessful writer, studying to become a lawyer. But, as the result of a bet with his brother, he accepted the challenge to write an adventure story as good as Stevenson's *Treasure Island*, and proceeded to write *King Solomon's Mines* – in a period of only six weeks, he later claimed.[2]

Although Haggard's earlier novels had failed, the enthusiastic advice of Andrew Lang and W.E. Henley persuaded Cassell's, who had also published *Treasure Island*, to accept the manuscript, and the book caused a sensation when it first appeared on September 30th 1885. Advertised as 'THE MOST AMAZING BOOK EVER WRITTEN', the story was warmly welcomed both by the reviewers and the general public alike. *The Athenaeum* called it 'one of the best books for boys – old or young – which we remember to have read', and the American *Book Buyer* said 'we cannot recall a bit of modern fiction to equal it'. Sales of the six shillings, one volume novel were quite remarkable. In England alone *King Solomon's Mines* sold 31,000 copies during the first twelve months, as compared with total sales of fewer than a thousand for Haggard's first two novels, while in America at least thirteen different editions appeared before the year was out.[3] The book has remained in print ever since, and remains a landmark, not only among all Haggard's works, but among nineteenth-century adventure stories generally.

Though Haggard had ambitions to be a public servant, he would not have been unhappy at this result. Born in Norfolk in 1856, the son of a barrister and country gentleman, he seems to have had an undistinguished childhood and adolescence, and, after failing an army entrance examination, was sent to a private 'crammer' in London in order to prepare for the Foreign Office entrance examination. Then, quite unexpectedly, his father found him a post on the staff of Sir Henry Bulwer, the Lieutenant-Governor of Natal in South Africa, and Haggard's experiences there from 1875 onwards seemed to have played a crucial role in his development. His duties introduced him to all sorts of people – Boer farmers, British politicians, Zulu natives – and he travelled about the country at a critical stage in its history, during which Britain annexed the Boer province of Transvaal, and fought the Zulu War of 1879 and the Boer War of 1880. He witnessed native ceremonies, talked to survivors of the Battle of Isandhlwana, where the Zulus defeated a British army, and saw his farm actually used for the peace negotiations at the end of the war of 1880.

But Haggard was unhappy at the political developments after the war, and, by now a married man with a son, returned to England with his family and began to study law. He had already written some magazine articles while in Africa, and now published several books while he was studying: *Cetewayo and his White Neighbours* (1882),[4] a serious account of the recent events in Africa, and two novels: *Dawn* (1884) and *The Witch's Head* (1885). Although the books received a few favourable notices, none sold at all well, so Haggard persevered with his legal plans and tried to re-enter the Colonial Service.

The tremendous popularity of *King Solomon's Mines*, however, as well as that of its immediate successors, *Allan Quatermain* and *Jess* (both 1887), persuaded Haggard to give up practising as a lawyer. Although he was never entirely happy with his career as an author and often longed for a life of public service, he accepted the situation, and concentrated upon earning his living through his writing. Other literary successes followed, amongst them being *She* (1887), the story of a beautiful, immortal queen; *Maiwa's Revenge* (1888), another story about Allan Quatermain; and *Cleopatra* (1889), a tale of ancient Egypt.

Though desolated by the death of his only son Jock in 1891, Haggard continued to write, but also began to play a part in public affairs. He stood unsuccessfully as a Parliamentary candidate in 1895, investigated the state of English agriculture in 1901, and served on various Parliamentary Royal Commissions. In 1912 he was knighted for his public services, and in 1914 revisited South Africa as part of a Royal Commission reporting on the British Dominions.

The novels continued to appear, and although there was some falling-off in the popularity of his work in the early years of the twentieth century, he produced a notable trilogy on the history of the Zulu people in *Marie* (1912), *Child of Storm* (1913) and *Finished* (1917). He enjoyed a particularly warm friendship with Rudyard Kipling in the last years of his life, before dying in 1925.

Rider Haggard published sixty-eight books altogether, including novels about contemporary life, such as *Love Eternal* (1918); works of non-fiction such as *Rural England* (1902); and historical novels such as *Cleopatra*. He is best remembered, however, for his stories about Africa. His early experiences there, the people he met, the journeys he made, the scenes he witnessed – all gave him a wealth of memories, anecdotes, and legends to draw upon. These not only provided him with the materials for his best novels but helped to shape his view of life.

King Solomon's Mines is a magnificent example of his work. The story begins onboard ship when Allan Quatermain, a big-game hunter sailing from Cape Town to Natal, meets two fellow-passengers, Sir Henry Curtis and Captain John Good. Curtis asks for Quatermain's help in searching for his younger brother, George, who has disappeared after going north in search of the fabulous treasures of King Solomon's Mines. Somewhat reluctantly Quatermain agrees to accompany the expedition, and, with the help of an impressive native, Umbopa, they make their way through real places into Matabele country, and then across desert and mountain into the fictitious Kukuanaland. A bloodthirsty tyrant rules here, with the help of his witch-like adviser, and when she demands the execution of Umbopa, civil war breaks out and a tremendous conflict follows. Eventually, Allan and his party triumph, but encounter many more surprises and dangers before returning home successfully.

We are, in other words, once again in the familiar world of the Adventure Story for Boys, a form which which grew rapidly in the nineteenth century, partly as a reflection of Britain's emergence from the Napoleonic Wars as a great military and imperial power. These stories, often exploiting the appeal of exotic parts of the Empire, such as Africa or India, and based upon an unquestioning assumption of British superiority over all foreigners, especially natives, developed those well-tried narrative patterns firmly established in the works of such writers as G.A. Henty. In their use of formulaic elements, it is clear that these stories owe a great deal to the structure of traditional folk and fairy tales, in which similar patterns tend to repeat themselves. V. Propp has shown, for example, how Russian folk-tales contain many features common to West European stories, such as the English tale of *Dick Whittington* or the universal *Jack the Giant Killer*, where a young hero, often with the help of a companion, and in possession of a magical gift such as a ring, leaves home to accomplish some great feat before returning triumphantly. Such stories, in their mixture of the realistic and the marvellous, their narration of the hero's journey as a Quest, and the frequently happy ending, may also owe something to the early romances, such as the tale of Galahad's search for the Grail in Malory's *Morte Darthur* (1485).[5]

The presence of this familiar structure of the folk-tale is very clearly seen in *King Solomon's Mines*. A preliminary section introduces the hero, establishes the purpose of the Quest, and describes the preparations for the journey. Then the hero and his helpers make their way to the appointed place, in this case literally a faraway kingdom, where they struggle with, and achieve victory over a villain, and finally make a successfully journey home. Rider Haggard's story-pattern is thus very familiar in its treatment of hero, Quest, struggle, and homecoming, containing the same elements as are found in many traditional tales and nineteenth-century adventure stories, essentially offering readers the same kind of psychological reassurance via familiar ingredients as are found there.

Rider Haggard, however, uses and develops these familiar elements with imagination, sophistication and feeling. Thus, while part of the pleasure the reader experiences when reading the book for the first time is recognition of the *familiar*, which brings that sense of reassurance so important to young readers, at the same time Rider Haggard's manipulation of these elements can make them seem *unfamiliar* and thus disturbing. In this way, by a combination of the familiar and unfamiliar, he creates the kinds of tensions appropriate to an adventure story.

Although Rider Haggard may have become a storyteller almost by accident, he thought intelligently about what he was trying to do and about the best means of achieving success, as his autobiography reveals. He was interested in writing romance, not realistic novels, and for that purpose, he said

> The really needful things are adventure – how impossible
> it matters not at all, provided it is made to appear possible –

and imagination, together with a clever use of coincidence
and an ordered development of plot, which should, if possible, have a happy ending, since few people like to be
saddened by what they read [6]

King Solomon's Mines is full of wonderfully imaginative inven-
tions – the map drawn in the old explorer's blood, the character of
the witch Gagool, the eclipse, the Hall of the Dead – all rendered
credible by a variety of techniques skilfully deployed, such as the
use of apparently authoritative editorial footnotes, and the facsimile
of the map and of Don José's letter. What convinces the reader of the
veracity of the tale above all, however, is the tone of the sensible, level-
headed, rather cautious middle-aged narrator, Allan Quatermain, for
this invites the reader's complete confidence.

The use of the hero as narrator is not completely new in the
nineteenth-century adventure story – Jim Hawkins tells his tale in
Stevenson's *Treasure Island*, for instance – but the fact that here he is
a man of 55 rather than a youth is the first of the variations Haggard
plays on the adventure-story formula, and, as the tale continues, he
rises to almost every challenge. Allan Quatermain's companions, Sir
Henry Curtis and Captain Good, are given marked individuality. Sir
Henry is a chivalrous aristocrat of heroic mould, whose brotherhood
with Umbopa is frequently insisted upon, in ways which many Victorians may have found disconcerting. Captain Good, on the other
hand, with his vanity over his personal appearance and his white legs,
would be almost a comic figure by contrast, were it not for his tragic
relationship with the young native woman Foulata.

The journey is described with a wealth of convincing details from
the moment the party fit out the expedition in Durban, through the
thousand miles to Sitanda's Kraal and the disastrous elephant hunt,
and then the account of the crossing of the desert to the final assault
on the freezing mountains and the descent into Kukuanaland. The
expedition's arrival in Kukuanaland brings another variation on the
formula of the folk-tale, for, whereas the traditional hero almost in-
variably has some type of supernatural assistance – a Chinese lamp,
some magic beans, an extraordinary cat – Allan Quatermain's party
are able to impress with the 'magic' of Captain Good's false teeth
and Quatermain's rifle-shooting.

Rider Haggard introduces another dramatic variation into the traditional structure of the adventure story by way of the sudden change
in the role of Umbopa. Allan Quatermain has been suspicious of him
from the beginning. What is he up to? Is he a potential traitor? But

various hints have been given to the reader that Umbopa is greater than he seems: Sir Henry Curtis admires and trusts him, for example. And then in chapter VIII we learn of the disappearance of the last King of Kukuanaland's baby, and in chapter X Umbopa reveals himself as the missing true heir to the throne.

Infandoos and the other chiefs ask for a sign that Ignosi, to give Umbopa his real name, is their proper ruler, and this enables Haggard to repeat the use of 'magic' through Captain Good's promise of an eclipse and its devastating effects. The confrontation between Ignosi's followers and Twala's army, wonderfully told in chapters XII to XIV, leads to the expected triumph, but then Rider Haggard enriches his tale with unexpected complexities by introducing a new crisis created by Allan Quatermain's party's search for the treasure-hoard and by Gagool's treachery. Even then Haggard's narrative invention is not exhausted, for, in the final chapter, the expedition, which had initially set out in search of Henry Curtis's long-lost brother but seems to have forgotten all about him, makes one last breath-taking discovery.

All of this is superbly done. Rider Haggard believed that the writing of adventure stories should be 'swift, clear, and direct, with as little padding and as few trappings as possible', and he practised what he preached.[7] He believed that if a book had what he called 'grip', his word perhaps for narrative energy and suspense, it excused all faults, and to obtain this he felt that a story should be written rapidly, so that the writer could preserve its atmosphere while it was being evolved. 'The way to write a good romance is to sit down and write it almost without stopping', he said.[8] In this way he makes his readers feel the heat of the desert, see an elephant charging, and hear the native regiments salute by drumming their shields with their spears.

Allan Quatermain (1887), another African romance about the great hunter and his companions, follows similar lines. The story begins as a quest when Allan grieving for the loss of his son Harry, decides to leave his Yorkshire home and set out for Africa once more with his old friends from the great journey in *King Solomon's Mines*, Sir Henry Curtis and Captain John Good. This time their search is not for treasure but to discover whether the tales of a great white race living north of Mount Kenia are true. From North-East Africa the party strike inland, acquiring a remarkable Zulu warrior, Umslopagaas, on the way. They have a series of exciting adventures, fighting a fierce battle with Masai warriors, undergoing a terrifying subterranean journey, and discovering the lost civilisation before they are caught up in a passionate love-triangle, and finally become engulfed in a ferocious civil war.

Using Quatermain as his narrator again, Haggard gradually draws the reader into the familiar structure of the traditional romance with great originality and insight. The search for a mysterious civilisation has haunted travellers and explorers throughout the ages, and Haggard describes the quest with wonderfully dramatic and poetic touches, made all the more convincing because it is the level-eyed Quatermain who narrates them. The grim encounter with the Masai, the defence of the fortified mission station, the escape from the Rose of Fire, and Umslopagaas's breath-taking exploits with his battle-axe Inkosi-kaas, all demonstrate those qualities which Robert Louis Stevenson called 'the plastic parts of literature', by which he meant the power of the writer to embody character, thought or emotion in some action or attitude that is striking to the mind's eye. Stevenson cited as memorable examples Robinson Crusoe recoiling from the footprint in the sand and Ulysses bending his great bow at the end of the *Odyssey*.[9]

What gave Rider Haggard's romances their power and popularity in the closing decades of the nineteenth century, however, was more than this; it was the way such stories as *King Solomon's Mines* and *Allan Quatermain* gave powerful expression, often through symbolical journeys into Africa and the past, to late-Victorian concerns with evolution, race and sexuality.

Right from his childhood Haggard had been acutely conscious of the imminence of death. His daughter tells the story of how, when he was barely 13, he woke up one night in his moonlit bedroom, and looked at his hand:

> How odd it looked in the moonlight, dead – dead. Then it happened. He realised that one day that hand would be limp also, that he could not lift it any more – it would be dead. The awful, inescapable certainty hung over him like a pall of misery. He felt it would be better if he died at once – he wished he were dead, rather than have to live with that in front of him.[10]

In addition to this tendency towards a melancholy temperament, Rider Haggard grew up in the post-Darwinian climate of opinion. The publication of *The Origin of Species* in 1859 seemed to many people to challenge Christian belief and to reveal a world in which the fittest to survive were not necessarily the noblest or the best. At home, Haggard, the son of a country squire, who was passionately devoted to the land, saw these beliefs confirmed in the collapse of British agriculture in the last decades of the nineteenth century. Haggard prided himself upon his knowledge of agriculture and the countryside, topics he had researched and nearly always wrote well about, especially in *A Farmer's Year* of 1901 and his *Rural England* (1902). In the last years of the nineteenth century the importation of cheap food from overseas and a succession of bad harvests brought a severe depression to British farming. Many went bankrupt and thousands left the land. Lord Ernle, for example, describes how a hamlet in Wiltshire, which had contained a chapel, fourteen cottages and a school in the 1880s, was 'grass-grown' and almost obliterated by 1921. Between 1872 and 1900 over 2 ½ million acres of arable land were turned over to grass and pasture, and in 1895 the price of wheat fell to its lowest figure for 150 years. All these changes signalled the end of a way of life which with all its social customs had existed for centuries.[11]

What Haggard saw in Africa confirmed his pessimism, for it is clear that in the decline of earlier civilisations found in many of his African romances Haggard also found powerful images of contemporary decline and transience. The ruins the explorers find surrounding King Solomon's Mines, perhaps based upon the recent archaeological discoveries of the Great Zimbabwe, suggest the decay of an earlier civilisation. In *Allan Quatermain* the travellers come across the remains of many cities, which speak eloquently not only of a glory that has disappeared but of a future decline:

> Gone! Quite gone! The way that everything must go. Like the nobles and the ladies who lived within their gates, these cities have had their day, and now they are as Babylon and Nineveh, and as London and Paris will one day be. Nothing may endure. That is the inexorable law. Men and women, empires and cities, thrones, principalities, and powers, mountains, rivers, and unfathomed seas, worlds, spaces, and universes, all have their day, and all must go.[12]

Haggard's account of the lost civilisation of the Zu-Vendi in *Allan Quatermain* furthermore enables him to offer a critique of trends within Victorian Britain, and to offer an alternative vision of society. Anti-capitalist and anti-industrialist himself, Haggard cannot resist praising the superiority of the agriculturally-based civilisation of the Zu-Vendi, with its feudal organisation and its social classes of territorial nobility, middle classes and well-to-do peasants, all clearly distinguished by their dignified and attractive modes of dress. These kind and light-hearted people also care little about money, we are told. Haggard cannot help contrasting this country's mild and just laws, which treat offences against people more severely than crimes against property, with the English system, which does the opposite; and he is also surprisingly tolerant of polygamy, and even of heavy taxation, which seems to fund an early form of unemployment benefit. It is not surprising that Sir Henry Curtis intends to try and stop foreigners from entering this secluded kingdom, and that he is dedicated to protecting its upright and generous-hearted people from the blessings of barbarism. 'I have no fancy to hand over this beautiful country to be torn and fought over by speculators, tourists, politicians and teachers, whose voice is as the voice of Babel', he says.[13]

In depicting the ruling house of his imaginary kingdom, however, Haggard cannot help revealing certain Victorian attitudes towards women and sexuality. The Zu-Vendi are ruled by two sisters, Nyleptha, who is fair with golden hair and grey eyes, and Sorais, who is dark, with black hair and cruel lips. The contrast between what Leslie Fiedler has called the Fair Maiden and the Dark Lady, the sinless blonde and the passionate brunette, has a long history. Walter Scott compares Rowena with Rebecca in *Ivanhoe* (1820), and J. Fenimore Cooper similarly portrays the sisters Cora and Alice in *The Last of the Mohicans* (1826).[14] However, Haggard's use of the same motifs in *Allan Quatermain* may have gained particular intensity from Victorian male anxieties about the emergence of the 'New Woman'. To give just two examples, London University began to admit women to degrees in 1878, while Ibsen's *A Doll's House*, with its portrayal of the rebellious Nora, appeared a year later. Like many of his contemporaries who resisted female suffrage, Haggard seems to have been disturbed by fears of the combination of clever women and sexuality. Nyleptha is spotless and almost passive, but Sorais is both attractive and proactive. She boldly declares her passion for Curtis, but when she cannot get what she wants she throws her lot in with the Archpriest Agon and the ambitious prince Nasta, out of a mixture of envy and revenge. Sandra Gilbert and Susan Gubar have argued that Haggard mediates various anxieties about female power in his adult novel *She* (1887), and it is difficult to avoid feeling that here in *Allan Quatermain* Haggard is suggesting that Nyleptha is good because she is passive and 'feminine' in showing weaknesses, but that Sorais is forceful and threatening, and so must be destroyed.[15]

What is also clear is how often a pattern of defeat runs through all Rider Haggard's books. Although the romances may appear to end in triumph, Haggard's stories observe what Graham Green has called 'the melancholy end of every adventure'.[16] Both Allan Quatermain and Umslopagaas die at the end of *Allan Quatermain*; Ayesha destroys herself in the flames in *She*. Eric Brighteyes plunges over a cliff to his death and Nada the Lily is immured in a cave. Antony and Cleopatra commit suicide in *Cleopatra*, while Isobel is killed in a Zeppelin raid and her husband dies of grief in *Love Eternal*.

Even in *King Solomon's Mines*, despite the apparently successful (and quasi-imperialistic) restoration of order in Kukuanaland, and the safe homecoming of Allan Quatermain and his party, one is aware of a melancholy note. There are so many deaths, not only of the villains, Twala and Gagool, and their supporters, but also of the regiment of 'Greys' and Foulata, and the faithful servants, Khiva and Ventvogel. Allan Quatermain's wife is long dead, and his son seems far away. The tone is surely elegiac.

Most powerfully of all, Rider Haggard found in the history of black people, particularly the Zulus, an almost perfect metaphor to express his profound sense of human tragedy. Although, as Wendy Katz has pointed out, Rider Haggard shared many of the racist assumptions of his Victorian contemporaries, revealed, for example, in Quatermain's discomfort over Captain Good's relationship with Foulata, his admiration for natives goes well beyond contemporary attitudes.[17] Haggard knew perfectly well that the African way of life was not perfect; it was often arbitrarily cruel and crudely superstitious, but Haggard was able to appreciate and express the richness of its social organisations and customs, and the dignity of its people, in ways which were not surpassed until the novels of the great Nigerian writer Chinua Achebe began to appear after World War II.

Rider Haggard not only wrote out of personal experience, from his own work and travels in Africa during the years in which Britain fought the Zulu War of 1879, but also benefited from knowing many of the figures who took part in the dramatic events he described – Zulu warriors such as Mazooku and Umslopagaas, and British statesmen such as Sir Theophilus Shepstone (Secretary for Native Affairs in Natal) and Sir Melmoth Osborne (British resident in Zululand). Thus he was almost uniquely qualified to convey in the form of popular fiction the history of the rise and fall of the Zulu people, in a series of novels beginning with *Nada the Lily* (1892), and ending with the trilogy *Marie, Child of Storm* and *Finished*.

Nada the Lily is a violent and passionate tale about the young Zulu warrior Umslopagaas and his love-affair with the beautiful white maiden, Nada the Lily. Haggard uses poetic licence to suggest that Umslopagaas was the son of Shaka, the first great Zulu leader at the beginning of the nineteenth century. So we read of Shaka's rise to greatness and the military genius by which from 1816 he converted his small and insignificant clan in the Transvaal into one of the greatest. We learn of his great love for his mother, and his grief at her death, when he caused thousands to perish. Finally, Shaka's two brothers Dingaan and Umhlangana kill him, and eventually Dingaan becomes king.

The story is amplified in *Marie, Child of Storm* and *Finished*, Haggard's trilogy on the history of the Zulu people. *Marie* is an adventure story about Haggard's old hero, Allan Quatermain. In the 1830s, we are told, Allan fell in love with Marie, the daughter of a Boer settler, and became involved in the Boers' attempt to deal with the Zulus and find land in Natal. But Dingaan, the Zulu king, proves to be unreliable. Despite Allan's warnings, the Boer leader and historical figure Piet Retief tries to negotiate with the Zulus, but is betrayed and brutally massacred along with his supporters at Weenen, the Place of Weeping.

Child of Storm, the second story in the trilogy, is set in the 1850s, during the reign of Dingaan's successor, Panda. Allan Quatermain becomes involved in the civil war which erupts between the two Zulu brothers Cetewayo and Umbelazi over the succession to King Panda. Allan actually prefers Umbelazi and fights for him in the battle between the brothers at Tugela River, but Cetewayo wins a great victory and becomes King Panda's successor.

Peace was not, however, to be the lot of the Zulus under their new king. Just before Shaka was killed by his two brothers in *Nada the Lily*, he made a great prophecy:

> Do you slay me, thinking to possess the land and to rule it? I tell you it shall not be for long. I hear a sound of running feet – the feet of a great white people. They shall stamp you flat, children of my father! They shall rule the land that I have won, and you and your people shall be their slaves![18]

Finished, the last book in Haggard's trilogy, shows how Shaka's prophecy came true. The story opens in 1877 with the British annexation of the Transvaal (an event at which Rider Haggard was actually present) and tells of the adventures of Allan Quatermain and his friend Maurice Anscombe, as they gradually become involved in the war between the Zulus and the British. Allan sees a good deal of King Cetewayo and actually attends the Great Council where the Zulus reject the British ultimatum, which demanded heavy fines and the dismantling of the Zulu army. When the British army under Lord Chelmsford then marched on the Zulus, they left their defences poorly organised, and suffered a great reverse at the Battle of Isandhlwana, when the Zulus killed well over a thousand of Lord Chelmsford's force, though at great cost to themselves.

Allan manages to escape from the battlefield, only later hearing about the heroic defence of Rorke's Drift, at which no fewer than eleven Victoria Crosses were won. After the Zulus are finally defeated at the Battle of Ulundi and Sir Garnet Wolseley sets up a British-controlled government in Zululand, Allan returns to Cetewayo's kraal and again meets the king who is now dying – an apt symbol of his people, for Shaka's prophecy has come true and the greatness of the Zulu race is indeed finished.

When this happened, Haggard felt that a great civilisation had been destroyed – a fact Andrew Lang recognised when he called *Nada the Lily* 'the epic of a dying people'.[19] Haggard depicts the Zulus with all their vices as well as their virtues, but he lends particular emphasis to their courage and their loyalty. He has no doubt that with their decline and that of their traditional way of life, something of value has been lost, certainly when compared with their modern plight. As he wrote in *Child of Storm*,

> ... by what exact right do we call people like the Zulus savages? Setting aside the habit of polygamy, which, after all, is common among very highly civilised peoples in the East, they have a social system not unlike our own. They have, or had their king, their nobles, and their commons. They have an ancient and elaborate law, and a system of morality in some ways as high as our own, and certainly more generally obeyed. They have their priests and their doctors; they are strictly upright, and observe the rites of hospitality ... Now everything is changed, or so I hear, and doubtless in the balance this is best. Still we may wonder what are the thoughts that pass through the mind of some ancient warrior of Chaka's or Dingaan's time, as he suns himself crouched on the ground, for example, where once stood the royal kraal, Duguza, and watches men and women of the Zulu blood passing homewards from the cities or the mines, bemused, some of them, with the white man's smuggled liquor, grotesque with the white man's cast-off garments, hiding, perhaps, in their blankets examples of the white man's doubtful photographs – and then shuts his sunken eyes and remembers the plumed and kilted regiments making that same ground shake as, with a thunder of salute, line upon line, company upon company, they rushed out to battle.[20]

In his vivid and powerful romances Rider Haggard found a wonderfully dramatic form through which to articulate his sense of human transience. More than that, when confronted by situations which it is impossible to understand properly, or to do anything about, Haggard could see no alternative other than a disciplined stoicism in the face of the ceaseless tragedies which the world seemed to offer. We see this when Umslopagaas heroically defends the Queen's stairway with his great axe at Milosis in *Allan Quatermain*, and when Khiva, the Zulu boy, fruitlessly attempts to save his master from an elephant-charge in *King Solomon's Mines*. 'Ah well,' says Umbopa, 'he is dead, but he died like a man.'[21]

At the end of the great Cello Concerto by Sir Edward Elgar (1857-1934), fellow-countryman, imperialist and almost exact contemporary of Rider Haggard, the jaunty rondo pauses for a vein of almost heart-breaking lyricism at the sadness of Elgar's vision, before the orchestra reasserts itself with a defiant but noble stoicism. It is this stoicism which Rider Haggard admires in the face of unavoidable disaster, as when the 'Greys' prepare for their last heroic stand, facing certain defeat:

> I looked down the long lines of waving black plumes and stern faces beneath them, and sighed to think that within one short hour most, if not all, of those magnificent warriors, not a man of whom was under forty years of age, would be dead or dying in the dust. It could not be otherwise; they were being condemned, with that wise recklessness of human life that marks the great general, and often saves his forces and attains his ends, to certain slaughter, in order to give the cause and the remainder of the army a chance of success. They were foredoomed to die, and they knew it. It was to be their task to engage regiment after regiment of Twala's army on the narrow strip of green beneath us, till they were exterminated, or till the wings found a favourable opportunity for their onslaught. And yet they never hesitated, nor could I detect a sign of fear upon the face of a single warrior. There they were – going to a certain death, about to quit the blessed light of day for ever, and yet able to contemplate their doom without a tremor. I could not even at that moment help contrasting their state of mind with my own, which was far from comfortable, and breathing a sigh of envy and admiration. Never before had I seen such an absolute devotion to the idea of duty, and such a complete indifference to its bitter fruits.[22]

It is a limited response but not an unworthy one.

Chapter Six

Some Questions about *Kidnapped*: Stevenson and the Act of Union

Now Scotch is the only History I know....
(Robert Louis Stevenson, *Vailima Letters*)[1]

Rider Haggard deals with the issues of the age, such as Darwinism and Imperialism, in a fairly overt way. Other writers, by contrast, such as Stevenson, Nesbit and Philip Pullman do this more indirectly, apparently distancing themselves from contemporary questions by using the form of fantasy or the historical novel. In the case of *Kidnapped* (1886), we can see that Stevenson's treatment of the relations between England and Scotland is revealed through his interest in two close but contrasting personalities.

Robert Louis Stevenson (1850-1894) made frequent use of collaborators. Both his stepson Lloyd Osborne and his wife Fanny Stevenson helped him with his books, and he discussed plans for collaboration with both W.E. Henley and Andrew Lang. A similar state of interdependence often appears in his novels. The friendship of Jim Hawkins and Long John Silver in *Treasure Island* (1883) and of David and Alan in *Kidnapped* are obvious examples.

While many of his books deal with conflicts between clearly defined parties – pirates versus honest sailors, English versus Scots, York versus Lancaster – there is also a good deal of changing sides in the course of the adventures. Long John starts off as an honest sea-cook before leading a mutiny. He then deserts the mutineers to rejoin the honest men, but finishes up by 'jumping' Captain Smollett's ship. Dick Shelton in *The Black Arrow* (1888) switches his allegiance from the House of Lancaster to the House of York, while Alan Breck Stewart deserts King George's army to join the Jacobites at the Battle of Prestonpans. James in *The Master of Ballantrae* (1889) seems to have the best of both worlds, fighting for Bonnie Prince Charlie while spying for the Hanoverian king.

The effect of this allegiance-switching in Stevenson's books is reinforced by the frequent use characters make of disguise. 'Disguise is the spice of life', says Michael in *The Wrong Box* (1889), and almost all Stevenson's other characters would agree with him.[2] In *The Black Arrow* Joanna passes herself off as a boy; in *Catriona* (1893) the heroine pretends to be David's sister; St. Ives, in the novel named after him, spends most of his time hiding from the British; Dr. Jekyll is transformed into a completely different personality.

All of this intrigue, allegiance-switching and disguise, together with the duality of many of his central characters indicates Stevenson's preoccupation with the problems of identity and morality. He sees man as constantly shifting and changing, and all the more difficult, therefore, to come to terms with. This varies from such obviously wicked criminals as Mr. Hyde and Deacon Brodie (a historical Edinburgh figure who became a house-breaker at night-time) to the more equivocal characters of Long John and Alan Breck, whose behaviour and virtues constantly fluctuate.

Long John Silver, a central character in *Treasure Island*, is a pirate, thief and murderer, quite ruthless in pursuit of Captain Flint's treasure. But, on the other hand, he is cheerful, brave, resourceful, and, above all, kind to Jim, a kind of substitute father. Stevenson constantly reminds us of the inconsistencies and ambiguities of human nature. He is always challenging our powers of moral evaluation. Who is really good or bad? How can one compare loyalty with courage? This man in particular seems to be brutal, but he can also be kind.

Stevenson's preoccupation with the ambiguities of human character and behaviour may to some extent derive from the paradoxes of his own life. Born in Edinburgh, the son of a prosperous civil and marine engineer, he was a sickly child, confined to his bed for long periods, but he grew up to become a famous traveller, often undertaking arduous journeys and finishing up in Samoa, even when quite ill. In his youth he was a rather wild Bohemian student at Edinburgh University, and quarrelled bitterly with his parents when he rejected their Christian faith. But he later became devoted to his father, and even took his widowed mother with him when he settled in Samoa, where they enjoyed family prayers together. Wishing to become a serious writer from his youth, he dashed off some of his best work, such as *Dr. Jekyll and Mr. Hyde* (1886), in a few days. And despite being an inveterate traveller, Stevenson remained passionately devoted to Scotland all his life, though knowing well, for example, that the

Edinburgh in which he grew up was an extraordinary mixture of high-minded prosperity and sordid criminality.[3]

Along with *Treasure Island* and *Dr. Jekyll and Mr. Hyde*, *Kidnapped* has always been singled out as representing Stevenson's work at its finest. 'Stevenson's ability to tell a story cannot be seriously disputed, and he never told a better one than this particular book', said the poet Patricia Beer.[4] Even more strikingly, Henry James, in a magisterial review of both *Dr. Jekyll* and *Kidnapped*, emphatically preferred *Kidnapped*, saying that it is 'a signal proof of what the novel can do at its best and what nothing else can do as well … it can illustrate human affairs in cases so delicate and complicated that any other vehicle would be clumsy'.[5]

Some of the reasons for the book's success are obvious. It abounds, for example, in those plastic qualities which Stevenson especially favoured. *Kidnapped* adds to this gallery, as when David's Uncle Ebenezer sends David outside in the dark to climb the stair-tower, causing him almost to stumble to his death in the unfinished building; when David, shipwrecked on the islet of Earrair, cries out for help and hears himself laughed at; and when, in the flight through the heather, Alan and David spend a day being scorched on the sun-baked rocks hiding from the redcoats.

As in many of his adventure stories, Stevenson uses the romance-structure as the foundation for his tale. David is like a young folk hero, and the death of his parents triggers his journey from the Ettrick Forest to search for his uncle. The folk hero's magical gifts here become a Bible, a shilling, and a recipe for making Lilly of the Valley Water, and the requisite first complication of the narrative occurs when David's uncle tries to murder him. David's journey continues when he is kidnapped aboard a ship, the *Covenant*, but here another traditional feature of the folktale appears when David acquires a companion, the Jacobite tax-collector Alan Breck Stewart. Alan gives David another magical token in the form of a silver button. Further complications to David's journey follow with the wreck of the *Covenant* and the murder of Red Fox which David witnesses. The story rises to its great climax as David and Alan fly from arrest for the murder, and David eventually achieves the success expected in all such romances by establishing his identity as the true heir of the House of Shaws, ultimately reclaiming the family wealth. As if to emphasise the folktale connection, Stevenson remarks 'So the beggar in the ballad had come home'.[6]

Like many other writers using the traditional structure of the folktale, Stevenson varies the predictable elements with unexpected deviations. In *Kidnapped* Stevenson presents the reader with a plot of greater complexity than most folktales, giving us at least three crises, and fooling the reader by introducing magical gifts – the bible, the shilling and the recipe – which are never used, while a later gift, the silver button, is of greater importance.

But Stevenson was not interested simply in writing romantic adventure stories for their own sake. He was intrigued by moral questions, and he used the romance-form in order to discuss serious issues. How seriously he regarded the romance-form he made clear in an essay he wrote about Victor Hugo:

> Romance is a language in which many persons learn to speak with a certain appearance of fluency; but there are few who can ever bend it to any practical need, few who can be said to express themselves in it.... Victor Hugo occupies a high place among those few. He has always a perfect command over his stories; and we can see that they are constructed with a high regard to some ulterior purpose, and that every situation is informed with moral significance and grandeur... His romances are not to be confused with 'the novel with a purpose' as familiar to the English reader: this is generally the model of incompetence; and we see the moral forced into every hole and corner of the story, or thrown externally over it like a carpet over a railing. Now the moral significance, with Hugo, is of the essence of romance; it is the organising principle.[7]

One of the most significant elements Stevenson introduced into *Kidnapped* is, of course, the historical dimension. *Kidnapped* is set in the year 1751 and deals with events in Scotland after the tragically unsuccessful Jacobite Rebellion of 1745. The historical facts are that, despite the Act of Union of 1707, which tried to combine England and Scotland into a United Kingdom, many Scots continued to support the House of Stuart and the Jacobite Cause. There were rebellions against the British government in 1708, 1715, 1719, and, most famously, in 1745, with Bonnie Prince Charlie being defeated at the Battle of Culloden a year later. The British government then took punitive action against Scotland, depriving the rebel chiefs of their land, forbidding the wearing of kilts and the playing of bagpipes, and settling loyal troops in the villages to prevent further uprisings. (This is one of the points of the bagpipe competition between Alan and Robin Oig in chapter 25.) Stevenson is concerned with depicting the state of Scotland in this period, with the clans helpless and humiliated, and poverty and hardship. And what he does most skilfully is to depict these scenes through the eyes of a non-sympathiser, young David Balfour, a Unionist who is loyal to King George and the Hanoverian Succession, but gradually comes to admire the courage and loyalty of the Jacobite rebels. It is David who feels the Highlanders' poverty so keenly and describes the countryside infested with beggars in chapter 15. David is full of admiration when he discovers that Alan is actually collecting money from the impoverished Stewart clansmen, who have already paid their taxes to King George. " 'I call it noble,' I cried. 'I'm a Whig or little better; but I call it noble.' "[8]

Stevenson was seriously interested in history. His first published work – printed at his father's expense when he was sixteen – was the history of a seventeenth-century battle entitled *The Pentland Rising: A Page of History 1666* (1866). In 1881 he actually applied for the Professorship of History at Edinburgh University, and later, when he settled in the South Seas, he became deeply involved in the political history of Samoa, publishing an account of its difficulties with the international powers as *A Footnote to History* in 1892. Ann Colley has pointed out, for example, how Stevenson used his keen awareness of Scottish history, with his knowledge of the clan system, to understand the structure of society among the South Sea islanders.[9]

In describing the Appin Murder of Colin Campbell, the 'Red Fox', and the hunt for his assassin in *Kidnapped*, Stevenson was writing about real events. (The identity of the real murderer is still unknown and debated to this day.) Stevenson does more than just narrate historical events, however; he depicts them with political intelligence. He describes the collapse of the way of life in the Highlands, and shows great sympathy with its splendidly heroic qualities and the loyalty of the clans. But he also shows the weaknesses and contradictions of that system in the despotism of the leaders and the bloodthirsty and self-destructive rivalry between the clans – the Campbells and the Stewarts, for example, not to mention the Massacre at Glencoe in 1692. Alan Breck's gallant but reckless behaviour is a vivid illustration of these complexities. Thus, although Stevenson admires many of the achievements of the clan-system, he does not uncritically glorify the past, instead depicting the reason for the decline and English supremacy. What Georg Lukács said about Scott's historical novels might be applied equally to Stevenson:

> Scott did not become a Romantic, a glorifier or elegist of past ages. And it was for this reason that he was able to portray objectively the ruination of past social formations, despite all his human sympathy for, and artistic sensitivity

to, the splendid, heroic qualities which they contained. Objectively, in a large historical and artistic sense: he saw at one and the same time their outstanding qualities and the historical necessity of their decline.[10]

The contrasting characters of David Balfour and Alan Breck Stewart, and their fluctuating relationship, is the other great variation of the romance-structure which Stevenson introduces into *Kidnapped*. Alan is no stereotyped faithful, unquestioning companion of folktale and legend, but a fully-rounded human being, heroic and gallant, yet also reckless and vain. He offers to carry David over the moors when he is too tired to walk, but does not hesitate to gamble his money away when David is sick. Stevenson's skill in handling this strained relationship is beyond praise, particularly in those magnificent chapters of 'The Flight in the Heather', when he shows the two friends exchanging insults until they have drawn swords to each other, and are only then forced to recognise their fundamental brotherhood and love.

Many critics have noticed the contrasting polarity between the two characters – David calm and prudent, and Alan dashing and reckless – and have suggested a larger meaning for the contrast. Ian Bell, for example, says that 'In David Balfour and Alan Breck he [Stevenson] gave substance to two sides of his own character, adventurer and rationalist, man of duty and man of action.'[11] Emma Letley, in her introduction to the World's Classics Edition of *Kidnapped* and *Catriona*, suggests that David represents considerable features of Scottish Lowland culture, while Alan typifies the contrasting Highland culture.[12] Frank McLynn synthesises the approaches of Letley and Bell. In his eyes, David is the limited and realistic Lowlander Stevenson felt himself to be, while Alan represents the romantic hero his creator would have liked to have been.[13]

Yet one also wonders if in depicting the two companions – David, Protestant, realistic, slightly priggish, English-speaking (an almost surrogate Englishman); and Alan, Jacobite, dashing, reckless, Gaelic-speaking – Stevenson may also be articulating some of the cultural and socio-economic tensions between England and Scotland in the late nineteenth century. Is the love-hate relationship between David and Alan also a reflection of Stevenson's sense of the relations between England and Scotland in Victorian Britain? Is the foundering of David's brig *The Covenant*, named after the great Scottish declaration of religious independence from the Church of England in 1638, meant to remind readers of an earlier clash between Scottish and English cultures?

In the second half of nineteenth-century Britain there began to be much talk of Home Rule. It was not Home Rule for Scotland that was gaining support, however, but Ireland. These discussions intensified after the Phoenix Park Murders in Dublin in 1882, and Prime Minister Gladstone's move towards giving Ireland independence. Stevenson was horrified by this. As Christopher Hardie shows in his essay 'The Politics of Stevenson', Stevenson was fundamentally a Tory and a Unionist.[14] In 1887 he even contemplated moving his family to Ireland in order to defy the Home-Rulers, and a year later he wrote an attack on the Irish Movement entitled *Confessions of a Unionist.* Stevenson was afraid of the anarchy and chaos that he thought would follow any threat to the Union. But ironically in 1886, the very same year that *Kidnapped* was published, the first Scottish Home Rule Association was set up.

In 1853, however, the National Association for the Vindication of Scottish Rights had already been established with a very different agenda. Its aim was to preserve and to strengthen Scottish identity but within an essentially British framework It wanted to remain loyal to the Act of Union of 1707 but also ensure the survival of a distinctively Scottish culture. And this seems to have been Stevenson's position. Although he admired Scottish virtues and depicts English harshness in *Kidnapped*, there is no obvious yearning for independence. He remained a Unionist. Despite their passionate disagreements, our last and enduring image of David and Alan is of them struggling over the hills together. 'We're neither one of us to mend the other – that's the truth!' says David. 'We must just bear and forebear, man Alan!'[15] They are bound together by deep affection and practical needs, despite all their disagreements.

'*Kidnapped* can be seen as a "condition of Scotland" novel', says J.R. Hammond, comparing it to *Middlemarch* and Disraeli's *Sybil*,[16] and this is obviously true, but one can also ask if it is Stevenson's novel about the State of the Union. By 1891 Stevenson was settled with his family at Vailima in Samoa, and told his friend Sidney Colvin that he was thinking of writing some history, but what? He continued,

> Now Scotch is the only History I know; it is the only history reasonably represented in my library; it is a very good one for my purpose, owing to two civilisations having been face to face throughout – or rather Roman civilisation face to face with our ancient barbaric life and government, down to yesterday, to 1750 anyway.[17]

Chapter Seven

The Railway Children **and the Strange Death of Liberal England**

> If Christ should come to London,
> Come to London today,
> He would not go to the West End,
> He would come down our way.
> He'd talk with the children dancing
> To the organ out in the street,
> And say he was their Big Brother,
> And give them something to eat.

> (E. Nesbit, 'Inasmuch as ye did it not',
> *Ballads and Lyrics of Socialism, 1883-1908*)[1]

The Railway Children (1906) is a pivotal book in Edith Nesbit's career. Before it was serialised in *The London* magazine in 1905-1906, she was best known as the author of half a dozen happy family comedies, realistic but sometimes with an element of fantasy in them, such as *The Treasure Seekers* (1894-1895) and *The Phoenix and the Carpet* (1903-1904). But something happened, and after the publication of *The Railway Children* the mood of her books changed. There is much unease and darkness in the stories that followed.

Life had never been entirely comfortable for Edith Nesbit. Born in 1858, she lost her father before she was four, an event so painful that the motif of lost parents occurs in other books such as *The House of Arden* (1908) as well as *The Railway Children*. Despite her father's death, Edith enjoyed a largely happy childhood, spent partly in France and Germany, until the family settled at Halstead in Kent in the 1870s. By then she was writing poetry and beginning to get it published in magazines. She married Hubert Bland, a businessman, in 1880, and her literary efforts were redoubled when her husband fell ill not long after their marriage. Edith needed to support him and their young son Paul. During the next twelve years, while looking after her family and supporting her husband's activities for the socialist Fabian Society, where she became friendly with such figures as Bernard Shaw and H.G. Wells, Edith produced a series of works – novels, poetry, anthologies, and short stories. Although she did some writing for children during this period, however, her work lacked individuality; it was only the experience of talking over her childhood memories with a young admirer, Oswald Barron, that seems to have tapped a source of inspiration inside her. In 1896 Edith published some reminiscences of 'My School-Days' for the *Girl's Own Paper* and at about the same time began to write a series of amusing and inventive stories about the adventures of the Bastable children, which were published as *The Story of the Treasure Seekers* in 1899. Such books as *The Wouldbegoods* (1901) and *Five Children and It* (1902) soon followed and established E. Nesbit as one of the finest and most popular children's writers of the twentieth century.

Life, however, continued to present problems. As well as writing and bringing up three children of her own, Edith also brought up two other children fathered by Hubert, to whom, however, she remained devoted. In 1910 Hubert fell seriously ill with heart trouble and the next few years became increasingly unhappy as Edith's amazing energy and her literary earnings both fell away. Hubert died in 1914, and during World War I Edith was forced to take paying guests into her home at Well Hall, and to sell flowers and vegetables from her garden in order to cover her living expenses. In 1917, however, Edith married Thomas Terry Tucker, captain of the Woolwich Ferry. He persuaded her to leave Well Hall, and they settled more comfortably in Kent near the village of St. Mary's in the Marsh. Here she died on May 4th 1924.

E. Nesbit came from a large family herself and enjoyed family life, so it is not surprising that so many of her children's books tell stories about families, whether the young people become involved in fantastic adventures with a strange creature called a Psammead who can make wishes come true in *Five Children and It*, or take part in more realistic adventures such as the Bastables enjoy in *Story of the Treasure Seekers*.

One of the happiest memories of E. Nesbit's youth was of the time when she lived at Halstead Hall in Kent. Across the field at the back of the house ran a railway, and Edith and her brothers often ran down to the track and walked along the sleepers to the nearest station. Perhaps Edith was reminded of those days when an old friend

Sergei Stepniak, a Russian exile who had escaped to Britain from the cruelties of the Czarist regime, was killed while walking on a railway line in 1896. The political aspects of her ruminations on her Russian friend's life could only have been amplified when, in 1904, thoughts of political injustice rose to the forefronts of everyone's minds when a French Appeal Court began reviewing the controversial evidence against Alfred Dreyfus, the army officer who had been sent to Devil's Island, allegedly for betraying his country's military secrets to Germany.[2]

Given these recent events and her childhood memories, it is not surprising that the idea of writing a story about children, railways and wrongful imprisonment should have coalesced in E. Nesbit's mind, and, with *The New Treasure Seekers* finished in late 1904, the first instalment of *The Railway Children* appeared as a monthly serial in *The London* magazine in January 1905. It was concluded in January 1906, the same year in which the story first appeared in book form. It has remained in print ever since and was the subject of an immensely popular film directed by Lionel Jeffries in 1970. It was and remains 'a much-loved book', in the words of John Rowe Townsend's authoritative *Written for Children*.[3]

The Railway Children is one of E. Nesbit's realistic works, and it belongs to that genre of children's literature known variously as the family or domestic story, which originated in the moral or evangelical tales of Maria Edgeworth and Mrs Sherwood at the beginning of the nineteenth century, and was later developed, often through serialisation in magazines or periodicals, by such writers as Charlotte M. Yonge and Mrs J.H. Ewing in Britain, and by Louisa M. Alcott and Susan Coolidge in the United States. The basic ingredient of the family story is the use of a realistic mode, more concerned with describing domestic events than romantic adventures, and misunderstandings between members of a family than battles with pirates. These stories usually involve middle-class families, with relations and servants playing some, usually a minor, part, and the main emphasis is upon the lives of the children. As a result of some crisis, the children often find themselves isolated in some way – perhaps the parents are dead or absent from home for some reason – and so the youths are thrown together without much supervision. The mother is killed in an accident in Charlotte Yonge's *The Daisy Chain* (1856), for example, and Mr March is away from home during the Civil War in Louisa M. Alcott's *Little Women* (1868). These stories also often rely upon the moral development of the children as one of their narrative devices – will Jo March ever learn to exercise self-control? – but many of these tales also suggest ways in which the children not only support but in some cases even help to rehabilitate the adults in their lives. The younger generation often redeem the old, as Ethel May helps her bereaved father in *The Daisy Chain* and Mary helps to reconcile the Old Squire and her father in Mrs Ewing's tale of *Mary's Meadow* of 1886.

The Railway Children contains many of these elements and clearly belongs to the same genre. After the crisis of the father's disappearance at the beginning of the story, Roberta (Bobbie), Peter, Phyllis and their mother move from London to a cottage in the country. Left to their own devices, because their mother has to support them by earning a living as a writer, the children gradually make friends with workmen and passengers on the nearby railway. They have a series of realistic adventures, looking after their mother when she falls ill, helping to prevent a railway accident, and organising a birthday party for their friend Mr Perks. In the process not only do the children learn to behave more thoughtfully, but Roberta also helps to restore her missing father to the family.

The structure of the story is thus rather formulaic, but Nesbit introduces unexpected variations into her tale, and one of the unusual features that gives it freshness is her use of the railways as part of the context in which the story is set. The Edwardian period saw the railways at their peak, dominating the transport system of Britain to an unexpected degree. The number of passengers using trains actually quadrupled between 1870 and 1912, and many of Nesbit's readers would have responded with a thrill to her unusual background for a family story, and especially to her accounts of the railway station, the uniformed railway workers, the mysterious technology of signals and lines, and, above all, the sights and sounds of the steam engines. Although there is no evidence that Nesbit actually researched the topic, her childhood memories, combined with discussions with her friend, the journalist Oswald Barron, whom the family credited with inspiring the story, as well as her own observations, enabled her to give an accurate picture of Edwardian railways. Even the small technical details about couplings in chapter 3 and engine controls in chapter 4, though abbreviated, are correct. Those readers who find the social context of the novel too vaguely delineated have missed the subtle distinctions between station-master, driver, fireman, porter and signalman suggested here.[4]

Although part of the appeal of E. Nesbit's book lies in this depiction of the railway, the major reason for the enduring quality of the story lies in its treatment of the children. Here Nesbit was something of a pioneer, for nineteenth-century children's books, often written out of a stern moral didacticism, had tended to depict children either as angels or devils. Even Lewis Carroll's Alice of 1865 might seem to be too good to be true for some readers.

E. Nesbit was not only a mother herself, however; she also had enlightened opinions about the upbringing of children. (It is interesting to note that both her daughter Iris and Iris's half-sister Rosamund attended a progressive Froebel school from 1892 onwards.) Nesbit believed that children are neither incredibly virtuous nor irredeemably wicked, but are individuals, with a mixture of qualities, and that their development was best assisted by benevolent tolerance rather than by authoritarian repression. She understood the importance of apparently worthless play for children, and shows us Roberta, Peter and Phyllis trying to garden, playing with a model steam engine, and making swallows' nests with clay. She depicts children's follies and quarrels – and here even the much-praised Bobbie is not without fault – as matters to learn to avoid rather than as acts of monumental sin. It is perhaps largely because of the style and tone of E. Nesbit's realistic treatment of children that Julia Briggs describes her as 'the first modern writer for children'.[5]

The railway children are portrayed with such enormous skill because Nesbit seems to have an intuitive understanding of the feelings and the behaviour of her child characters. She comes nearest to explaining this gift in her book *Wings and the Child* (1913), where she related it to what can only have been the most acute sense of her own childhood:

> You cannot hope to understand children by common-sense, by reason, by logic, nor by any science whatsoever. You cannot understand them by imagination – not even by love itself. There is only one way: to remember what you thought and felt and liked and hated when you yourself were a child. Not what you know now – or think you know – you ought to have thought and liked, but what you did then, in stark fact, like and think. There is no other way.[6]

Thus, as happens to the children in many other of Nesbit's mature works, Roberta, Peter, and Phyllis are freed from the constraints of adults, in this case because of the absence of their father and the preoccupations of their mother, to regulate their own lives, to visit the railway, to talk to strangers, to go down to the canal, to go round the village collecting for what they think is a good cause. Only occasionally and gently does E. Nesbit comment on their actions, largely through the counsels of the children's mother.

Nesbit depicts the children as individuals with a sensitive aware-ness of the difference in their ages. Phyllis, the youngest, always 'meant extremely well', we learn on the very first page. Her warm feelings are expressed through unselfconscious physical contact, and she is always quick to kiss and embrace as a sign of reconciliation. She not only treats Perks, the friendly porter, who feels aggrieved at not being told of the Russian refugee, in this way, but also old grumpy Mrs Ransome, when she agrees to contribute to the children's birthday collection. Any tendency to over-sentimentalise Phyllis's baby-like innocence, however, is kept firmly in check by the constant reminders that she has fallen over her undone bootlaces once again.

Peter has his tenth birthday early in the story. Indeed, the explosion of one of his presents, the model engine, presages the forthcoming tragedy. As in E. Nesbit's other books, the children are well-read – Bobbie refers to *Macbeth* and even Phyllis comes up with a mangled quotation from a poetry book – but Peter not only quotes Kipling and Macaulay but often insists on interpreting life in story-book terms. Comedy often arises from the contrast between the grandiloquent language Peter uses and the more ordinary experience he is actual-ly dealing with. When the girls think of asking their mother about Peter's 'mining' exploits, for example, he does not simply ask them not to, but prefers to exclaim melodramatically, 'I've trusted you to the death. You know I'm going to do a lone adventure'.[7] Similarly, though he behaves with commendable coolness when rescuing the boy injured in the tunnel, he cannot resist adding the words, 'Fear not, you are in the hands of friends'.[8] Noel Streatfeild has suggested that Peter remains an elusive figure, perhaps because E. Nesbit was still grieving over the death of her own son Fabian, who had died aged 15 in 1900, but Peter's literary impersonations, his mining expeditions, his youthful pluck, and his boyishness – one thinks of the way he teases the girls with his crude bloodthirstiness and eagerly befriends Jim in the last chapters – give him a strong identity.[9]

But Bobbie clearly emerges as the most striking of the three child-ren. She is, as Julia Briggs has remarked, 'a child at the crossroads'.[10] On the one hand, a young girl, barely older than Peter, she is unsure of herself, not only vulnerable to Peter's teasing but someone who actually does faint when she has to halt the train to prevent it crashing into the landslip. On the other hand, she is growing up and taking on serious responsibilities, looking after the younger children, sending for the doctor when her mother is ill, and organising assistance for the Russian refugee. Most important of all, when she discovers the reason for her father's absence, she manages to help to secure his return, despite the grief she carries. No wonder E. Nesbit confesses, 'The more I observe her the more I love her'.[11]

The plot of *The Railway Children* deals essentially with middle-class people, within the genre of a family story with a happy ending. The Edwardian Age in which it was written, however, although apparently a period of prosperity and glamour, was also one of growing tensions and potential conflict at home and abroad, and it is not surprising to find signs of this within the story. The most powerful expression of tension between stability and disaster in E. Nesbit's story is articulated through the theme of injustice, which is forcefully illustrated not only by the father's sudden arrest and departure from his loving home at the beginning, but is then reinforced by the parallel episode of the Russian refugee in later chapters. The heading to Chapter 5, 'Prisoners and Captives', might make a subtitle for the whole book.

This sense of a stable home brutally shattered by the unjust removal of the father is mainly conveyed through Bobbie's perceptions and feelings, and the moment of recovery is realised with such wonderful inwardness and intensity – ' "Oh! my Daddy, my Daddy!" That scream went like a knife into the heart of everyone on the train'[12] – that one cannot doubt that it derives its force from Nesbit's feelings about the loss of her own father when she was young. But the emotion conveyed is more than autobiographical, for the fear of parental loss and sudden deprivation when young is surely universal.

But as well as the loss of their father, the children also encounter other problems: they experience money difficulties; their mother falls ill; they meet a sick Russian; and they find a boy injured on a cross-country run. E. Nesbit is interested in how a family of young children behave in critical situations.

It is clear that she believes in patience, resourcefulness, good humour and self-help. The mother stands as a model for this throughout the book, brave at her husband's disappearance, resourceful in writing to earn a living, inventive in her poems and treats for the children, and wise in her advice. There is a particularly touching moment when she asks the children not to walk along the railway line, but is too honest to deny that she did it herself when she was young. Nowhere is her quiet heroism better expressed than in the opening chapters when she is confronted by one crisis after another, and nothing illustrates it more endearingly than the courageous improvisation and humour she displays when the family arrive at the cottage, Three Chimneys, late at night to find it deserted with only the rats to disturb the silence. ' "What fun!" said mother in the dark, feeling for the matches on the table.'[13]

Fred Inglis argues that there is a moral patterning in *The Railway Children*, and that the children develop through various stages of the story.[14] Thus, although Peter's intentions are good, E. Nesbit makes it quite clear in the first stage of the book that his 'mining' of the railway coal is equivalent to stealing and is wrong. In the second stage, the children learn that, although it is wrong to beg, it is permissible to ask for help in an emergency, especially if you offer to repay it, as the children offer to repay the Old Gentleman for the hamper of food he sends their sick mother. In the third stage of the story the children become more *active* agents, preventing a railway accident, assisting the Russian refugee, and rescuing a baby from a fire. In helping Perks, the friendly porter, to celebrate his birthday they continue learning, and, in a finely wrought chapter, discover that it is sometimes more difficult to do good than might be imagined. For Perks provides more than comic relief, and E. Nesbit shows him reflecting the class divisions in Edwardian England, when he resists what he believes is the condescending charity of the villagers and the children. 'If a man didn't respect hisself, no one wouldn't do it for him', he says,[15] and it is only the children's loving innocence that saves the day.

Although there is clearly something in Fred Inglis's interpretation of the novel, it is perhaps a little too schematic. E. Nesbit is always too alert to the real nature of children to depict them progressing quite so neatly. She rarely idealises them, and it is entirely typical of her realistic and deflating irony that she depicts Bobbie and Peter quarrelling, and Peter cutting his foot quite badly in Chapter 10, only a few pages after their mother has been praising them for learning not to fight so much.

Of course, E. Nesbit does not probe very deeply into the disagreeable aspects of economic life or class conflict in *The Railway Children*. Although the family have to learn to do without both jam *and* butter on their bread for a time, true poverty is avoided. Society is such that the mother and her children are always recognised as middle-class and treated with the respect E. Nesbit thinks they are entitled to, even when Peter is caught stealing coal. (Would a working-class child have been treated in the same way?) It may be that, despite her early involvement with the Fabian Society, Nesbit could not help reflecting her own middle-class origins. Yet one has to say that, in her depiction of the unsympathetic, exhausted signalman (unsympathetic because exhausted?) and the dignified refusal of Perks to accept what he thinks is charity, E. Nesbit helped to widen the social range of children's books.

E. Nesbit also believed in Providence. Without ignoring the disagreeable aspects of life, *The Railway Children* shows that she was an optimist, and believed that children should have a view of the world in which, in addition to their own efforts at work and co-operation, there is the possibility of generosity and goodness from others. Because of their goodness, the children bring out goodness in other people. Of course, it is possible to argue that the mother is too perfect, and that the Old Gentleman is too conveniently to hand when there are real crises, but in *The Railway Children* E. Nesbit seems to want her young readers to feel that there is loving kindness and benevolence in the world. Such coincidences as the discovery that the boy rescued in the tunnel is the grandson of the Old Gentleman, as well as the character of the Old Gentleman himself are better considered as quasi-symbolic evidence of a beneficent universe rather than as realistic elements in the story.

E. Nesbit's earlier stories had been sunny and optimistic. The tales of everyday life, such as *The Treasure Seekers* and *The Would-begoods*, focus on the exploits of a middle-class family, the Bastables, as described by one of the children, Oswald, and his self-glorifying version of events often contrasts ironically with what really happened. Although the children's mother has died and there is some genteel poverty, these books are high-spirited comedies. Despite their good intentions, the children regularly blunder into hilarious mishaps, which always turn out all right at the end. Nesbit's fantasies, such as *Five Children and It* and *The Phoenix and the Carpet*, are similarly light-hearted, portraying middle-class children, who, as the result of encountering magic in some form, such as meeting a sand-fairy or a phoenix, are able to experience exotic adventures by sprouting wings and learning to fly, for example.

But as the Edwardian Age moved towards its close, British society changed and E. Nesbit's books became increasingly sadder. Her husband Hubert Bland had been a founding member of the Socialistic Fabian Society, we remember, and Edith herself had played a considerable part in its activities, serving on its Pamphlets Committee, for example. She was friendly with such figures as G.B. Shaw, H.G. Wells and Annie Besant, the woman who had led the support for the match girls' strike at Bryant and May's in 1888. Edith made her sympathies quite clear by organising elaborate Christmas parties for the slum children of Deptford, and by writing poetry about the plight of the industrial poor such as 'Inasmuch as ye did not … ', published in *Ballads and Lyrics of Socialism 1883-1908.*

In his book *The Strange Death of Liberal England* (1936) George Dangerfield argues that in the Edwardian period there occurred an erosion of the values which had made Victorian Britain so successful, particularly a belief in the importance of democratic discussion and compromise. He pointed to the increasing militancy of the Trade Unions, the violence of the Suffragette Movement with Emily Davidson's death at the 1913 Derby, and the threat of civil war over Ireland, where Unionists resisted Parliamentary attempts to offer Home Rule. Dangerfield's individual points have been challenged in detail, but the thrust of his argument has received substantial support. Despite its nostalgic image as a 'Golden Age', the Edwardian era was in fact a period of considerable turmoil.[16] The standard of living declined, with real wages falling from a peak around 1900 to their lowest level in the years 1911-1912, and with 40 million working days lost by strikes in 1912 compared with 2 million in 1907. In agriculture alone, it has been calculated that in 1913, with five exceptions, 'the average earnings in every county were below the poverty line'.[17] The new Liberal government under Asquith did introduce some well-meaning reforms, bringing in Old Age Pensions in 1909, and in 1911 a National Insurance Act to pay for medical services and Unemployment Insurance to provide payment for unemployed workers. But these measures, however welcome, were seen as palliative.[18] Finally, in August 1914, Britain declared war on Germany in what was to become the tragedy of World War I, effectively putting a full stop to life in the United Kingdom as it had been.

E. Nesbit showed increasing signs of social and political unease in her fantasy *The Story of the Amulet*, which appeared in 1906 just after *The Railway Children*. This is a fantasy about a group of middle-class children who, through the discovery of a magic amulet, are able to travel through time to the Past. The story displays Nesbit's usual comic skills as she narrates the children's adventures, wherein they visit Babylon and ancient Egypt. But when they bring the Queen of Babylon back to their own Edwardian London, they are disconcerted by her comments on the state of the poor in Mile End Road:

> And now from the window of a four-wheeled coach the Queen of Babylon beheld the wonders of London. Buckingham Palace she thought uninteresting; Westminster Abbey and the Houses of Parliament were little better. But she liked the Tower, and the river, and the ships filled her with wonder and delight.
>
> 'But how badly you keep your slaves. How wretched and poor and neglected they seem,' she said, as the cab rattled along the Mile End Road.

'They aren't slaves; they're working people,' said Jane

'Of course they're working people. That's what slaves are. Don't you tell me. Do you suppose I don't know a slave's face when I see it? Why don't their masters see that they're better fed and better clothed. Tell me in three words.'

No one answered. The wage-system of modern England is a little difficult to explain in three words even if you understand it – which the children didn't.

'You'll have a revolt of your slaves if you're not careful,' said the Queen.

'Oh, no,' said Cyril; 'you see they have votes – that makes them safe not to revolt. It makes all the difference. Father told me so.'

'What is this vote?' asked the Queen. 'Is it a charm? What do they do with it?'

'I don't know,' said the harassed Cyril; 'it's just a vote, that's all! They don't do anything particular with it.'

'I see,' said the Queen; 'a sort of plaything.'[19]

Nesbit's social criticism intensified in *The House of Arden* (1909). This is another time-fantasy about two Edwardian children, Edred and Elfrida, who live in a Castle which is in some decay. Through their friendship with a strange creature, the Mouldiwarp, who can do magic, they too are able to travel to the Past and have exciting adventures. They return to Napoleonic times, meet an eighteenth-century highwayman, and become involved in the Gunpowder Plot. When they try to bring their Jacobean cousin Richard back with them to the twentieth century, however, he prefers to remain in the Past:

'Why don't you want to come with us to our times?'

'I hate your times. They're ugly, they're cruel,' said Richard.

'They don't cut your heads off for nothing anyhow in our times,' said Edred, 'and shut you up in the Tower.'

'They do worse things,' Richard said. '*I* know. They make people work fourteen hours a day for nine shillings a week, so that they never have enough to eat or wear, and no time to sleep or to be happy in. They won't give people food or clothes, or let them work to get them; and then they put the people in prison if they take enough to keep them alive. They let people get horrid diseases, till their jaws drop off, so as to have a particular kind of china. Women have to go out to work instead of looking after their babies, and the little girl that's left in charge drops the baby and it's crippled for life. Oh! I know. I won't go back with you. You might keep me there for ever.' He shuddered.[20]

The decay of Arden Castle symbolises the ways in which the land-owners and speculators are ruining modern Britain. The children are urged to restore the Castle and look after their poor tenants, but they have no means to do so, and, although they manage to rescue their missing father, the general thrust of the story ends in defeat. It is as if E. Nesbit saw the need to transform Britain but could find no convincing way forward.

Harding's Luck (1910) is even more realistic and pessimistic. Although strongly linked to and intended as a sequel to *The House of Arden*, *Harding's Luck* is strikingly different in that it places almost the whole focus of the story upon that rare figure in Nesbit's tales, a working-class hero, in this instance named Dickie Harding. He is a poor, lame orphan, whose only friend is a burglar-tramp called Mr Beale, and they live, more or less, as beggars. In her opening chapters Nesbit excels in depicting Dickie's milieu in Edwardian London, and it is a long way from the comforts of the Bastables:

> Dickie lived at New Cross. At least the address was New Cross, but really the house where he lived was one of a row of horrid little houses built on the slope where once green fields ran down the hill to the river, and the old houses of the Deptford merchants stood stately in their pleasant gardens and fruitful orchards. All these good fields and happy gardens are built over now. It is as though some wicked giant had taken a big brush of yellow ochre paint, and another of mud-colour, and had painted out the green in streaks of dull yellow and filthy brown; and the brown is the roads and the yellow is the houses. Miles and miles and miles of them, and not a green thing to be seen except the cabbages in the greengrocers' shops, and here and there some poor trails of creeping-jenny drooping from a dirty window-sill. There is a little yard at the back of each house; this is called 'the garden', and some of these show green – but they only show it to the houses' back windows. You cannot see it from the street. These gardens are green, be-cause green is the colour that most pleases and soothes men's eyes; and however you may shut people up between bars of yellow and mud colour, and however hard you

> make them work, and however little wage you may pay
> them for working, there will always be found among these
> people some men who are willing to work a little longer,
> and for no wages at all, so that they may have green things
> growing near them.[21]

But Dickie, through Magic, is able to travel to the Past and so becomes involved with the old Arden family, and when he returns to the
Present becomes friends with Elfrida and Edred, the children from
Nesbit's earlier book. Dickie helps to reform his old tramp friend
and to restore the modern Arden family's fortunes by discovering a
lost treasure. It even turns out that working-class Dickie is the real
Lord Arden and the true heir to the Castle. But in the end, because
he feels guilty about depriving his new friends, Elfrida and Edred, of
their home and anticipated rights, Dickie decides to disappear and
return to the Jacobean Age.

Harding's Luck is a brilliant and at times poignant example of
time-travel fiction. But what makes the story so powerful is Nesbit's
anger at the squalor of the lives of the Edwardian inhabitants of
New Cross and Deptford, with the poverty and pawnshops and
petty crime. Even the Past by comparison seems more ordered and
beautiful. It is as if, following John Ruskin and William Morris,
Nesbit is offering a critique of modern Britain, but could only suggest
that a remedy might be found through the alternative fantasies of
acquiring unexpected (and unearned) wealth or retreating to an
idealised Past. It is significant that when the Arden family find the
treasure, they do use some of it to renovate the appalling workers'
cottages on their estate, but this is hardly a political programme.[22]

Although Nesbit's later works, particularly *The Magic City* (1910)
and *Wet Magic* (1913) continued her search for better societies,
in the differing forms of a toy-world and an underwater fantasy,
sales were very disappointing after the great success of her earlier
works. Despite some brilliant ideas in *The Magic City*, where the
children build an elaborate imaginary city out of wooden blocks and
plasticine, they go through a rather arbitrary series of adventures and
encounter an extremely unpleasant Nurse, who at one point succeeds
in destroying their city. *Wet Magic*, the story of some children's
experiences underwater after they befriend a mermaid, is simply
muddled, particularly in a confusing battle-scene where real people,
fictitious characters and even book titles are all mixed up together. A
combination of social disillusion and personal difficulties gives these
later works a sense of fatigue and even defeat.[23]

The Railway Children of 1906, however, boldly demonstrates a positive faith in the possibility of human growth and happiness, and, affirming the fundamental kindliness and generosity of human behaviour – from parents and old gentlemen, from railway-workers and shopkeepers – resolves tensions with tact and great good humour. The pain is there, but E. Nesbit was able to create a vision of a benevolent and caring society, leaving her readers, like Bobbie, to go quietly away at the end and think about the meaning of the story.

Chapter Eight

From Evangelism to Feminism: The Works of Amy Le Feuvre

'What are you doing now?' he inquired as he passed down the stairs. Milly turned round, her little face flushed, and eyes looking very sweet and serious.

'I was just waving to God, Uncle Edward. I thought I saw Him looking down at me from the sky.'

Sir Edward passed on, muttering inaudibly, – 'I believe that child lives in the presence of God from morning to night.'

(Amy Le Feuvre, *Probable Sons*, 1894)

Don't you know that a modern girl will not be managed by anyone, least of all her husband.

(Amy Le Feuvre, *Jock's Inheritance*, 1927)[1]

As the years passed, the optimism of Edith Nesbit's earlier stories began to give way to a mixture of escapism and social critique as she increasingly questioned the values of the Edwardian period. The changes in Amy Le Feuvre's works, however, occurring over the course of a writing career of over thirty years, although almost as radical as Nesbit's, do not seem to be based upon any conscious act of rebellion. They are more associated with her apparently comfortable alignment with developments in society during her lifetime, particularly with regard to religion and the changing policy of her main publisher, the Religious Tract Society.

The Religious Tract Society was a publishing phenomenon. Founded in 1799 as a major offspring of the Evangelical Movement, its main aim originally was to publish cheap religious tracts for distribution to adults in Britain and overseas. *The Dairyman's*

Daughter by the Rev. Legh Richmond, which first appeared in the magazine *The Christian Guardian* in 1809, was one of its earliest and greatest successes, for this simple, pious story of a young woman's strong Christian faith as she faced an early death sold over four million copies in tract form in the first half of the nineteenth century.

By the 1820s the Society began to publish books specifically aimed at young readers, and in 1824 started a monthly magazine for children: *The Children's Companion: or, Sunday Scholar's Reward.* By 1831 the RTS Catalogue listed nearly three hundred publications for the young, and, as it continued to expand its activities, the Society began to publish works about geography, history and science, alongside its evangelical and moral tales.

These early stories were heavily influenced by the religious origins of the RTS, and indeed the Society suggested the kinds of qualities they should contain. An emphasis upon scriptural truth and some account of a sinner's way to salvation were strongly recommended, with an emphasis upon a plain and direct prose style. The works of Mrs Sherwood and her sister Mrs Cameron, such as Sherwood's *The History of the Fairchild Family* (1817) and Cameron's *Cleanliness is Next to Godliness* (1823), showed the powerful influence of the Evangelical tradition at this time, even though the RTS did not publish these particular books.

Later writers, usually women, developed this tradition further in the nineteenth century. 'Hesba Stretton', the pen-name of Sarah Smith (1832-1911), achieved amazing sales figures with her realistic and often poignant stories of poor street-children such as *Jessica's First Prayer* (1867) and *Alone in London* (1869). *Jessica's First Prayer*, for example, sold two and a half million copies by 1911, the year Hesba died. Other writers working in the same vein included Maria Louisa Charlesworth (1819-1881), best-known for her evangelical family novel *Ministering Children* (1854), and Mrs O.F. Walton (1849-1939). Mrs Walton's best-known story *Christie's Old Organ, or Home, Sweet Home* (1874) is the pious, sentimental tale of how the young street-urchin Christie befriends a poor, old organ-grinder, and after the old man's death is helped by a benefactor to become a scripture-reader among the urban poor. This and Mrs Walton's other great popular success, *A Peep Behind the Scenes* (1877), a realistic picture of circus life, remain in print to this day, showing the enduring power of the evangelical literary tradition.[2]

The strength of the Christian faith which inspired and powered this tradition was, however, deeply shaken by a series of assaults on religion in the course of the nineteenth century. In 1838 Charles Lyall's

Elements of Geology seemed to challenge the account of the Creation given in the *Book of Genesis*. Charles Darwin's *Origin of Species* of 1859 raised even greater doubts. Intellectuals such as Henry Sidgwick and Leslie Stephen began to articulate their difficulties, and Matthew Arnold's poem 'Dover Beach' of 1867 gave most eloquent expression to his anxieties about the survival of the Christian religion:

> The Sea of Faith
> Was once, too, at the full, and round earth's shore
> Lay like the folds of a bright girdle furl'd.
> But now I only hear
> Its melancholy, long, withdrawing roar,
> Retreating, to the breath
> Of the night-wind, down the vast edges drear
> And naked shingles of the world....
>
> And we are here as on a darkling plain
> Swept with confused alarms of struggle and flight,
> Where ignorant armies clash by night.[3]

Perhaps the clearest signs of this decline in religious faith and the growing secularisation of society can be found in the actual statistics of church attendance. Here the evidence is overwhelming. According to the Census Report of 1851 on Religious Worship, just under eleven million people attended church on Sunday March 30th 1851, but the number of Communicants on Easter Sunday in 1918 had fallen to just over two and a quarter million. (Today the number is just over one million.)[4] The Sea of Faith's melancholy, long, withdrawing roar was being heard everywhere.

The publications of the Religious Tract Society began to reflect the increasingly secular nature of society in the later years of the nineteenth century. *The Boy's Own Paper*, as already noted in chapter three, was started by the RTS in 1879, to provide sound and healthy reading for boys, and soon achieved enormous popularity, with a readership of over half a million by the 1880s. But, although the magazine did contain some articles on religious subjects, its successful contents were predominantly a mixture of natural history, competitions, advice about games and such hobbies as stamp-collecting, serialised adventure stories by such authors as W.H.G. Kingston and school stories by Talbot Baines Reed. Reed's popular school story *The Fifth Form at St. Dominic's*, serialised in 1881-1882, makes an interesting comparison with *Tom Brown's Schooldays*, for in Hughes's story of 1856 the role of the chapel and of religion is paramount, while in Reed's later work, though Christian values are still present, there is far less didacticism and much more good humour and good-natured tolerance. It was a sign of the times that the *BOP* even concealed the fact that it was being published by the Religious Tract Society.

The Girl's Own Paper was launched a year later with a similar mixture of contents, but aimed at a female readership. It sold even more copies than the *BOP*, with popular serials by such authors as Evelyn Everett Green (1856-1932) and Jessie Mansergh, better known as Mrs G. de Horne Vaizey (1856-1917). But the tone of this fiction, although didactic and promoting such virtues as benevolence, industry and unselfishness, is far removed from the intense spirituality of earlier RTS publications. Mrs de Horne Vaizey's stories, such as *Peggie O'Shaughnessy* (1902), are about lively young heroines, who are wild but kind-hearted, and these tales reveal considerable humour.

For as society's values changed, the increasingly secular nature of Victorian life was reflected in its literature. Indeed, this whole process of gradual change can be revealed and explained by considering a number of what might be considered representative evangelical texts publishing during the course of the nineteenth century. Such tracts as Legh Richmond's sin-obsessed rural account of *The Dairyman's Daughter* of 1809 were replaced by more city-based redemptive works such as *Jessica's First Prayer* and *Christie's Old Organ*, and the stories of Talbot Baines Reed and Mrs G. de Horne Vaizey clearly reflect the emergence of ethical but more secular values at the end of the century.

The career and works of Amy Le Feuvre (1861-1929) perfectly illustrate the way the times were changing. Amy (christened Amelia Sophia) was born in Lewisham on 3rd February, the third child and second daughter of Edmond Philip Le Feuvre, who worked for Her Majesty's Customs. The family, whose origins seem to have been in the Channel Islands, came from the prosperous and respectable middle classes. Her father was Secretary of the Evangelical Alliance in Blackheath, and her maternal grandfather an Anglican Rector in Lincolnshire. Amy grew up in a large family with an older sister Charlotte (born 1858) and an older brother William Philip (born 1860), as well as two younger sisters Edith (born 1863) and Henrietta (born 1870) and a younger brother Frederick (born 1868).

William qualified as a doctor at Guy's Hospital in London in 1888 and went off to work in South Africa, combining his medical practice with missionary work. But Amy seems to have been educated priv-ately, partly by an aunt to whom she was sent when her parents spent some time in Germany, and also by a governess. She began writing at the age of nine, her brother William tells us, and it does not look as if her lack of schooling hindered her in any way, judging from her books, which contain many references to literature, painting and music.

Despite the evidently traditional nature of her upbringing, however, Amy seems to have been an unusually independent young woman for her times. In 1887 she visited her uncle, a Lieutenant-Colonel in the Royal Engineers based in Aldershot, and, while there, a family friend recruited her as a helper at the Soldiers' Home and Institute which existed to provide support for the troops. This kind of practical welfare work obviously appealed to the young woman, and she continued to do philanthropic work for the army in Chatham, Plymouth and finally Okehampton for many years.

About the time of her visit to Aldershot, Amy seems to have begun writing professionally, for her first book – entitled *Eric's Good News*, for which the RTS paid her £15 – was published in 1894. Reflecting Amy's interest in army matters, this simple tale is about a young invalid Eric, who is befriended by Captain Graham, and, in discovering his own Christian faith, helps to save Captain Graham too. *'Probable Sons'*, published the same year, and this time earning Amy £30, is equally devout. Sir Edward Wentworth, a selfish, rich bachelor, is dismayed to learn that he has to look after his dead sister's young daughter Millicent. But, according to the fashion of many earlier evangelical tales, the angelic child gradually wins her uncle over to the Christian faith.

Once Amy's career was launched, there was no stopping her. Around 1900 the young unmarried woman seems to have moved herself to Devon and settled into a cottage on the edge of Dartmoor, where she helped run a Soldiers' Home for the Okehampton Artillery Camp. From this point forward, tales, often published in such magazines as *Sunday Hours*, and full-length stories, sometimes serialised in the *Girl's Own Paper*, flowed from her pen. Le Feuvre never made a lot of money from individual books – in 1905 Hodder paid her an advance of £100 for her novel *Bridget's Quarter-Deck*, for example – but her collective earnings mounted up. (This was partly because her popular books were frequently reprinted. *Teddy's Button*, for example, first published in 1896, was still being published by the Lutterworth Press in 1990, and sales of this book alone are said to have exceeded a million copies.) In 1913 she moved to Portland Lodge in Exeter and stayed there until her death in April 1929, when she was buried in Okehampton Churchyard. She had published over eighty books altogether, many of them translated into languages as wide-ranging as Arabic, Czech, French, German, Icelandic, Italian and Japanese. As evidence of her success, in 1928, the year before she died, the Religious Tract Society negotiated an agreement to pay Amy an annuity of £300 to cover existing royalty payments; and the gross value of her estate at her death was over £10,000.[5]

Amy Le Feuvre's fiction is always set in the modern world, is broadly realistic once one accepts its sentimental idealism, and always has a background of Christian belief. Le Feuvre began her career as a strongly didactic writer within the evangelical tradition of Hesba Stretton and Mrs Walton, and this is particularly obvious in her books for younger children. Right from the time of James Janeways's *A Token for Children* of 1671, Christian writers had produced narratives in which by the purity of their lives (and deaths) young children had brought salvation to their elders. This *motif* of the angelic and redeeming child had become increasingly powerful from the romantic period at the beginning of the nineteenth century when the youth, with all the trappings of romanticism – innocence, physical attractiveness and precocious wisdom – regularly appeared in evangelical literature. Hesba Stretton's Jessica and Mrs Walton's Christie demonstrated how the young can bring their elders to salvation. Cedric's rehabilitation of his irascible grandfather in Mrs Hodgson Burnett's *Little Lord Fauntleroy* of 1886 was a recent, if more secular, example of the same process, and this work, both as a novel and then a play, enjoyed immense popularity.

The presence of the angelic child with the capacity, through childish innocence and wisdom, to rescue reprobate and fallen adults is one of the recurring motifs of Amy Le Feuvre's works. The little invalid Eric brings Captain Graham back to the Bible in *Eric's Good News*, and Millicent draws her selfish Uncle Sir Edward back to God in *'Probable Sons'*. In one of the most comprehensive demonstrations of this theme, Betty Stuart in *Odd* of 1897 brings salvation to many of the book's characters through her wonderfully unaffected innocence – a father who has lost a young child, a family shaken by a financial scandal, an old sexton and an elderly invalid. Through her own trust in God, Betty brings light to the gloomy lives of many others. *Dicky's Brother*, a short tale of 1923, almost reads like one of the earlier temperance tracts, as it tells how ten-year-old Dicky persuades his brother, the soldier Walter, to renounce alcohol and to find God. Finally, in *Mimosa's Field* (1953), a story published long after Amy's death in 1929, young Mimsie learns about God from a friendly landlady, and then, through her own simple faith, manages to convert her own intellectually sceptical father.

The trouble with much of this kind of plot, of course, is not only that it becomes too hackneyed and predictable, but that Le Feuvre is not always able to persuade her readers that such actions are credible. The children are too idealised and the sinful adults too easily converted. Real life can be more challenging, we feel. When Milly tells her Uncle Edward 'I was just waving to God', in *'Probable Sons'*, one feels that it is childish charm which is being admired rather than realistic faith. 'Amy Le Feuvre was something of a specialist in this line', as Judith Rowbotham wryly observes.[6]

Amy Le Feuvre's children are not always so idealised, however. In particular, where she is writing about large families rather than individual children, Amy Le Feuvre often portrays them more realistically and even amusingly. This is so even when the family background is predominantly religious. In *A Thoughtless Seven* (1898), for example, although a friendly neighbour tries to give the children Christian guidance while their parents are away, what one remembers about the story is the way the large middle-class family get bored and squabble with each other, are frightened by a thunderstorm, and enjoy a seaside holiday, where they have a boating adventure. All of this is told in a direct straightforward manner by fifteen-year-old Mary, one of the children.

This use of a child-narrator reminds the reader of Edith Nesbit's young narrator-hero Oswald Bastable, although *A Thoughtless Seven* lacks any of Oswald's unconscious irony. But it is noteworthy that the Bastable children had first appeared in *The Treasure Seekers* in magazines in 1894-1895, and then in *The Wouldbegoods* in 1900-1901, just as Amy Le Feuvre's literary career was beginning. The influence of Nesbit's comic family stories are even more apparent in some of Le Feuvre's later books, in particular a trilogy about the Marjoribanks family: *'Us, and Our Donkey'* (1909); *Us, and Our Empire* (1911); and *'Us, and Our Charge'* (1916).

'Us, and Our Donkey' is the story of the Rev. Marjoribanks and his five children, told by the teenage daughter Grissell. After their mother dies, the father becomes the Rector of a village in Lincolnshire – rather like Amy's own grandfather – and the children take on various jobs, fishing, selling vegetables, making and selling toffee, in order to raise the money to buy themselves a cart and donkey. They enjoy various adventures, all narrated in a light-hearted manner, as when the donkey runs away and gets stuck in a ford. The children's efforts to recover the donkey when it is stolen by some local ruffians makes an entertaining climax to the story in which is embedded, although fairly lightly, the larger context of the father's efforts to

bring his children up as good Christians by using the Latin motto
of the knight buried in the Parish Church – *Semper fidelis, semper
paratus*. The narrator Grissell is a more serious version of Oswald
Bastable, though there is little of Oswald's self-regarding heroism.
Le Feuvre's formula in these tales might perhaps be summed up by a
simple phrase – Evangelicanism plus Nesbit.

Us, and Our Empire continues the adventures of the Marjoribanks
family. The book is dedicated to the Earl of Meath, who helped es-
tablish Empire Day in 1916, and opens with Kipling's poem 'Land
of Our Birth'. We are moving away from the intense Evangelical
feeling of the early nineteenth century, and can see how much Amy
Le Feuvre was affected by the imperial ethos of the pre-war years.
The Marjoribanks children become pre-occupied with the idea of
praising and working for the good of the British Empire. They form
an Empire League in the village and get into various scrapes as they
try to recruit members. Le Feuvre pokes gentle fun at their more gran-
diose ambitions, and when the children try to manhandle a republican
agitator, their father reminds them that a man is free to say what he
likes in England. The story is clearly deeply committed to the idea of
British imperialism, but attempts to marry it to the Christian faith in
the words of Grissell at the end:

> It is very nice to be a citizen of our British Empire, but
> that will only last as long as we are on this earth. It's ten
> hundred times better to be a citizen of God's empire, for
> that lasts forever.[7]

'Us, and Our Charge', the third and last of the stories about the
Marjoribanks family, is even more affected by contemporary events.
Again it is related by the young Grissell and reminds us of Nesbit's
books about the Bastable family. The story opens with the death of
the children's father and the family moving to Scotland to live with
their grandfather. The first half of the tale is about the children's
adventures with Pat, a mischievous Irish boy, who enjoys playing
practical jokes. But the tone of the book changes dramatically from
chapter ten when World War I breaks out. At first the children are
intensely patriotic, and Grissell shows a disturbing enthusiasm
for 'the excitement and the glory of the big war in front of us'.[8]
The painful reality of the war soon grows more tangible, however,
and, when the girls help to look after wounded soldiers at a nearby
hospital, and then hear that Pat, who joined the army, has been killed
in the trenches, Grissell finds that she is no longer able to go on with
her diary. Although the children try to keep to their father's charge,

'Hold fast that which is true', one cannot help feeling that patriotism and support for the army are becoming more dominant values.

The increasingly active roles of Grissel and her sister Lynette following the outbreak of World War I give rise to considerable discussion of the roles girls and women might play in such a situation. The children's grandfather opposes any action at all, saying 'I want no Amazons here. Sit at home and work and pray for the absent ones, that is all we want our girls and women to do'.[9] In helping out at the hospital, however, Grissell and Lynette display a very different ethos from their grandfather, which is buttressed by the figure of the hospital matron, Miss Fawcett, from whom they receive sensible advice about looking after the wounded, about the importance of being able to make poultices as well as light puddings, and especially of the need to help soldiers suffering from nervous disorders as well as physical damage.

The fact is that the times were changing again, and that Amy Le Feuvre's fiction reflects these changes even in what at first sight seem like her most conventional work. Girls' education had begun to develop dramatically after the establishment of schools specifically for them by Miss Buss and Miss Beale in the 1850s, and John Stuart Mill's great essay on *The Subjection of Women* of 1869 contributed to the changing climate of opinion. The High School Movement for Girls spread rapidly from the 1870s, and in 1872 and 1878, Cambridge and Oxford Universities, respectively, founded their first colleges for women. The emancipation of women received a further major boost in 1882 when the Married Women's Property Act legalised women's possession of property, and from then on more and different careers became possible for young girls and women, not just as governesses and female companions, but as clerks, journalists, nurses, teachers and typists. Mrs Emmeline Pankhurst founded the Women's Social and Political Union in 1903 to press for female suffrage, and, during World War I women gained even more power and freedom, though not yet the vote, as they moved into an ever wider range of new and responsible jobs. It is no coincidence that the hospital matron in *'Us, and Our Charge'* is named Lydia Fawcett, for it inevitably reminds the reader of Millicent Garrett Fawcett, one of the great leaders of the movement for female suffrage, and the mother of Elizabeth Garrett Andersen, the first British woman to qualify as a medical doctor in Paris in 1870. In Amy Le Feuvre's lifetime female emancipation took enormous strides, and though it is perhaps not explicit, she did reflect and explore the significance of this movement in her writings.

Amy was herself a remarkably independent and successful woman. As early as 1897 in *On the Edge of a Moor*, she had written a novel, perhaps mirroring her own life to some degree. After a family financial crisis, Rhoda, a young unmarried woman, decides to fend for herself by leaving the family home and settling in a cottage in a poor and remote Devon village. She has just enough money from her family to live on, and resolves, as she tells a neighbour, 'to help some of these poor country people to live happier, fuller lives – not to exist like mere animals, but to know something of what they were sent into the world for.'[10] She visits the sick, assists the village postmistress, starts a Bible Class, boards two poor children from the East End of London, and intervenes with a landlord on behalf of a distressed tenant. The story reads like a very idealised account of the life Amy herself was trying to live. But, although Rhoda succumbs to convention and marries the (now reformed) landlord at the end of the tale, what impresses is the rather touching picture of a spirited, unmarried, young woman, living on her own, and by her own efforts bringing comfort to the lives of the impoverished villagers.

The Making of a Woman (1903) is the story of Jean Desmond, an educated young woman whose life is stifled by her wealthy but dour grandfather. A friend persuades the grandfather to pay Jean a small income, and she goes off to learn and practice art first in London and then Paris. Although she obtains some commissions, life is hard and Jean's character gradually matures and becomes less ego-driven. She returns home to nurse her sick old grandfather, and finds religion. The story ends with her becoming a missionary's wife.

Other stories, such as *A Girl and her Ways* (1925), *Jock's Inheritance* (1927) and *Adrienne* (1928) follow similar patterns. Such books, usually aimed at older girls, and published by Hodder & Stoughton and Ward, Lock, rather than the RTS, reflect the changing social values that emerged after World War I. Gentian, the heroine of *A Girl and Her Ways*, for example, dismisses her fiancé because she does not love him, and tries to earn a living as a female taxi-driver, before she finds faith in God, and marries the man she really loves. Orris, the protagonist of *Jock's Inheritance*, has to earn a living by managing a woman's club in London and then by cataloguing a large private library. She is a typical Le Feuvre heroine, quietly attractive, slightly studious, unselfish and religious, but with considerable independence and self-esteem. When she agrees to marry Jock at the end of the story, she tells him:

'Don't you know that the modern girl will not be managed
by anyone, least of all by her husband.'

'I thank God daily that you are not modern,' said Jock.

'Even so,' said Orris demurely, 'I cannot always be managed, Jock.'[11]

Her Kingdom (1929) epitomises Amy Le Feuvre's later work perfectly, with its combination of a diluted evangelical didacticism and a modern feminist romanticism. The story begins like a Mills and Boon love-story when the orphaned heroine Anstice enters into a loveless marriage. She agrees to look after Justin's three motherless children in exchange for a share of his prosperous home. Two elements give the tale its distinctive flavour, however, one modern and one related to the evangelical tradition. For, despite her apparently compromised situation, Anstice retains a strong independence. She is a twentieth-century woman, earning her own living, able and willing to look after herself, seeking to survive in a difficult situation, and afraid of no one. Drawing on her quiet common sense and selflessness, she believes in trying to do good, befriending her husband's wayward children, helping the infirm, old country folk, supporting a depressed neighbour, reconciling two quarrelling sisters, and bringing her husband and his lost sister together again. Not surprisingly, she finds love with her husband in the end, but not before he has come to accept her religious beliefs. In the wake of World War I, the tradition of the Victorian family novel, with its conventionally happy ending and religious message, is just about breathing, but its decline is evident, and the thrust of a nascent modern feminism has a real presence. Society, in other words, is changing, and literature is changing along with it.

Having begun her literary career as a strongly didactic writer within the evangelical tradition of Mrs Sherwood and Mrs Walton, Amy Le Feuvre used her talents to portray children and young women more realistically than the idealised stereotypes of many of her predecessors. In this way she reflected some of the changes of her lifetime. Her limitations as a writer, however, prevented her completely escaping from or even seriously questioning the narrative conventions and formula of so many late-nineteenth-century novels. In her gentle pictures of independent young women, however, perhaps she may be regarded as a modest precursor of later developments. The year of her death (1929) was also the year Virginia Woolf published *A Room of One's Own*.

* * * * *

Checklist (All books were published in London unless stated otherwise)

1894   *Eric's Good News*: RTS.
1895   *'Probable Sons'*: RTS.
1896   *Dwell Deep; or, Hilda Thorn's Life Story*: RTS.
1896   *Teddy's Button!* : RTS.
1897   *On the Edge of a Moor*: RTS.
1898   *Odd:* RTS.
1898   *A Puzzling Pair:* RTS.
1899   *His Big Opportunity*: Hodder & Stoughton.
1898   *Bulbs and Blossoms:* RTS.
1898   *A Thoughtless Pair*: RTS.
1899   *The Carved Cupboard*: RTS.
1899   *Roses*: Hodder & Stoughton.
1899   *Legend-Led*: RTS.
1900   *Odd Made Even*: RTS.
1900   *Brownie*: Hodder & Stoughton.
1900   *Olive Tracey*: Hodder & Stoughton.
1901   *A Cherry Tree*: Hodder & Stoughton.
1901   *Heather's Mistress*: RTS.
1902   *A Daughter of the Sea*: Hodder & Stoughton.
1903   *The Making of a Woman*: Hodder & Stoughton.
1903   *Two Tramps*: Hodder & Stoughton.
1903   *Jill's Red Bag*: RTS.
1904   *His Little Daughter*: RTS.
1904   *A Little Maid*: RTS.
1905   *Bridget's Quarter Deck*: Hodder & Stoughton.
1905   *The Buried Ring*: Hodder & Stoughton.
1906   *Christina and the Boys*: Hodder & Stoughton.
1906   *The Mender:* RTS.
1906   *Miss Lavender's Boy and Other Sketches*: RTS.
1907   *Robin's Heritage:* Hodder & Stoughton.
1907   *Number Twa!:* RTS.
1907   *The Chateau by the Lake:* Hodder & Stoughton.
1908   *A Bit of the Rough Road:* RTS.
1908   *'Me and Nobbles'*: RTS.
1909   *'Us, and Our Donkey'*: RTS.
1909   *A Country Corner:* Cassell.
1909   *'His Birthday; A Christmas Sketch'* RTS.

1910   *Joyce and the Rambler:* Hodder & Stoughton.
1910   *A Little Listener:* RTS.
1911   *Us, and Our Empire:* RTS.
1912   *Tested!:* S.W. Partridge.
1912   *Four Gates:* Cassell.
1912   *Laddie's Choice:* RTS.
1913   *Some Builders:* Cassell.
1913   *Her Husband's Property:* RTS.
1914   *Harebell's Friends:* RTS.
1914   *Herself and Her Boy:* Cassell.
1914   *Works:* RTS.
1915   *Daddy's Sword:* Hodder & Stoughton.
1915   *Joan's Handful:* Cassell.
1916   *Dudley Napier's Daughters:* Morgan and Scott.
1916   *A Madcap Family; or, Sybil's Home:* S.W. Partridge.
1916   *'Us. and Our Charge':* RTS.
1917   *Tomina in Retreat:* RTS.
1917   *'Joy Cometh in the Morning':* RTS.
1918   *A Happy Woman:* RTS.
1918   *Terrie's Moorland Home:* Morgan and Scott.
1919   *The Chisel:* RTS.
1920   *The Discovery of Damaris:* RTS.
1920   *Little Miss Moth:* S.W. Partridge.
1921   *Martin and Margot:* RTS.
1922   *The Most Wonderful Story in the World; a Life of Christ for Little Children:* Hodder & Stoughton.
1922   *Oliver and the Twins:* RTS.
1923   *Dicky's Brother; or,'thou hast destroyed thyself, but in me is thine help':* Pickering and Inglis.
1923   *The Children of the Crescent:* RTS.
1924   *The Little Discoverers:* Oxford University Press.
1924   *My Heart's in the Highlands:* Ward, Lock.
1925   *Granny's Fairyland:* Sheldon Press.
1925   *A Girl and her Ways:* Ward, Lock.
1926   *Chats with Children; or, Pearls for young people:* Pickering and Inglis.
1926   *Noel's Christmas Tree:* Ward, Lock.
1926   *Three Little Girls:* J.F. Shaw.
1927   *Andy Man: a story of two simple souls:* Pickering and Inglis.
1927   *Jock's Inheritance:* Ward, Lock.
1928   *Cousins in Devon:* RTS.
1928   *Adrienne:* Ward, Lock.

1928 *Around a Sundial: and, Dicky's Brother:* Pickering and Inglis.
1929 *Alick's Corner:* RTS.
1929 *Her Kingdom: a story of the Westmoreland Fells:* Ward, Lock.
1930 *Under a Cloud:* Ward, Lock.
1931 *A Strange Courtship:* Ward, Lock.
1931 *Rosebuds. Choice and original short stories:* Pickering and Inglis.
1933 *Stories of the Lord Jesus: (*By Lettice Bell and Amy Le Feuvre.) A.B. Shaw.
1953 *Mimosa's Field:* Lutterworth.

(The publication of this work so much later than the author's other books is something of a mystery. The publishers suggest that a relative might have found the manuscript long after Le Feuvre's death and submitted it to the publisher. The contract for the book signed by C.S. Le Feuvre is dated November 5th 1947.)

Chapter Nine

Imperialists of the Air: Flying Stories 1900-1950

A lonely impulse of delight
Drove to this tumult in the clouds.
> (W.B. Yeats, 'An Irish Airman Foresees his Death')

I know nothing about the technical problems of air transport Services, but as a Conservative who had been brought up in the days of Rudyard Kipling, Joseph Chamberlain and Milner, I saw in the creation of air routes the chance of uniting the scattered countries of the Empire and Commonwealth.
> (Viscount Templewood, Secretary
> of State for Air, 1922-1929)[1]

Individual authors, such as Barbara Hofland and Charles Kingsley responded to changes in society in different ways, sometimes reflecting its dominant values, and sometimes, as in the case of Rider Haggard, questioning them. If we look at children's literature over a period of time, or examine a particular genre, we can see the same kind of varying reactions. The children's books of the 1930s, as we shall see, tended to be mainly in harmony with the previous values of that decade, but also contained a handful of diffident writers. The genre of flying stories, which became popular in the first half of the twentieth century, similarly tends to reflect the spirit of the age, but contains even fewer dissenting voices.

The emergence of flying stories in the early years of the twentieth century can be seen not only as an extension of the traditional adventure story established by Marryat, Ballantyne and Henty, but also as response to specific technological developments occurring in aviation at the same time. The purpose of this chapter is to consider the relationship between these historical developments and the literature which accompanied and was stimulated by them, to define the characteristics of that literature, and to discuss the political and imperial values which these flying stories offered.

After the first Zeppelin flight in 1900, aviation made rapid progress in the early years of the twentieth century. In December 1903 Orville Wright made the world's first controlled and sustained flight by a power-driven aircraft; in 1908 S.F. Cody made the first official flight in Britain; and in 1909 Louis Blériot flew across the English Channel.

World War I accelerated the development of aviation, though mainly in destructive ways. Airship and aeroplane attacks killed nearly 1,500 people in bombing raids on Britain by 1918, for example, while public admiration was particularly focused on those pilots who in such planes as the Sopwith Camel harassed and attacked the enemy. A new word was coined for outstanding aerial champions – the 'ace' – and such men as Billy Bishop and the German pilot von Richthoven were almost idolised as 'the cavalry of the clouds...the knighthood of the war', in Prime Minister Lloyd George's words.[2]

The creation of the Royal Air Force in 1918 inevitably continued to raise the public consciousness about the military potential of aircraft. In 1920, for example, Lord Trenchard, the first Chief of the Air Staff, used the RAF to put down a rising in Iraq, and his political chief, Sir Samuel Hoare, campaigned vigorously, by publicising long-distant flights, and by establishing University Air Squadrons and Light Aeroplane Clubs, to create what he called 'an air sense' throughout the country.[3]

Equally important was the development of civil aviation, as intrepid flyers strove to emulate the exploits of the Wright Brothers and Blériot, and economic interests sought to exploit the commercial possibilities of swift air travel. Alcock and Brown's flight across the Atlantic in 1919, Lindbergh's great Atlantic solo in 1926, and Amy Johnson's record-breaking journeys in the 1930s all increased public awareness of the drama and romance of flying, while the organisation of regular commercial air services between London and Paris in 1919, and then by the Dutch airline KLM to the East Indies in 1924 showed what was practicable. Furthermore, 1924 was the year in which various small British companies amalgamated to form Imperial Airways, which from 1926 began to create routes between many different parts of the Empire – from London to Karachi and Delhi in 1929, to Cairo and Capetown in 1932, and to Singapore a year later. This steady growth, accelerated by the enormous importance of aviation in World War II, and the tremendous expansion of civil aviation since then, had by the 1950s made flying a commonplace experience for many people.[4]

'Real flight and dreams of flight go together', however, as Thomas Pynchon reminds us in his novel *Gravity's Rainbow*,[5] and flying stories began to appear in Britain in increasing numbers from the end of the nineteenth century, first of all reflecting the early pioneering days of aviation, then concentrating on stories of combat inspired by the events of World War I, and later proliferating in the form of stories about the use of planes for record-breaking, for exploration, and for apprehending criminals in the 1920s and 1930s. Though flying stories continued to be popular in the Second World War, a fairly steady decline seems to have set in by the 1950s, as writers of the older generation disappeared, and the new writers of adventure stories preferred to work in the more traditional mode of historical romance, or to experiment in fantasy and science fiction. It is significant that even the one great exception to this decline, W.E. Johns, who did retain his popularity into the 1960s, turned to writing science fiction himself from 1954.[6]

The earliest writers in the pre-1914 phase owe a good deal more to fantasy and invention than to precise scientific knowledge. Such authors as Jules Verne and H.G. Wells had imaginatively explored the possibilities of space travel in such books as *From the Earth to the Moon* (1865) and *The First Men in the Moon* (1901), undoubtedly reflecting current speculation. Writers such as Harry Collingwood, 'Herbert Strang' and Percy F. Westerman pursued similar ideas in their children's books. Harry Collingwood, for example, in his *The Log of the 'Flying Fish'* (1887), a story deeply reminiscent of Jules Verne, portrays the exploits of a group of adventurers who, with the help of Professor von Schalckenberg, build a flying machine which can not only take off vertically but also undertake underwater ex-peditions, because it is constructed from a newly-discovered metal, 'aethereum', and can produce electricity and an expansive gas from crystals.[7]

Some of Herbert Strang's earlier books reveal similar elements of fantasy, though combined with growing authenticity. *The King of the Air* (1908), for example, depicts an airship which is shaped like a bird but also power-fuelled, and it also shows how a flying machine can be used to rescue threatened diplomats and to bomb hostile 'natives'.[8]

Perhaps Blériot's successful flight across the English Channel in 1909 stimulated the growing realism in these stories, however, for following his exploit, the fantastic accounts of gyro-cars, hydrofoils and rockets began to be replaced by more technically convincing tales about aeroplanes and airships. The career of Percy F. Westerman (1876-1959) illustrates the change most clearly. Westerman was prevented from following the naval career he hoped for by poor eyesight, and settled instead for clerical work as an Admiralty clerk in the Portsmouth Dockyard. A natural outdoorsman, he spent his spare time sailing and cycling all over Britain, and turned his hobbies to good account by writing about them for such magazines as *The Motor Boat, Hobbies* and *Yachting Weekly*. His first books, such as *A Lad of Grit* (1908), were historical tales, written in the vein of G.A. Henty, and often published by Henty's old publisher Blackie, who may indeed have regarded Westerman as Henty's successor. But, though Westerman's first love remained the sea, he began to introduce elements of new technology, whether real or imaginary, into such stories as *The Flying Submarine* (1912), and soon began to produce not only more authentic stories of naval warfare but also of aerial adventure in such books as *The Secret Battleplane* (1916).

Winning his Wings: a story of the R.A.F. (1919) is not only a key book in Westerman's career, but also totally characteristic of the way flying stories were developing. Set in the later stages of World War I, it describes the career of eighteen-year-old Derek Daventry, a new cadet at Training School, with accounts of his first flight, passing out as a pilot, and shooting down his first German plane in a raid over London. Posted to France, Derek helps to hold up the German advance on Paris, and experiences many other adventures before he is shot down, and invalided back to England where he is awarded the DSO.

Descriptions of Derek's first flight – the take-off, coping with an air pocket, setting a compass course, plunging through the clouds, negotiating a bumpy landing – of training with fellow-cadets, of Channel-crossing, of life on the squadron, and of carrying out running repairs, are all narrated in uninspired but serviceable prose, and point the way forward for other writers. Westerman wrote well over a hundred other books after *Winning his Wings*, including sea stories, mysteries and historical tales, but realistic flying adventure stories always formed an important part of his prolific output.

In the 1930s, indeed, Westerman produced a whole series of adventure stories about a flying detective, Colin Standish. In *The Amir's Ruby* (1932) and *The Westow Talisman* (1934) Standish, a senior pilot of Far Eastern Airways, is employed on special flights to bring valuable heirlooms, which criminals are planning to steal, safely back to Britain. As a result of the success of these missions, Standish is invited to become a sub-inspector in the newly-formed Royal Air Constabulary, and in such stories as *Standish of the Air Police* (1935), *Ringed by Fire* (1936) and *Standish Gets His Man* (1938) achieves an equally successful series of coups.[9]

During the 1930s, however, flying stories by W.E. Johns (1893-1968) began to appear, which eventually were to become even more popular than Westerman's. Unlike Westerman, Johns had actually seen a good deal of active service in World War I. Originally a soldier who experienced trench warfare in Gallipoli, Johns transferred to the Royal Flying Corps in 1917, and was a member of the 55th Squadron involved in bombing raids on Germany. Shot down in 1918, he finished the war in a prison camp, but remained in what became the RAF until 1927, obtaining further flying experience in India and Iran, and even claiming that he once interviewed Ross (i.e. Lawrence of Arabia) during a period when he was working as a recruiting officer in London.

Johns began to submit aviation pictures, articles and stories to various periodicals, and in 1932 published 'The White Fokker', his first story about Biggles, the pilot who would become his most enduring creation, in the magazine *Popular Flying*. 'Biggles' is the nickname of James Bigglesworth, at this time a teenager but already a Flight Commander on active service in France during World War I. Members of Biggles's squadron are regularly being ambushed and killed by a German Fokker D. VII, and though Biggles eventually managed to trap and shoot down the German pilot, what Johns emphasises is not just the skill of his hero but the cruelty of war, including its psychological damage, as this extract reveals:

> Bigglesworth, commonly called Biggles, a fair-haired, good-looking lad still in his teens, but an active Flight Commander, was talking, not of wine or women, as novelists would have us believe, but of a new fusee spring for a Vickers gun which would speed it up another hundred rounds a minute … He had killed a man not six hours before. He had killed six men during the past month – or was it a year? – he had forgotten. Time had become curiously telescoped lately. What did it matter anyway? He knew he had to die some time and had long ago ceased to worry about it. His careless attitude told one story, but the irritating little falsetto laugh which continually punctuated his tale told another.[10]

In these early stories Biggles is no stereotyped, tight-lipped hero, but a patriotic, skilful and highly-strung young man, who several times comes close to tears, even hysteria, when comrades are lost. In the magazine stories, collected in such books as *The Camels are Coming* (1932), *Biggles of the Camel Squadron* (1934) and *Biggles Learns to Fly* (1935) Johns successfully conveys the way many flyers felt and thought, with their mixture of idealism and simulated flippancy in those days of improvised flying when the average life-expectancy of a new pilot was about three weeks. Critics of Johns do him a disservice when they ignore these early books.

The problem for Johns was where to go once he had exhausted his war experiences. *The Cruise of the Condor* (1933) suggests the way his career was to develop, for it describes the adventures of Biggles and two of his wartime comrades, the Hon. Algernon Lacey and flight-sergeant Smyth, after the war, when they go on a treasure-hunt into the wilds of Brazil. Later books, such as *The Black Peril* (1935) and *Biggles Flies Again* (1938) show him reverting to more conventional plots, with the addition to the group of fifteen-year-old Ginger Hebblethwaite, and recurring appearances of an old German antagonist Eric von Stalheim. At the same time Biggles gradually hardens into an increasingly masterful hero, impervious to almost all dangers.

Although Johns was considered too old for flying duties in the Second World War, he became a lecturer at the Air Defence Cadet Corps and produced some specialist books for the Air Ministry, but his career as a writer of fiction took on a new lease of life with such books as *Biggles Defies the Swastika* (1941) when Biggles resumes active service. He also invented a heroine Squadron Officer Joan Worralson ('Worrals') of the Women's Auxiliary Air Force about whom he wrote a separate series of stories. After the Second World War Johns continued to write about Biggles, usually in the Flying Branch of the C.I.D., in such books as *Sergeant Bigglesworth C.I.D.* (1946) and *Biggles Gets his Men* (1950). By the time Johns died in 1968 he had written 102 books about Biggles and 11 about Worrals.[11]

But although Johns was clearly the dominant and most popular author of flying stories from the 1930s to the 1950s, he was by no means alone. Reacting no doubt to the growing interest in aviation, and stimulated by the success of such pioneers as Strang and Westerman, many other writers began to produce flying stories in remarkable abundance in book form and in magazines.

Although *The Boy's Own Paper* still relied upon romantic adventure fiction rather than contemporary realism for most of its stories, it did include many features about aviation among its non-fiction, such as articles about air pockets and instructions on modelling monoplanes, as well as photographs of such famous pilots as Mrs

J.A. Mollinson (formerly Amy Johnson). Occasionally, too, serials such as George E. Rochester's *The Flying Beetle* appeared among its more traditional tales of boarding-school life or historical romances, and its articles about cricket and cycling.

The Modern Boy, which was launched by the Amalgamated Press in 1928, was a two-penny weekly which appeared every Saturday in quarto, rather than the *BOP's* folio size, and with a three-toned pictorial cover. For two pence readers (adults as well as juveniles perhaps) got thirty pages of serials, photographs, features, and usually a strip cartoon retelling the story of a recent film. Johns wrote regularly for it, and George E. Rochester actually had a flying Western – *The Smugglers of Rustler Ranch*, featuring Chickenfeed Wilson, the flying sheriff – published in 1935. When Johns's serial *Winged Menace* (reprinted in book form as *The Black Peril*) ended on April 13th 1935, it was immediately followed by Percy F. Westerman's Standish serial *Ringed by Fire*, which started on April 20th. Though it would be wrong to describe *The Modern Boy* as entirely devoted to flying stories, for it also contained such items as *The School for Slackers* by Charles Hamilton (i.e. Frank Richards) and Colin Robertson's *Fire on the Film Set*, it was clearly an important source for them in the 1930s.

The Amalgamated Press, although best remembered for its school stories in the *Gem* and *Magnet*, also published many other periodicals which featured flying stories, such as *Chums*, *Pilot* and the *Schoolgirl*. The latter, mainly aimed at girl readers, of course, had a series about the adventures of the two flying sisters, Joan and Kit Fortune in the 1930s. In 1940 the Press's *Champion* magazine began stories about one of the best-known flying heroes, 'Rockfist Rogan', an ace-pilot who was also a boxing champion. (By contrast, D.C. Thomson's 'Big Five' story-papers, the *Adventure*, the *Rover*, the *Wizard*, the *Skipper*, and the *Hotspur* do not seem to have produced so many flying stories in this period.)

Popular Flying, which began in April 1932, under the editorship of W.E. Johns, was an even more important source. Published by John Hamilton, and costing sixpence a month, it contained sixty-four pages which not only usually included flying stories by such authors as Johns and perhaps 'Arthur Cave' (i.e. Christopher St John Sprigg), but features on such topics as 'The Air Force Overseas', 'Airports of the Future' and 'How Record Flights are Planned'. As well as contributing fiction, Johns wrote a regular column of comment from 'The Editor's Cockpit' in each issue.

Flying, a weekly which began in April 1938 and was also edited by W.E. Johns, cost three pence, and had a much greater emphasis on factual articles than either *The Modern Boy* or *Popular Flying*, including discussion on such topics as 'Aerial Advertising' and 'Who Did Kill von Richthofen?' But though Johns did contribute an air-thriller *Murder by Air*, featuring another hero named Steeley, he ceased to work for the magazine after December 31st 1938 because of his sustained attacks on Air Ministry Policy. Johns also ceased to be the Editor of *Popular Flying* in 1939 after a series of editorials attacking the government for its policy of appeasement.

In addition to the fiction which appeared in magazines and periodicals, flying stories were published in book form, of course, and almost every publishing house seems to have realised how popular they were, and so had their particular aviation authors. A. & C. Black published such books as *Pirates of the Air* (1937) by M.E. Miles and Jack Heming's *The Air Spies* (1936) in its 'Air Adventure' series. S.W. Partridge published Rowland Walker's *Captain McBlaid of the Air Police* (1932) and (some) Percy F. Westerman in its 'Great Adventure' series; Sampson Low, Marston published the flying stories of Michael Poole, such as *Couriers of the Air* (1936), and a remarkable series by Eileen Marsh about female aviators, such as *Lorna – Air Pilot* (1937). The Oxford University Press published flying stories by Air-Commodore L.E.O. Charlton, J.F.C. Westerman (Percy's son), and (some) W.E. Johns, including such titles as *Biggles Flies North* (1939).

Most remarkable of all was the publisher John Hamilton, however, who seems to have set out to corner the market in the 1930s, and played a crucial part in the development of aviation publishing. Established in 1925 by Charles H. Daniels and his wife Mary, the firm of John Hamilton recognised the growing interest in aviation, and began to specialise in books with air subjects. In 1932 it launched the magazine *Popular Flying*, aimed at the adult market, and asked Johns to become editor. A magazine expected to sell 12,000 copies monthly soon reached sales of over 32,000, and its success encouraged Hamilton to start a second magazine in 1934 called *Wings*, which contained flying adventures both in fact and fiction.

The John Hamilton Company published books on aviation in general, biographies and autobiographies of famous pilots, including accounts of famous German war heroes, as well as aviation history, and technical and instructional works on such topics as air navigation, gliding and aircraft modelling. The firm produced picture postcards of famous aeroplanes (each pack of seven costing a shilling) and more ambitious artwork. The catalogue for George E. Rochester's *The Flying Beetle* of 1935, for instance, contains advertisements for five water-colours by Stanley Orton Bradshaw of such aerial scenes as 'The Dog Fight' (2s. 6d.mounted or 1s. 6d. unmounted); and sepia prints by Howard Leigh of war-time aeroplanes such as the Sopwith 'Pup' at two shillings each. Although the firm published a certain amount of general fiction, with an emphasis upon 'thrillers', as well as a series of International Cook Books, it was with these flying stories that it achieved particular success. The famous 'Ace' series contained over seventy different full-length stories (selling at 3s. 6d. per volume) by such writers as Covington Clarke, J. Railton Holden, and W.E. Johns. Sadly, John Hamilton ceased publishing in 1941 after the firm was (rather ironically) bombed out of business, and the company's warehouses were damaged by fire. Although it lingered on for a time, the firm produced no more flying stories. During its brief existence, however, it had played a major part in raising the popular consciousness of aviation.[12]

From the 1930 until the 1950s it is clear that flying adventure stories became enormously popular. As well as books by W.E. Johns, Percy F. Westerman and Herbert Strang, works appeared by a bevy of other authors, including John Allan, Lucas Beresford, T.C. Bridges, A. Harcourt Burrage, Captain Michael Cely, E. Keble Chatterton, Covington Clarke, Air Commodore L.E.O. Charlton, Lt Colonel Driggs, F.E. Edsted, S.C. George, R.A.H. Goodyear, J.T. Gorman, W. Hansbro, Jack Heming, J. Railton Holden, David T. Lindsay, A.S. Long, M.E. Miles, John Noy, Jan Penhay, A.O. Pollard, Michael Poole, George E. Rochester, John Templer, the anonymous 'Vigilant', Roland Walker, J.F.C. Westerman, Alan Western, A. Whitehouse and Eric Wood. They established what looks like a minor literary genre.[13]

A small number of women writers, such as Dorothy Carter, C.M. Drury and the already-mentioned Eileen Marsh, also wrote flying stories, often about female pilots. (Ida Melbourne, however, who wrote *The Flying Sisters* (1935), was actually the pseudonym for Eric Lythe Rosman.[14])

Few of these writers, it has to be said, show any great originality in their works, although there were some exceptions. Air Commodore L.E.O. Charlton (1979-1958), for example, had a distinguished career in both the army and the Royal Air Force before retiring to write in 1928. *The Bush Aerodrome* of 1937, for example, though suffering from an over-complicated plot, shows both technical knowledge and freshness in its account of a British family's adventures when they build an aerodrome and set up an autogyro business in West Africa. John Templer, whose real name was John B. Townsend (1901-1958), had also served in the RAF and contributed stories to *The*

Modern Boy. A friend of Johns, Templer specialised in Air Police stories, with Flight Lieutenant L. Jayson, known as 'Jaggers' in such books as *Jaggers, Air Detective* (1936) and *Jaggers Swoops Again* (1937). Templer's creation of a flying detective seems likely to have influenced Johns, for his hero 'Biggles' becomes a policeman in his later stories such as *Sergeant Bigglesworth C.I.D.* (1947).

Such originality, however, is unusual among the hosts of flying stories published in the inter-war years. Many of them fall into very recognisable and formulaic patterns. What then are the characteristics of the flying story, and what does it tell us about imperialism in this period? The genre can usually be defined quite easily in terms of plot and characters, although there are naturally a number of individual variations. The hero is normally a young person, usually old enough to learn to fly and serve in the war or to undertake similarly hazardous adventures. An important feature of many stories is the hero's actual induction into the skills of aviation. In J.F.C. Westerman's *Menace from the Air* (1938), Ralph and his friend Tom are novices when the book begins, and the second chapter is devoted to 'Learning to Fly'. After that the hero generally moves through other initiations, such as the solo flight, cross-country journeys, being forced down, engaging an enemy, whether he is at war or in the midst of some other adventure, until the story's successful conclusion. One of the genre's conventions is to place considerable emphasis on the hero's companions, including ground staff, and on the airbase, whether it is an airport with hangars and customs offices or a more primitive landing strip improvised somewhere unexpectedly.[15]

What is quite notable about the characters in these stories, however, with the exception of the presentation of Biggles in Johns's earliest books, is their remarkable lack of individual characterisation. Popular interest in the exploits of pilots from World War I onwards has sometimes been seen as a natural reaction to the feeling that individualism was being crushed by the mass destruction of modern war. C.E. Montague, for example, in his autobiographical account of World War I says, 'At Agincourt the whole of our force … lay handy in one bivouac…. But now? Two million men can never be a happy few [but] … Air fighting came to be pretty well the old duel, or else the medieval melée between little picked teams.'[16] But the heroes of Westerman, L.E.O. Charlton, and J.R. Holden, are almost indistinguishable from each other. It is almost as if even in that area of fiction where heroes might still be expected to operate, individual personalities were beginning to disappear. Percy F. Westerman indeed seems to half-recognise the fact when he describes Derek Daventry, the colourless hero of *Winning his Wings* as 'one of many of the new type…the aerial warriors of Britain'.[17] Instead of individual characterisation, much greater emphasis seems to be placed upon the group to which the central character belongs, whether it is on active service, such as Biggles's famous 266 Squadron, with his cousin Algy, to be later joined by flight-sergeant Smyth, or Jerry Dearling and his team of secret service agents in Jan Penhay's *The Secret Flight Squad* (1937), or even some kind of civil aviation business such as Joe and Paul Yates operate with their father in L.E.O. Charlton's *The Bush Aerodrome* (1937).[18]

One can, of course, relate this apparent decline of the hero to the process Lucien Goldmann called 'reification'. He argues that the later periods of western capitalism, especially the imperialist period between 1912 and 1945, can be identified by the gradual disappearance of the hero and by the emergence of a world increasingly dominated by objects with their own autonomy.[19] It is certainly true that the new technology of aeronautics plays a prominent part in the genre of flying stories, from the twenty-page description of an airship in Collingwood's *The Log of 'The Flying Fish'* (1887) to the account of the spacecraft with which W.E. Johns ended his writing career in such books as *Kings of Space* (1954).[20] J.F.C. Westerman's description of a new plane in *The Air Record Breakers* (1937) is a fairly modest example:

> To the casual observer, it was just an ordinary monoplane, but an expert would have quickly picked out several unconventional points. Streamlining was carried out to a fine degree of perfection, the small fuselage had seating accommodation for four people, the wing span was very short in comparison with its other measurements, but the wings themselves were abnormally thick and wide. The ailerons appeared normal until a second glance showed that there were no control wires operating them. Nevertheless, they moved easily and smoothly when Dick climbed into the pilot's cockpit and handled the controls.[21]

Although Johns actually included a glossary of technical terms for his early flying stories, explaining the meaning of such words as 'blipping', it is the way writers describe the combination of man and machine which is noticeable. Despite the references to the control-stick, the rudder and the engine cowling, in this incident from George E. Rochester's *The Scarlet Squadron* (1938), for example, it is what the hero does with his plane that matters when he is pursued by a Chinese assailant:

I pulled viciously on the control-stick, jerking on full rudder. The machine swung with a jar that might well have
strained every strut and flying-wire. But I kept her so, and
as I completed a small circle in the air at an acute banking
angle, Kiu Lo tore past me.

It was my chance. As swiftly as I could I kicked the
rudder bar straight and whipped back the control-stick to
centre. The machine answered gallantly and right on the
tail of Liu Lo I started in pursuit, my gun roaring a staccato
accompaniment to the pulsating thunder of the engine.

He banked, his nose downwards. But I had anticipated
the move, for in very truth I was so close that it was about
the only course left to him. The range was too short for
me to miss and as he banked he laid his flank open to my
gun.

I pressed slightly on the rudder. The machine swung
and, in the act, the bullets from my synchronised gun rip-
ped through his fuselage from behind the cockpit to the
engine cowling.[22]

Even so, technology, objects and planes are very important, and
become animated and take on a life of their own occasionally, as here
the machine 'answered gallantly', almost like a human companion.
Elsewhere E. Keble Chatterton describes a flying-boat in these terms
in his 1932 story *Scouts of the Sky*: 'To see her twist and turn was a
lesson in perfect mobility. No insect could have been more mobile.'
Similarly, in J.T. Gorman's *Gorilla Gold* of 1937, an autogiro is said
'to wink back at her master from every scrap of white metal about
her', and *Couriers of the Air* (1936) describes some criminal aircraft
pursuing the young hero's monoplane in terms of a fox-hunt: 'The
Gnat had become the fox of the air and the pursuing planes were the
hunters, glorying in the joy of the chase.' On the other hand, even
Biggles becomes a mechanical object in *Biggles Defies the Swastika*,
when Johns says, 'For the next two months he became a machine, a
part of the aircraft.'[23]

With this apparent dissolution of characterisation and a greater
emphasis upon technology, it is clear that there is some reification
present in flying stories, but with it there goes an occasional joy in
flying which is at times almost transcendental. This near-religious
impulse, seen most notably in W.B. Yeats's fine poem 'An Irish
Airman Forsees his Death', is often expressed in clumsy language
in the flying stories, far from the simple directness of Cecil Lewis's

Sagittarius Rising (1936) or Antoine de Sainte-Exupéry's poetic *Wind, Sand and Stars* (1940). Those were adult works, but the youthful reader might have some glimmer of a similar feeling as he read of Jerry Dearling's joyful return to the air after illness in *The Secret Flight Squadron* or of Derek Daventry's first solo flight in *Winning his Wings*:

> The ecstasy of it all! To find himself controlling a swift aerial steed, to handle the responsive joy-stick, and to make the machine turn obediently to a slight pressure on the rudder-bar. Anxiety was cast to the winds. The sheer lust of flight in the exhilarating atmosphere gripped the cadet in its entirety.[24]

Whatever the reasons, emphasis upon the activities of a group of flyers rather than individuals also helped to give flying stories opportunities for more complicated plots than traditional adventure stories sometimes employed. When a group is involved in a battle or in solving a mystery, it is possible for members of that group to take on different tasks, or to pursue their activities separately, and thus multiply the number of concurrent adventures. W.E. Johns, in fact, developed absolutely formulaic plots along these lines when he moved on from stories about World War I, in which Biggles is the sole hero, to later books, such as *Biggles – Air Commodore* (1937), for example. Here Biggles, Algy and Ginger Hebblethwaite set out to discover why some merchant ships have been sunk under mysterious circumstances in the Indian Ocean. When they separate to begin their search, Ginger and Algy crash in the jungle, and Biggles has to rescue them; but later, when Biggles and Ginger are lost on an island, it is Algy who has to do the rescuing. Although the device was obviously used to create suspense, its use became very predictable; indeed, its very proliferation marks it as another characteristic of stories where men are seen as members of a team rather than as individuals.

The plots of most flying stories tend to fall into one of two categories – either exploits set in the First or Second World Wars, or exploits involving criminals or mysteries of some kind, perhaps a search for a missing aviator or lost treasure. What is significant about most stories, however, is the way they are based upon a total acceptance of the dominant social and political values of the period. Though Johns could depict, with more skill than he has sometimes been given credit for, the sufferings experienced in World War I, there is no suggestion anywhere that its causes might have been questioned. Indeed, in a famous letter to Geoffrey Trease written in 1946 he claimed 'I teach the spirit of team-work, loyalty to the Crown, the Empire and to rightful authority'. George E. Rochester's hero of *The Flying Beetle* says almost the same in his famous and repeated pledge – 'For God – for King – for Country!'[25]

It is unlikely, as Bernard Porter points out, that Britain had any great desire to expand its vast colonial empire in 1914, and though the outcome of the First World saw the acquisition of mandated territories in Palestine, Iraq and Transjordan, as well as taking over Tanganyika from Germany, Britain's main aim in the post-war years was simply to hold on to its existing imperial power in a period of increasing nationalism. In Ireland, Egypt, Iraq, and especially India protests grew and various concessions had to be made, although usually only after initial resistance to change. During this same period Britain's economic decline continued, and many politicians saw imperial trade, by encouraging emigration and through imperial preference, as a way of dealing with this. Leopold Amery, Colonial Under-Secretary from 1919-1921, and Colonial Secretary from 1924-1929, was a staunch advocate of imperial economic policies, and the Empire Day Movement, the Empire Marketing Board, and the press campaigns of Lord Beaverbrook and Lord Rothermere all kept these ideas alive in the 1920s and 1930s.[26]

In view of the literary connections between modern flying stories and the traditionally conservative and imperialistic adventure stories of G.A. Henty and Herbert Strang, it is not surprising that there is also a clear ideological inheritance. These works of the new technological age are related quite clearly to their late-Victorian predecessors in their defence of Britain's political and therefore imperialistic status quo, and expression of attitudes of British racial supremacy to foreigners, especially if they were black.

Major T. Gorman's *Gorilla Gold* of 1937 is fairly typical, for, although the villain is English, the book is notable for its treatment of the African 'natives', who are either evil and cowardly like the Zande tribe, or childlike and loveable like the pigmies. As Bob Dixon points out, 'Racism is a constant and ... inevitable feature of empire-building, since it seems impossible to subject people to an alien rule without believing in their inferiority'.[27] It is certainly true that the stories of writers as diverse as J. Railton Holden, Michael Poole and J.F.C. Westerman offer simple, stereotyped views of foreigners, whether they are black or white. And while it becomes tedious to labour the point, what is particularly disappointing in the work of W.E. Johns is the way his attitude seems to have shifted from a recognition of good and bad Germans, just as there are good and bad Englishmen, in his earlier war stories, to his fairly general dismissal of most non-Europeans as 'dagos', 'half-castes' and 'wogs' elsewhere. Even as early as *Biggles Flies Again* in 1934, Johns was writing fairly frequently in this vein:

The Greek laughed a short, unpleasant laugh.

'Do you think you are in a position to dictate terms?' he scoffed.

'I certainly do, or, not being entirely a fool, I should not have returned to this den of thieves.'

'What is to prevent me killing you now?' asked the Greek, with an evil smile.

'Come here and I'll show you,' said Biggles imperturbably, crossing to the window. The other followed. 'I'm going to show you what will happen if I'm not back in my machine in half an hour,' he went on, waving his handkerchief through the window.

The 'Vandal,' circling above, swept down in a steep dive near the palm-grove. A sheet of orange flame leapt upwards and a deafening detonation shook the palace to its foundations. The 'Vandal' made a quick stalling turn and Smyth could be seen crouching low over a Vickers gun.

Rat-tat-tat-tat-tat-tat. Rat-tat-tat-tat-tat. The sand flew up in a long line as the mechanic put half a belt of ammunition into the ground as the machine roared past.

Biggles saw the Arabs running for cover. 'My friends have had quite a lot of experience at this sort of thing', he observed casually, 'and if anything happens to me I can promise you that neither this building nor any man on the oasis will be standing by the time they've finished. The dhow in the offing will also make a handy target. Furthermore,' he bluffed as an afterthought, 'I have told them if they want any assistance to call up R.A.F. machines by radio from Aden and Khartoum. Every gunboat within five hundred miles will pick up the call and hurry along to see what it's all about.'

'Where did you get that gun?' snarled the Greek, with an evil scowl; 'it wasn't –'

'Bosh!' snapped Biggles. 'Do you think we show passengers all our equipment?'

'Well, what are you going to do about it?'

The mention of the Royal Air Force and the gunboats seemed to shake the Greek, for his face turned a pale olive-green....[28]

The use or mention of the Royal Air Force in so many stories inevitably associates them with an implicit political ideology. Indeed
this connection between flying and imperial interests was further
strengthened by the inevitable if indirect relationship of many British
flyers with the government-subsidised Imperial Airways, with its
evocative roll-call of imperial air-routes from London to Cairo, to the
Cape, to Karachi, to Singapore and to Australia. Readers are always
reminded, in Jack Heming's words, that planes link Britain 'to the
furthest corners of the Empire'.[29] Another very obvious illustration of
this connection between flying and imperialism is the title Viscount
Templewood, Secretary of State for Air from 1922-1929, gave his
autobiography of those years in office: *Empire of the Air: The Advent
of the Air Age 1922-1929*.

What to modern readers is even more remarkable than the insistence on air links or endemic notions of racial superiority, however, is
the alarmist, ultra-defensive reaction to any threats, real or imaginary,
to the Empire – a reflection perhaps of the post-1918 anxiety to retain
Britain's imperial power in a period of growing unrest. Some stories
show an awareness of nationalism, but it is rarely discussed openly.
Eric Wood's *Wings Over India* (1938) is perhaps the most explicit,
probably because in telling the story of how the RAF suppressed a
rising on the North-West Frontier of India, the author felt some explanation was necessary:

> The key-pin of all the troubles had been a young gentleman
> named, after the fashion of his people, the Fakkir of Madda.
> He was a Moslem, had been educated in England, and,
> like so many of his kind, had returned home firmly con-
> vinced that the British Raj had no right in India, which
> should be 'free' and independent. Occidental learning had
> only increased the Oriental fanaticism of the Fakkir of
> Madda. He was a one-idea man. He failed to see, perhaps
> deliberately closed his eyes to the fact, that if the British
> left India that country of strange romance and enormous
> wealth, with its teeming multitude of potential consumers,
> would become the cockpit of grabbing nations – some of
> whom, by insidious propaganda, fostered ideas of freedom
> and hoped, and waited, for the day when spasmodic erup-
> tions would give place to extensive and extending war-like
> operations.[30]

Given the connections between flying, the imperial air-routes
and the RAF's responsibilities of national defence, which included

overseas duties, it seems natural enough that many flying stories should have been set in Africa or the Middle East, and that they should reveal attitudes of British racial superiority. What is still extraordinary to discover, however, is how, in one flying story after another, what begins as an investigation into an apparently conventional crime, involving robbery or smuggling perhaps, soon uncovers an international conspiracy planned by sinister foreigners to overthrow Britain and to destroy the whole Empire.

Jack Heming's *The Air Spies* (1936) is a characteristic tale of how a youthful enthusiast, Bill Smith, achieves his great ambition of learning to fly, when he is rewarded by a millionaire for returning his wallet. After qualifying as a pilot in record time, Bill is employed by the millionaire as an agent to help 'defeat the Empire's enemies'. Not only are foreign criminals plotting to steal the plans of a new aeroplane, but they are doing so to humble the Empire. In the end the leader, Radiloff, who seems to bear a considerable resemblance to Lenin, tries to stir up discontent by smuggling cocaine to large gatherings of the working-classes somewhere near Redcar, but young Bill, the millionaire, and their planes are able 'to smash the Communist plot'.[31]

Taken in isolation, the story could be dismissed as a literary aberration, but Johns's *The Black Peril* (1935) similarly describes how Biggles defeats a Russian-led conspiracy to build secret military installations along the East Coast of Britain; indeed, Biggles and Co. actually land in Soviet Russia to foil the attempt. J. Railton Holden's *Wings of Revolution* (1934) is the story of how three brothers, with some adult help, foil a Red (Communist) plot to take over first Egypt and then the rest of the world. Rowland Walker's *Captain McBlaid of the Air Police* (1932) has similar subject matter, beginning as a search for a mysterious submarine, and ending by describing the crushing of an international conspiracy, led by an evil genius called Damiensk. J.F.C. Westerman's *Menace from the Air* (1938) unfolds a similar plan to take control of Europe by means of an airship. The young hero Tom disputes the villain's plot:

> 'one airship, however invulnerable, could not hope to conquer Europe. Why, England alone could finish her off somehow before long!'
> 'England is our greatest difficulty,' came the admission. 'As a result, she is the first to be dealt with. But she will stand no chance against our weapons.'[32]

The fear of foreign conspiracies and invasions, sometimes bordering on paranoia, found in these stories, might be interpreted as an expression about the rise of fascism and Nazi Germany. But it is worth emphasising that many of them seem to equate the threats of foreign invasion with Russia or with 'Communism', though usually in vague, unanalysed terms, rather than fascism. The Zinoviev letter scare of 1924 – when a forged letter, purporting to have come from Zinoviev as head of the Communist International, and inciting British workers to revolt, was published in the British press – had whipped up an already existing fear of Bolshevism at least in some quarters. It was this fear of foreign-incited class revolt that is reflected in books such as *Wings of Revolution, The Black Peril* and *The Air Spies*, rather than anxiety about Hitler. The classic example of the flying story rife with conspiracy-driven anxiety is George Rochester's *The Flying Beetle*, which, though published by Hamilton in book form in 1935, had first been serialised in the *Boy's Own Paper* as early as 1926, the same year, of course, as the General Strike. *The Flying Beetle* is an extraordinary story which owes something to the influence of John Buchan and Baroness Orczy combined. It opens with a masked chief summoning a group of leading criminals to help him destroy England and her Empire: 'you boast, you English, that you have an Empire on which the sun never sets. But the day will come when the Empire shall be rent asunder. The day will come when her colonies will have broken away.'

Fortunately this leader, a wealthy country gentleman named Sir Jasper Haines, employs as his secretary his apparently effete, book-reading nephew, Harry Davies, who, always dressed in black, not only manages to outwit him, but also has the courteous (and characteristically British?) habit of leaving a calling-card behind after his exploits, signed 'The Black Beetle'. A master of disguise and a superlative airman, Harry Davies pilots a black aeroplane, and is always able to defeat Sir Jasper's endeavours – to smuggle arms to Indian rebels, for example – but, most important of all, he is the staunchest patriot, whose prayer book bears the inscription – 'For God – for King – for Country'.

Aggressive, patriotic, deeply conservative, racist, Rochester was almost as prolific as Johns and P.F. Westerman in the 1930s, and produced many similar books about international conspiracies such as *The Despot of the World* (1936) and *The Scarlet Squadron* (1938). The latter is another noteworthy example of the Flying Beetle's zeal in defending Britain, this time against a sinister foreigner who boasts:

> 'The hordes of China are about to rise,' he went on, and something in his voice told me he spoke the truth, 'and

with China in arms, the whole of Asia will flock to our banner. India will become ours in a night, and we shall sweep westwards till we call a halt only in mighty London itself! What of your flag then, you spy? What of your great Empire? Pah! A shambles and we the butchers!'[33]

Generalisations are dangerous, of course, and one can readily identify areas that would reward further research, such as investigating the prevalence of the kind of *economic* imperialism suggested by L.E.O. Charlton's African story *The Bush Areodrome*. It would be particularly interesting to compare the values of non-flying with those of flying stories over the same period in terms of imperialism. Were they more imperialistic or not? Finally, it could prove extremely rewarding to trace the different shifts of feeling towards empire between 1910 and 1950, because even if we say that the dominant ideology running through most of the flying stories can be broadly termed 'imperialism', we always have to remember Raymond Williams's words to the effect that that

imperialism, like many other words which refer to fundamental social and political conflicts, cannot be reduced, semantically, to a single, proper meaning. Its important historical and contemporary variations of meaning point to real processes which have to be studied in their own terms.[34]

Chapter Ten

The Retreatism of the 1930s: A Few Dissenters

To me, England is the country, and the country is England.
And when I ask myself what I mean by England ... England
comes to me through my different senses ... the tinkle of
the hammer on the anvil ... the corncrake on a dewy morning ... the last load at night of hay being drawn down a
lane as the twilight comes on ... the smell of wood smoke
coming up in an autumn evening....

(Stanley Baldwin, 'On England')

The first sound in the mornings was the clumping of the
mill-girls' clogs down the cobbled street. Earlier than that,
I suppose, there were factory whistles which I never wake
to hear.

(George Orwell, *The Road to Wigan Pier*)[1]

After the horrors of World War I (1914-1918) and the violent class-
conflict of the Great Strike of 1926, Britain seemed to withdraw from
militant confrontation and to search for some kind of national unity.
The National Government elected in 1931 and its successor in 1935
were pledged to preserve stability. Stanley Baldwin, Prime Minister
in 1923-1924, 1924-1929 and 1935-1937, was the appropriate leader
and symbol for a Britain 'desperate for a return to tranquillity and
social peace', as Kenneth Morgan reminds us.[2] Much of the country
prospered, particularly in Southern England and the Midlands, and
the majority of workers had no significant spell of unemployment
between 1929 and 1940. The population continued to rise. Home
ownership grew and there were over a million cars in private hands

which made visits to the seaside or the countryside a popular pastime for the more prosperous.[3]

This is the main reason why much of the children's literature of the thirties reflects a kind of quietism, what Peter Hunt has called 'a retreat from the realities of the world surrounding the child and the book'. And so, he says, the world of children's literature was largely 'the world of the comfortable middle class'.[4] The juvenile literary scene seems to have become dominated with works of fantasy, sometimes brilliant, but often gently escapist, even when professing to be realistic.

Thus, a representative list of children's books published in the 1930s includes:

1930   *Wireless in Toytown* by S.G. Hulme Beaman (1886-1932)
1931   *The Chalet School and Jo* by Elinor Brent-Dyer (1894-1969)
1932   *Darkie & Co.* by Howard Spring (1889-1965)
1932   *William the Pirate* by Richmal Crompton (1890-1969)
1933   *The Incredible Adventures of Professor Branestawm* by
            Norman Hunter (1899-1995)
1934   *Winter Holiday* by Arthur Ransome (1884-1967)
1934   *Mary Poppins* by P.L. Travers (1899-1996)
1935   *The Box of Delights* by John Masefield (1878-1967)
1935   *National Velvet* by Enid Bagnold (1889-1981)
1936   *Hedgerow Tales* by Enid Blyton (1897-1968)
1936   *Little Grey Rabbit's Party* by Alison Uttley (1884-1976)
1936   *Ballet Shoes* by Noel Streatfeild (1895-1986)
1936   *Wurzel Gummidge* by Barbara Euphan Todd (1897-1976)
1937   *Martin Pippin in the Daisy Field* by Eleanor Farjeon (1881-1965)
            The Hobbit by J.R.R. Tolkien (1892-1973)
1938   *The Sword in the Stone* by T.H. White (1906-1964)
            Orlando: the Marmalade Cat by Kathleen Hale (1898-2000)
1939   *The Ship that Flew* by Hilda Lewis (1896-1974)

Any decade which contains such books as *The Box of Delights* and *The Hobbit* must be considered successful, and incidentally raises questions about the suggestion frequently heard that that the Second Golden Age of Children's Literature began in the 1960s. One must also note, however, that the main strength of the period lies in its high quality fantasy from Hulme Beaman to T.H. White.[5]

Howard Spring (1889-1965) is a particularly interesting example because, although he was brought up in poverty and worked for a number of years as a journalist in South Wales, his children's books,

Darkie & Co. (1932), *Sampson's Circus* (1936) and *Tumbledown Dick* (1939) virtually ignore the society around him. Although they are realistic in the broadest sense, these tales are really jolly *picaresques*, which combine melodramatic plots and comic caricatures with considerable zest, but essentially accept the *status quo* without either systemic analysis or, it must be said, expressing any great discomfort. The impression one gets is that, apart from occasional mishaps, everyone is perfectly safe.

The children's literature of this period tends to reflect the values of the prosperous and untroubled part of the population, not really noticing the often violent struggles of the General Strike and the rise of communism and fascism. Adult literature of the time, such as the works of Auden, Graham Greene and Orwell, did notice these events, but it is as if children's writers deliberately chose to ignore them and retreat into comedy or pastoral fantasy. It goes without saying that children's writers must write as they will, and that there is no obligation on them necessarily to write realistically or produce propaganda about the age in which they live. One might, however, have expected to find more variety among the fiction published in what was a troubled period, as happened in the second half of the nineteenth century when, to give a few examples, realistic tales by 'Hesba Stretton' (the pseudonym of Sarah Smith [1832-1917]) and Charlotte M. Yonge appeared alongside the works of 'Lewis Carroll' (i.e. Charles Dodgson [1832-1898]) and Rider Haggard.

For although much of Britain did enjoy relative prosperity and stability in the 1930s, particularly in the south and industrial Midlands, there were also massive regional variations. Unemployment, often said to have blighted the whole of Britain in this period, was in fact most devastating in those areas dependent on the older stable industries of textiles, iron and steel, and mining, such as Lancashire, Scotland, the North-East and South Wales. In 1936, for example, one in four workers in the Rhondda and almost one in five in Crook (County Durham) had been unemployed for a year or longer. While workers in the newer industries flourished, the older and less-skilled workers suffered, especially where there was also poor housing and health provision. Andrew Thorpe calculates that unemployment never fell below a million during this period, and quotes the wife of a sixty-two-year-old miner saying that they 'would be better dead than go on like this'.[6]

The picture in agriculture was more complicated because, while there was some government help in the form of protection imposed from 1931-1932, and direct subsidies to producers of wheat and sugar beet, which made conditions better for some, there was also much poverty and debt. In June 1933, for example, the number of workers employed in agriculture fell below 600,000 compared with over one million in 1931, and the number of farmers declared bankrupt reached 600 in 1932 compared with 44 in 1920.[7]

Because of these regional and industrial variations, and the contrasts between poverty in some parts of Britain and prosperity in others, one could say that in the 1930s Britain was almost as divided into two nations as it had been in the 1840s. It is, therefore, not surprising that some children's writers of this period, though not very many, did reveal unease at the social and economic difficulties and inequalities.

The most popular reading of the 1930s, as represented by magazines such as the *Gem* and the *Magnet*, published by the Amalgamated Press, and the *Hotspur* and the *Rover*, published by D.C. Thomson, mainly concentrated upon adventure stories and school yarns, and were essentially escapist. Yet they did raise social issues from time to time, particularly in stories about working-class 'scholarship boys', who struggled (usually successfully) to cope with their middle-class and sometimes snobbish schools. Although 'Frank Richards' (i.e. Charles Hamilton [1876-1961]) notoriously avoided any mention of religion, sex, strikes or unemployment in his stories in the *Gem* and *Magnet*, there were a succession of working-class 'scholarship boys' alongside Harry Wharton and Billy Bunter at Greyfriars School.[8]

Eleanor Grahame's *The Children who Lived in a Barn* (1938) is one of the few books which reflects some of society's tensions in this period in a muted but more sustained way. Grahame (1896-1984), whose family came from rural Scotland but moved to Essex when she was four, worked as a medical student for a time before moving first into a bookshop and then to the post of children's book editor for Heinemann and then Methuen. When Penguin Books started their series of Puffin Story Books for children in 1941, Eleanor Grahame was appointed their first editor and for more than twenty years played a critical role in their development, as Stuart Hannabuss has observed, building up a discriminating list of fine children's books. She was extremely sensitive and well-informed authority on children's literature.[9]

The Children who Lived in a Barn is in fact a modern version of a *Robinsonnade*, given a realistic setting in British in the 1930s. The story is essentially about the adventures of the Dunnett family who live in the village of Wyden. When the grandfather is taken ill abroad, the children's parents have to fly out to help him, leaving their five children, aged between 13 and 7, to look after themselves. But their unpleasant landlord threatens to evict the children from their cottage and they find refuge in a barn offered by a kindly farmer. When the children don't hear from their parents, and there are rumours of a plane crash, they know they will have to cope on their own. They clean up the barn and learn to prepare their own meals. When the holidays end, the children return to school. Thirteen-year-old Susan has to do the cooking and the laundry, while the others do odd jobs in their spare time to earn money. The Rector's wife arranges for the children to be regularly inspected by the District Visitor, and other members of the village offer interference or help in various ways. Finally, a friendly journalist, learning of the children's plight, writes a newspaper article about them, which the parents read by chance while recovering from their flying accident overseas. The parents are safely reunited with their children and the threatening adults are defeated.

Although the story looks at first as if it is going to offer a rural idyll, once the reader accepts the implausible disappearance and then reappearance of the parents, the book becomes a convincing picture of real life. When the children lose their cottage and have to manage on limited resources, they have to learn to look after themselves, find food, fuel and clothes, learn to cook their meals, and to cope with the problems of everyday life without much money or parental help. Life is particularly harsh for Susan, the eldest girl, for she has to shoulder most responsibility. Threatened by the District Visitor, she has to make sure that the barn is clean and tidy, and that the children attend school regularly and neatly. There is a vivid account of her doing the family washing in a copper boiler between 4 and 8 a.m., before she gets herself off to school. She has difficulty dealing with her energetic and sometimes uncooperative younger brothers and sisters. And, though they do receive a small allowance from their absent father's bank account, there is always a shortage of money. Even eleven-year-old Bob feels the pressure – 'money, money, money! Cried a voice inside him. *We must have money!*'[10]

But, as well as this picture of the children struggling against practical and economic problems, the story also shows an interesting awareness of the different social classes, with the middle class, represented by the Rector and his wife, the District Visitor and their landlord, revealed as interfering and cruel, while the villagers, especially the farmer and his wife, seem more friendly and supportive. The old tramp Solomon, clearly at the bottom of the social ladder, is the most sympathetic adult in the book. Eleanor Grahame's publisher, Routledge and Kegan Paul, worried about this aspect of the manuscript, but, as well as pointing to the presence of other sympathetic adults, Eleanor Grahame defended herself, saying 'I too was a little taken aback (sic) to find how poorly the grownups developed – and yet I think they are pretty true to life.'[11] The book well deserves its republication by Persephone Books (London: 2001, 2003), and Jacqueline Wilson's warm praise in the preface.[12]

Apart from the framing device of the parents' disappearance at the beginning and reappearance at the end of the story, *The Children who Lived in a Barn* is very simply organised in a series of episodes, and the work of Eve Garnett (1900-1991) is similarly very episodic. Although Eve Garnett trained as an artist at the Royal Academy Schools and her illustrations to Stevenson's *A Child's Garden of Verses* (Puffin, 1948) are still well regarded, she is best known for her three children's books about the working class Ruggles family. *The Family from One End Street* was first published in 1937 and won the Carnegie Medal that year. *Further Adventures of the Family from One End Street* was not published until 1956; though the story was begun in 1940, it was believed to have been destroyed by fire and not recovered until later. A third story, *Holiday at the Dew Drop Inn: a One End Street Story* was not written and published until 1962.

Eve Garnett came from a middle-class family and enjoyed an idyllic upbringing, but moving to London to study art in the 1920s seemed to have had a profound effect upon her. According to her nephew and biographer, Terence Molloy, 'Eve, besides being particularly touched by the plight of unemployed ex-servicemen, found her social conscience roused during frequent visits to the East End on seeing the deplorable condition of children in the slums'.[13] Some of her drawings of children won the admiration of the publisher John Lane, and she was commissioned to illustrate Evelyn Sharp's *The London Children* of 1927. This touching book, which simply describes the lives of poor working-class children in London in the late 1920s, contains many short accounts of children playing in the streets, including one of a docker's daughter sent from Wapping to convalesce in Devon, which clearly influenced Garnett's own writing.

Eve Garnett also devised and illustrated another important book on children entitled *Is It Well with the Child?*, published by Muller in 1938. There is little prose in this book, just a series of poignant and angry monochrome sketches illustrating the poverty of urban working-class life. The book's savagery often arises from the juxtaposition of an ambitious, public statement with a picture illustrating the reality of the working-class situation. Illustration No. XV, for example, quotes an Air Raid Precaution suggestion, as World War II approached, that 'One room in the house should be set apart and made gas-proof'. Eve Garnett's accompanying illustration shows a family of seven eating, sleeping and living in a single room. A quotation from *The Times* adds that 'There are over 110,000 families living in one-room dwellings in London alone.'[14]

Eve Garnett, therefore, brought a considerable awareness of the lives and conditions of working-class families to her children's books, and, as she made clear in her talk about accepting the Carnegie Medal for *The Family from One End Street*, she knew what she was trying to do:

> I have always thought, not perhaps very originally, that the reason one half of the world does not know how the other half lives, is chiefly because the half which might be expected to know is not interested. Once people are interested they are usually concerned to know, and it seems to me, like so many other useful things, this interest is best begun in the nursery – particularly nurseries like the one from which came the almost incredible but true story of the little girl who asked her nurse if it were really true that there were people who hadn't even one motor-car! This may be exceptional but it is true that the average child of well-to-do parents today – particularly the country child – is extraordinarily ignorant of the conditions under which less fortunate children live. One wonders why.[15]

The Family from One End Street is basically a happy family story about Mr Ruggles, a dustman, Rosie, his wife, who is a washerwoman, and their seven children. The book is very episodic in form with, more or less, each of the ten chapters concentrating on a simple domestic adventure involving one of the children. Lily Rose tries to help her mother, but accidentally uses a hot iron on an artificial silk petticoat which causes it to shrink. Kate, who has passed the exam to go to secondary school, loses but then recovers her new school hat. Jo sneaks into a cinema for a free visit, but is discovered by the musicians, who ultimately pay for him. Nine-year-old John is driven away in a car he has been asked to mind, but the kindly owners look after him and invite him to their son's party. The book ends with the whole family enjoying a Whitsun Bank Holiday in London at the Cart Horse Parade in Regent's Park.

Further Adventures of the Family from One End Street has slightly more structure. The first three chapters depict the family still living in London, but Lily catches measles, and Peg and Jo are ordered to convalesce in the countryside. Kate (now twelve) goes to look after them, and the book's middle chapters concern these children's adventures at the Dew Drop Inn with kindly Mrs Wildgoose. Meanwhile, back in London, Mr Ruggles achieves his life-long ambition to obtain and raise a pig; and the story ends when the convalescents return home only to discover that Kate has now developed measles herself. *Holiday at the Dew Drop Inn*, published in 1962, deals with Kate's holiday in the countryside, and is similar to the story in *Further Adventures*.

A lot of this is easy reading. The characterisation is thin, almost stereotyped at times, and the structure of simple, domestic episodes with little real development is fairly basic. The domestic crises, serious enough in themselves, are nearly always resolved quite easily, either by a stroke of good luck, as when Mr Ruggles finds some money in a rubbish-heap, or by the help of some kindly stranger, as when some friendly dockers send the runaway Jim safely home in a lorry.

Some critics, like John Rowe Townsend, have found Eve Garnett's attitude altogether too condescending. Here is what he says in his revised edition of *Written for Children* in 1976:

> [*The Family from One End Street*] seems to me too condescending to be altogether commendable. Mr and Mrs Ruggles are seen from above and outside. Even their names, and the choice of their occupations as dustman and washerwoman, make them seem slightly comic. People from higher up the social scale are terribly nice to the Ruggleses; and the Ruggleses know their place.[16]

There is some truth in this, and yet it does not do full justice to Eve Garnett's realistic portrayal of the difficulties of the Ruggles's poor working-class life – their struggles for shoe-repairs and their reliance on second-hand clothes, the costs of school uniforms and of doctors' bills, the problems over bus fares, the absence of bathrooms and electricity – all the daily grinding for sufficient money to bring up seven children. Yet these are happy stories, full of warmth and gentle humour, as the characters fall into and recover from various mishaps, and they are told with genuine affection and admiration for the family. Christopher Hopkins relates this to what, following W.E. Empson, he calls 'Proletarian Pastoral'.[17] He reminds us that there is a strong pastoral interest in Eve Garnett's stories. Mr Ruggles has always wanted to buy a pig, tries to save money for it, and at the end of *Further Adventures* finally realises his ambition. In *Further Adventures* not only Kate, but Jo and Peg as well spend time in the countryside, to which Kate returns in *Holiday at the Dew Drop Inn*. As part of this pastoral theme, Mr Ruggles and his family are presented as simpler and yet somehow more contented than we might expect from their situation. The reader follows their adventures with sympathy and humour. They seem poor but happy.

And yet Eve Garnett shows us that their world is more complicated than it appears in a number of disturbing episodes. When the friendly Lawrences invite John to their son's birthday party, he meets children from a different social class:

> 'Do you go to school?' she asked next. John nodded.
> 'I'm in the third form,' she continued. 'Where are you?'
> John looked puzzled. Forms were things one sat on.
> '*I'm* in a Standard,' he said.
> 'I thought that was a sort of flag,' said the girl. 'What does it mean?'
> John found it hard to explain. ' There's seven,' he said. 'I'm in four. My sister's in seven – she's got a scholarship,' he added proudly.
> 'I've a cousin who's got one,' said the girl not to be outdone. 'She's going to Oxford, is your sister going to Oxford?'
> 'No,' said John, 'she's going to Otwell Central.'
> 'It sounds like a railway station,' said the girl....[18]

Later on in the story Mr Ruggles finds an envelope containing some money amongst the rubbish, and when he returns it to the owner, an impoverished author, Mr Ruggles thanks him profusely for giving him two pounds reward:

> 'Don't,' said the author; 'I only wish it were more but times are difficult,' and he slammed the door after his guests. His cheerful mood had evaporated. Mr Ruggles's thanks bothered him. Eight human beings (for he supposed the baby was indifferent) achieving complete happiness and their life's ambition for five shillings a head; five shillings! *Thanks....* Did one pity or envy Mr Ruggles....[19]

Even the placid Ruggles is sometimes aware of a less contented working class, however. When he finds the lost money, he cannot help reflecting on the unfairness of life. 'I'm fair upset', continued Mr Ruggles. 'It's no wonder to me some chaps turn Communists; no wonder at all.'[20] Eve Garnett's book is more challenging than it might first appear. One cannot help noticing that *The Family from One End Street* was published in the same year as George Orwell's picture of appalling poverty in parts of Britain in *The Road to Wigan Pier*.

The political views of Geoffrey Trease (1909-1998) were even more direct. Although from a middle-class family in Nottingham, Trease abandoned his classics course at Oxford, took up social work in London, and began free-lance writing. Gradually adopting progressive views, after his marriage in 1933 Trease began to think of writing children's books. Then, as he explains in his engaging autobiography *A Whiff of Burnt Boats* (1971), Trease had a revolutionary idea:

> While in London I had come across a book translated from the Russian *Moscow Has a Plan*, in which a Soviet author brilliantly dramatised for young readers that first Five-year plan which had already captured the imagination of the adult world. I did not want to write books like that, I could not, but Ilin's had planted a time-bomb in my mind which now suddenly exploded into questions and ideas. Why were all our own children's books still rooted in the pre-1914 assumptions which serious adult literature had abandoned? In the boys' adventure story especially there had been no development since my own childhood. Such stories still implied that war was glorious, that the British were superior to foreigners, that colonial 'natives' were 'loyal' if they sided with the invading white man and 'treacherous' if they used their wits to counterbalance his overwhelming armaments. In historical tales the Cavaliers and the French aristocrats were always in the right, no matter what the teachers explained at school, and the lower orders, like the lesser breeds, figured only in one of two possible roles, as howling mobs or faithful retainers.[21]

Inspired by this idea, Trease developed his notion of a story about the legendary Robin Hood as a 'proletarian hero'. His revolutionary concept was welcomed by the left-wing publisher Martin Lawrence, and Trease's tale *Bows Against the Barons*, written to expose romantic and reactionary views of Merry England, was published in 1934.

In a long career Trease went on to write over a hundred books, including many adventure stories, but this has one of his best plots. Although he writes clumsily in places, Trease creates a credible hero in young Dickon, who escapes to Sherwood Forest after killing one of the king's deer which is ravaging his crops. There he meets Robin

Hood and the others who are critical of the King and his barons for ruling unfairly. Various adventures follow, as Dickon runs messages, escapes capture, and helps a Peasant's Revolt against Sir Ralph D' Eyncourt and his army. But in the end, when the outlaws become too successful, the Duke of Wessex intervenes and destroys them with a massive display of brute force. Robin himself dies, and Little John and Dickon make for the Derbyshire Hills, resolved to go on working to make Robin's dream come true of 'An England without masters'.[22]

Although vigorously written, *Bows Against the Barons*, perhaps because it was Trease's first book, is too simplistic, too reductive of the virtues and especially the vices of the antagonists. The melodramatic portrait of one of the book's villains, Sir Ralph D'Eyncourt, is typical:

> The Eagle of D'Eyncourt was home [from the Crusade] all right!
>
> Perched on the body of the land, red claws sunk deep in the flesh of the peasants, it drank the very life-blood of the surrounding country.
>
> Sir Ralph had brought many things back with him besides the faked relics he had purchased to put in his chapel. He had brought a secret and loathsome disease which was destroying him body and soul; he had brought new notions of luxury and cruelty, learnt in the rotting courts of Eastern Europe. And for these he must have more money and power, ever more money and power....
>
> For his feasting and drunkenness, the men must sweat and groan with plough and spade.
>
> For his music must the tiny children spend all day scaring crows or minding pigs.
>
> For his clothes of rich cramoisy and samite must the village women crawl ragged and shivering through the winter.
>
> For his pride must the best horses, the tallest men, the cleverest boys, waste their time dashing hither and thither to attend him.
>
> 'Well,' he would have bellowed at anyone who questioned him. 'It's all *mine*, isn't it?'[23]

Looking back on his first book, Geoffrey Trease later said:

> *Bows Against the Barons* was, as Margaret Meek has fairly written, 'genuine black-and-white' and I would not quarrel now with the verdict in her Bodley Head Monograph: 'At this time Trease believed that it was his duty to be

a propagandist of social and political realism in opposition to those writers who trafficked in improbability. We find his villains capitalist in utterance, and the heroes are downtrodden proletariat of the thirties rather than twelfth-century peasants, but as an example of shaking up the mix-ture and telling a clear yarn it has still much to offer.'[24]

Comrades for the Charter, published later the same year, shows a considerable advance, at least in avoiding so much stereotyping. It is the passionate story of two boys – one from the countryside, the other from Birmingham – who both become involved in the early Chartist struggles in Wales; but this picture of social unrest in the late 1830s, carried, as Trease himself admitted, 'more than a flavour of twentieth-century politics'.[25] Led and educated by an itinerant salesman and agitator John Tapper, the boys attend political meetings and so learn the injustices of nineteenth-century Wales. But they also get caught up in a series of adventures as they deliver messages, learn to avoid the police and help to identify a spy in their midst. They are present at the tragedy of the Newport Massacre of November 1839 when British redcoats butchered the protesting Chartists. But after the massacre the two boys and Tapper escape to the North, in order, as Tapper says, to 'Live to fight another day. Go on spreading the Gospel of Man.'[26]

Trease's novel about injustice and the needs to reform or risk the dangers of violent revolution speaks directly to the Britain of the 1930s, but the book is too didactic. John Tapper's political speeches are fine, but the meaning of Trease's novel is not sufficiently dramatised until the reader reaches the final pages. The story indeed reminds us that books need more than good intentions to make them live, as Frederick Engels's famous letter of 1888 to Margaret Harkness made clear.

Margaret Harkness sent Engels a copy of her socialist novel *City Girl*, and although Engels praised it, he reminded her that good (socialist) intentions were not enough to guarantee the creation of literature, and referred to the contrary intentions but artistic greatness of the reactionary novelist Balzac:

I have learned more [from Balzac] than from all the pro-fessed historians, economists and statisticians of the period together. Well, Balzac was politically a Legitimist; his great work is a constant elegy on the irretrievable decay of good society; his sympathies are all with the class doomed to extinction. But for all that his satire is never keener, his irony never bitterer, than when he sets in motion the very men and women with whom he sympathises most deeply –

> the nobles.... That Balzac thus was compelled to go against
> his own class sympathies and political prejudices ... that I
> consider one of the greatest triumphs of Realism, and one
> of the grandest features in old Balzac.[27]

The work of L.A.G. Strong (1896-1958) offers the same kind of passionate observation of life in the 1930s as Geoffrey Trease. Like Trease an all-round man of letters, Strong, after leaving Oxford had various spells of teaching before becoming a prolific author of novels, biographies and criticism.

The Fifth of November (1937) is based upon the familiar idea of time-travel. When the twentieth-century Spence family celebrate Bonfire Night, their eccentric Uncle Edward, is so appalled at the children's ignorance that he resolves to teach them about the history of Guy Fawkes and takes them to visit the Tower of London. But Uncle Edward and his nephew Dick begin to have dreams about the Gunpowder Plot and in their dreams watch the history of the conspiracy unfold before their eyes in a series of dramatic scenes. Contemporary life is suggested by various deft touches. The Spence children attend a London day-school because 'the slump of 1932 had hit the Spences hard', we are told.[28] But the main way by which Strong relates his fictional recreation of history to modern life is through an extended parallel; for the gist of *The Fifth of November* is to show how an oppressed people, in this case seventeenth-century Roman Catholics, may rise up in violence if they are harshly treated. This is Strong's parable about the neglect of the working classes in the 1930s.

Strong wrote another adventure story for children in the 1930s which is even more closely connected with the social distress of the day. *King Richard's Land* (1933, reprinted in 1938) is the tale of two cousins Nigel and Bruce who become involved in the Peasants Revolt of 1381. The orphans of aristocrats, they find themselves threatened by some angry villagers, but are rescued by the village leader Yeo. He explains the causes of the villagers's grievances to them – 'As long as our masters were our lawful masters – as long, that is, as they behaved lawfully – we had no quarrel with them. It's when they became our unlawful masters that the quarrel began'.[29] Yeo tells the boys how the Black Death made labour scarce, and, although Parliament then introduced fixed wages, it failed to fix the price of bread. So the two boys join Yeo's march to Canterbury, and then the great March of 60,000 demonstrators from there to London. Here young King Richard hears the people's complaints and promises to help them.

Reading of these events of the Middle Ages, it is impossible not to see the modern parallels. In 1922 the first National March of the Unemployed to London had taken place, but the South Wales miners marched on London again in 1927, and there was another great March from Scotland, Devon and Wales in 1929, followed by the third National March in 1930. The fourth National March in October 1932 was a protest not only against the Means Test but the cuts in unemployment benefits, and there were violent clashes as the crowd of 100,000 covered the area around Marble Arch and Hyde Park. The Welsh miners marched again in 1934, and there was what was called a National Protest March in 1936, the same year as the Jarrow Crusade presented its petition to Parliament.[30]

Strong's fine story of the Peasants' Revolt, with its resonance of contemporary marches, rather disintegrates into a more conventional historical romance at the end. The boys help to prevent an attack on the King, and eventually return home to look after their own estates. Strong's narrative collapses in a way which mirrors the collapse of the Revolt. Despite his fine words – 'I am your king. I will be your leader' – the king is unable to overrule Parliament and help the people; and they return to the countryside defeated.[31] One cannot help being reminded of King Edward VIII's ineffectual words – 'something must be done', when he visited the distressed Welsh mining villages in 1936.

For in that year great demonstrations in Wales saw 100,000 meet in the Rhondda and 50,000 in Aberdare, and amongst the protest about the economic conditions, references were also made to the Spanish Civil War which had broken out on July 18th-19th.[32] Contemporary civil wars seem an unlikely subject for British children's books, especially in the 1930s, but there was an unlikely and honourable exception in the work of W.E. Johns.

Johns, as we have seen in the previous chapter, began to write adventure stories about his flying hero 'Biggles' in 1932, initially drawing upon his experiences in World War I. Increasingly, however, Johns began to look for new material and began to write more conventional plots, although still with a flying background, such as *The Cruise of the Condor*, about a treasure hunt in Brazil. But Johns, although an adventure-story writer, was also deeply patriotic and took a keen interest in Britain's defences. In *The Black Peril*, which was serialised in *The Modern Boy* magazine from February 1935, Biggles and Co. thwarted an air-raid from Russia, for the threat of the Soviet Union worried many observers in the 1930s. (An unpublished story by Percy F. Westerman deals with the same topic.[33])

But Johns became more concerned with the rise of fascism, most particularly in its National Socialist incarnation in Germany from 1932, in light of Hitler's efforts towards rearmament at a time when the British government was trying to scale down defence expenditure. Johns used his position as editor of the magazine *Popular Flying* to attack the British government's policy of disarmament and he regularly argued for not only its halt, but a complete reversal. Johns was also fond of Spain, a country he had frequently visited, and when civil war began there in 1936, he bitterly denounced the British government's policy of non-intervention. In March 1939 he wrote

> The Spanish Government – by which I mean republican Spain – is as democratic as a government can be. It was elected by the vote of the people. That it was a Left Wing government makes not the slightest difference. It was the will of the people, and the soul of democracy lies in the simple fact that 'the people are always right.' But our government, being Right Wing, does not hold that view. So it prefers to see Spain slaughtered by its own sworn enemies rather than lift a finger to save it. There you have the truth of the affair.[34]

Biggles in Spain (1939) portrays Biggles and his pals becoming accidentally involved in the Spanish Civil War when their holiday cruise ship is bombed by a fascist plane, and a British secret agent asks them to deliver an important letter to the Foreign Office. They encounter various dangers, mainly from Franco's fascists, before they successfully complete their mission. There is the usual mixture of fast-paced episodes involving spies, kidnapping, air-battles and prison-escapes before the heroes triumph.

But what makes the book particularly interesting, of course, is its political context. Johns's acute awareness of the horrors of war is powerfully realised by his description of the bombing of Barcelona in chapter two. Although Johns tries to be impartial about the conflicting sides in the civil war, he cannot help leaning more sympathetically towards the Republican cause, and especially the International Brigade; and he is totally unsympathetic to the fascists, particularly the vicious agent Goudini – 'I know nothing about your war', says Ginger. 'I don't want to know anything about it, but I hope the side wins that represents the majority of true Spaniards'.[35]

Not surprisingly Johns's outspoken political views got him into trouble. He continued to argue for rearmament, and attacked Prime

Minister Chamberlain for the Munich Agreement in 1938. In March 1939, as we have seen, he criticised the British government again for its non-intervention in Spain. He had, however, been removed from editing the weekly magazine *Flying* in January 1939, and was now told that the May issue of *Popular Flying* would also be his last as editor.

Johns continued writing his Biggles books, of course. *Biggles in the Baltic*, his first story to have a Second World War setting, was serialised in March 1940. This tale opens with Chamberlain's poignant broadcast words – 'England is now, therefore, in a state of war with Germany', and Biggles murmurs, 'Well that's that. It looks as if we are in for another spot of war flying'.[36]

The retreatism of the 1930s was coming to an end.

Chapter Eleven

Anarchy, Didacticism and Politics: The 1970s and the 1990s

> Mrs Barbauld told me that she admired 'The Ancient Mariner' very much, but that there were two faults in it, --- it was improbable, and had no moral. As to the probability, I owned that that might admit some question; but as to the want of a moral, I told her that in my own judgement the poem had too much.
>
> (Samuel Taylor Coleridge, *Table Talk*)[1]

It is a commonplace in discussing American literature to draw attention to its moral seriousness, even when that literature appears to be at its most amoral and chaotic. Cooper's tales of Deerslayer and his Indian friends, Melville's exotic sea stories, and Hawthorne's romances of New England are all works to which Coleridge's own criticism of 'The Ancient Mariner' might be applied, the weakness being not, as Mrs Barbauld thought, the absence of any moral but rather the presence of too much moral. The same can be said of many other American writers. Is it any wonder, given this tradition, that Hemingway himself borrowed the titles of two of his best novels from the *Devotions* of John Donne and the *Book of Ecclesiastes*?[2]

The persistence of this tradition can be found in American children's books of the 1970s, especially by contrast with what was being published in Britain at this time. The 1960s and 1970s were, of course, a particularly turbulent period in American history, and full of contradictions, with extraordinary economic growth and technological change, accompanied by the struggles of the Civil Rights Movement, political assassinations and a controversial war in Vietnam. It was an era which saw, among many other social changes, the introduction of the birth control pill in 1960, a rise in divorce rates and the growth of single-parent families from 5.8 million in 1960 to 18 million in 1996, an increase in robberies from 107,000 in 1960 to 349,000 in 1970, the legalisation of abortion by the Supreme Court in 1973, and a massive spread of illegal drugs. All these issues were very frankly dealt with in American children's literature of the 1970s, but the thread of moral didacticism continued to run very clearly.[3]

The work of Betsy Byars is a case in point. Although her earlier books, such as *The Summer of the Swans* (1970) and *The Eighteenth Emergency* (1974) had a delicate restraint and pleasing irony, some of her later works moved much nearer to bibliotherapy. *The TV Kid* of 1976, for example, is a witty and accessible story about a young boy, Lennie, whose mother runs the Fairyland Motel, where, because of his deep-rooted insecurity and loneliness, he spends most of his time watching TV at the expense of making personal relationships and doing his schoolwork. He knows all the TV commercials off by heart, and makes up deep fantasies about winning quiz programmes and then buying a full-sized puppet for a companion. Behind the motel are some holiday houses which Lennie likes to visit in the autumn when the holiday-makers have left. Here one day he is bitten by a rattlesnake – a horrific experience – but he is saved by a passing policeman and taken to hospital. After a period of intense pain he begins to recover, but the experience has changed him. When a TV set is installed in his hospital room, he realises that the programmes present a very artificial view of life, and that the real things are his pain and his mother's love. He tells his mother about the science test he failed before his accident, and begins working on a new project to make up for it. The story ends with Lennie reading his project – the topic is rattlesnakes! – to two young girls whose parents are staying at the motel. For all the book's hardboiled witticisms and treatment of topical issues, in other words, Betsy Byars is clearly a serious-minded writer concerned not only with the personality of the child but also his need to integrate into the world around him. It is a sign of Lennie's progress that he is able to form relationships with the two young girls at the end of the story.

In *The Pinballs* (1977), to give another example, Byars portrays three children from disturbed backgrounds who are sent to a foster home. At first they have great problems relating to each other and the world outside. They are like the balls in a pinball machine, says Carlie, helplessly knocked about by everyone. (She is in the home after being beaten up by her *third* stepfather.) Gradually, however, the children learn to trust and love each other, and discover that life can be worthwhile. 'I guess even a blind pig can come up with an acorn every now and then', Carlie tells her eight year-old foster-brother Thomas J., when he finds her missing earring.[4] But it is all a little too insistently didactic, too neatly packaged right up to the statement of the moral at the end. 'Pinballs can't help what happens to them and you and me can', says Carlie, just in case the readers have missed the importance of learning responsible and socially-aware behaviour.[5]

Judy Blume's work is very similar. Although her books are usually written both in the first-person singular and the colloquial idiom of American teenagers, the moral lessons are quite overt. Perhaps because it is more genuinely autobiographical, *Starring Sally J. Freedman as Herself* (1977) is freer of didacticism than Blume's other works. But examples of Blume's more typically didactic novels are *Then Again, Maybe I Won't* (1971), which describes the problems of twelve year-old Tony Miglione as he gradually learns to cope with the strong feelings which threaten to make him ill, and *Blubber* (1974), which tells the story of a girl who unthinkingly participates in the bullying of a fat classmate until she finds herself victimised and learns the error of her ways. Even *Forever* (1975), Blume's controversially frank treatment of teenage sexuality, puts enormous emphasis upon learning personal and social responsibility, and contains a description of a visit to a family-planning clinic which is almost documentary in its effect (and intention?). As Patricia Craig said, *Forever* has at times 'a clinical, instructive quality'.[6]

There is, however, another tradition of writing in America, con-nected oddly enough with the figure of Henry James, who is not perhaps the first novelist who comes to mind when thinking of children's books. In such stories as 'The Lesson of the Master' (1888), and supremely in his great novel *The Ambassadors* (1903), he came to question those austere values we associate with Puritanism, and asserted the joy of experience, even when this joy challenged con-ventional American morality and seemed to threaten it with anarchy. Strether, the elderly and rather prim New England bachelor, is sent to Europe to bring his young friend Chad back to Boston and his business responsibilities. But in Paris Strether begins to discover the errors of his own unfulfilled life, and urges his other friend Bilham not to make the same mistake – 'Live all you can; it's a mistake not to. It doesn't so much matter what you do in particular, so long as you have your life. If you haven't had that what *have* you had? Do what you like as long as you don't make my mistake. For it was a mistake … Live!'[7] Readers of Mark Twain will recognise similar sentiments behind his notice at the beginning of *The Adventures of Huckleberry Finn* (1884): 'Persons attempting to find a motive in this narrative will be prosecuted; persons attempting to find a moral in it will be banished.'[8]

Given the strength of the achievements of Henry James and Mark Twain, it is ironical that such categorical imperatives seem to have been observed more in the restrained and genteel pages of British children's books in the 1970s than in the open spaces and radical experiments of American fiction. The whole tradition of quasi-surrealistic fantasy, going right back to Lewis Carroll's *Alice's Adventures in Wonderland* (1865) – and even earlier – is evidence of that, though the fact that this writing often takes the form of fantasy rather than realism suggests that British culture needed to go underground (almost literally!) in order to articulate its own anarchical and subversive values in ostensibly non-serious ways. Who could regard a little girl's adventures with playing cards, having fallen down a rabbit hole, as a serious questioning of authority? But, as Juliet Dusinberre has pointed out, by the time Lewis Carroll died in 1898, *Alice* had quite supplanted John Bunyan's *Pilgrim's Progress* (1678), the great *moral* allegory, in the popular imagination.[9] And this kind of writing has been an important strand in British children's books ever since, producing a good deal of literature, often challenging authority, which emphasises individual rather than social values and is comic, even farcical, in form.

Another nineteenth-century example of subversive literature is Rudyard Kipling's *Stalky & Co* (1899), which, like *Alice*, contains satire of earlier didactic writing, this time of such school stories as Thomas Hughes's *Tom Brown's Schooldays* (1857) and F.W. Farrar's pious and sentimental *Eric; or, Little by Little* (1858). Where Hughes in particular uncritically praised manliness, 'muscular Christianity' and the school spirit, Kipling admired his characters for their independence and anti-establishment ingenuity, their skill, for example, at *avoiding* games and going off for a quiet smoke. When Kipling's young school-boy heroes are reprimanded by a House Master for being unhygenic, they take their revenge by hiding a dead cat under the floorboards to stink the school out, and Kipling actually approves of their rebellious behaviour.

Richmal Crompton's *William* books continued that tradition from the 1920s. *Just William* (1922) was the first of a series of over thirty books, and in the activities of young William Brown and his gang of Ginger, Douglas, and Henry, not forgetting the dog Jumble, we see something of the same kind of cheerful anarchy found in *Stalky & Co*, as William, with ruffled hair and socks around his ankles – immortalised in the drawings of Thomas Henry – sides with tramps, jolly ladies and eccentrics against the world of parents, teachers and clergymen, and indeed all the materialistic values of Violet Elizabeth Bott's bourgeois family.[10]

Nearer to our own times is *The Bash Street Kids*, a comic strip created by Leo Baxendale and Ken Walmsley for the illustrated weekly children's magazine the *Beano* in 1953. Here is another group of children – Toots, Smiffy, with his protruding teeth and a nearly bald head, and Plug with his veritable fangs – clearly placed in a modern urban setting, often a classroom which the mortar-boarded teacher, a nice anachronism, unavailingly tries to control. The comedy is blacker and the anarchy far stronger than Richmal Crompton's, for this is a world where soot-bombs explode and the kids use racing-pigeons to make pigeon pie. Raymond Briggs exhibits similarly anarchic values in his early picture books for young children. *Father Christmas* (1973) depicts a grumpy, swearing misanthropist rather than the usual cheery and sentimental stereotype, and *Fungus the Bogeyman* (1977) celebrates the lives of Fungus, Mildew, and Mould, who live underground (again!) in regions of filth, and actually enjoy eating green eggs and washing in scummy water.[11] (This is not far from the world of the anarchical magazine *Viz* which started in 1979, such popular BBC television comedy programmes as *Monty Python's Flying Circus* which ran from 1969-1974, or *The Young Ones* which ran from 1982-1984.)

Gene Kemp's stories about Cricklepit Combined School share something of the same counter-culture, with their inclusion of bad language and bullying, and with jokes and riddles in practically every chapter. Indeed, Gowie Corbie, the hero of *Gowie Corby Plays Chicken* (1979), commits all kinds of wild and unpopular offences simply because he enjoys being a loner. He trips up and injures the captain of the school football team, pours glue over another boy's briefcase, and constantly bullies his helpless deskmate, Heather. Child of a broken home, with one brother dead and another in prison, he rejoices in his independence in an aggressive *patois*:

> Go and get knotted... I ain't done nuthin' for nobody 'cos nobody's done nuthin' for me. Not ever. And they never will. And I tell you this. You've gotter look after yourself in this stinkin' world, 'cos nobody else will, and anybody who tells you any different is talkin' crap.... [12]

Perhaps Gowie Corbie's violence frightened even Gene Kemp. He undergoes a most unconvincing reformation about two thirds of the way through the book, rather as if Betsy Byars wrote the ending with its affirmation of reintegrative values. But the damage has been done by then, and it is the ball-of-fire Gowie of the first ten chapters who will live in most children's memories, not least because of the vigour and relish with which Gene Kemp records his exploits.

Tyke Tyler shows no such reformation in her last term at the Cricklewood Combined School, befriending the form idiot and potential thief instead of more socially acceptable children; falling into a pond in an attempt to reclaim a dead sheep's bones; stealing examination papers; and finally climbing the school tower and wrecking it on the last day of term. Again, like the Gowie Corbie book, *The Turbulent Term of Tyke Tyler* (1977) is robust, original and funny, catching the authentic noises of the classroom in ways that remind one of *The Bash Street Kids*, and asserting the values of the child and his or her experiences against the adult hierarchy. It is no wonder that this book won the 1977 Carnegie Medal and also the Other Award given by the Children's Rights Workshop in the same year.

This kind of British children's literature seems to have three characteristics which distinguish it from the more didactic American stories, although the distinctions are not always precise. First, these anarchical books depict a hero or heroine, with a group of like-minded companions, who refuse to go along with the values of the establishment. However, they are not necessarily reformers or revolutionaries, and usually accept the social structure as established fact; they simply don't find it particularly helpful and do not seek to join it. What they want to do is to have a good time by asserting their own individuality, and to try and outwit the regime when the regime hinders or prevents this happening. This is why – and this is the second characteristic of this kind of writing – the central protagonists usually enjoy life. They have adventures and get into scrapes which are exhilarating and amusing. These characters are the heroes and heroines of *comic* books, aimed at being amusing. But, thirdly, these heroes and heroines do have values of their own: independence, initiative, originality, an unwillingness to conform, and a loyalty to others who share these values. These are their alternative values to those of the prevailing social system, and at times they threaten to subvert it.

Jan Mark's *Thunder and Lightnings* (1976), which also won the Carnegie Medal, is another example. It tells the story of Andrew, whose parents are relaxed, middle-class liberals, and of Victor, whose working-class mother is rigid and repressed, obsessed with neatness and tidiness. The novel has several themes: the problems of friendship across class barriers, the need to accept life as it is, and, above all, the integrity of the individual, whatever sort of society he lives in. It is Andrew, the clever boy going to university, who has to learn about courage and independence from Victor, the boy who can barely read. For when Andrew offers to teach Victor how to read, Victor rejects his well-meaning attempt in these terms:

> 'That's no good you trying to teach me anything.... If you start being good at something, people expect you to be even better and then they get annoyed when you aren't. That's safer to seem a bit dafter than you are.'
>
> 'But you're not daft,' said Andrew. 'I thought you were at first, till I knew you better. The same as the first time I saw you I thought you were fat. I didn't know you were dressed in layers. Why do you wear so many clothes? Don't you get hot?'
>
> 'Now and again,' said Victor, 'but I don't care.'
>
> 'But don't you care if people think you're stupid?'
>
> 'No I don't,' said Victor. 'Why be miserable just to make other people happy.'[13]

This is the voice of the genuine child maverick, of course, one heard repeatedly in Jan Mark's work, notably in *Hairs in the Palm of the Hand* (1981), where a young girl hilariously disrupts the school system and confuses the teachers by giving a series of false names. She even contrives to stir up protests about sexist teaching and inadequate classrooms before she reveals that she is not a pupil at this school anyway! And it is all very funny. 'Why be miserable just to make other people happy.' 'Live all you can; it's a mistake not to.'

For those readers who wondered if the anarchy of these books is irresponsible – and some readers, especially school-teachers, were embarrassed by the success of the *William* books, *The Bash Street Kids*, and *The Turbulent Term of Tyke Tyler* – it is important to recognise their popularity and to try to identify the reasons for it. Leo Baxendale, one of the originators of the anarchical *Bash Street Kids*, defended his creation in these terms:

> We live in a society that screws people up and screws people down. One section of the population are selected to be a competitive elite, screwed up to go careering through life like demented clockwork toys. A larger section are screwed down to the floor, demoralised into acceptance of lives and jobs below their potential and hopes. If you consider that each person, to himself or herself, is the centre of the universe, this screwing of people's lives must lead to frustrations, resentments, anger, and feelings of inadequacy boiling away inside. And ... these things feed my humour.[14]

This suggests very well how what looks like a peculiarly British response to a peculiarly British set of problems may also have wider
and more social implications than first appears. For example, Robert
Cormier's American school story *The Chocolate War* of 1974 is
about more than schoolboys too, although its powerful and painful
picture of school life might deceive some readers. What we are really
offered is a vivid account of the working of a power structure led
by an ambitious head teacher, and a sadistic elite of bullies who
combine in a deliberately systematic way in order to make everyone
else conform. One has either to accept the regime or to rebel against
it and be destroyed, as Jerry, the defeated hero, is. There is no hope
of the cheerful anarchy found in Kipling or Gene Kemp; and, though
the sequel, *Beyond the Chocolate War* (1985), shows some resistance,
when Obie challenges Archie, the leader of the bullying Vigils, he
gets nowhere. The story ends pessimistically with Archie's successor firmly installed in power to extend the system and brutalise it
further.[15]

This account of some American and British children's books of
the 1970s is inevitably limited. As a counter, one could point to the
presence of such didactic British books as Bernard Ashley's well-
meant story of a black boy, *The Trouble with Donovan Croft* (1974)
or Jan Mark's bleaker (and less successful?) attempts at science fiction, such as *The Ennead* of 1978, as ways of qualifying the broader
picture suggested here. But even so there does appear to have been a
greater interest in didactic forms among American children's books
of the 1970s, alongside the persistence of more anarchic forms
among British books with their emphasis upon independence and
non-conformity.[16]

Whether this tells us something about British and American societies in the 1970s and 1980s is an interesting matter for speculation.
But an extension of subject matter including very recent changes in
society, such as the growth of single-parent families, together with
an emphasis upon didacticism, seems to have been a characteristic of
American children's fiction, alongside a resurgence of vitality in the
anarchic tradition in British writing, however much we may wish to
qualify this broad picture.

Was this didacticism in American fiction simply a continuation of
the Puritan tradition introduced by the seventeenth-century colonists,
or that desire for the American mind to be practical and productive (in
de Tocqueville's word, 'earthward'), or was it more simply related to
the great modern explosion in church membership, perhaps connected
with World War II, which rose from 64 million in 1940 to 114 million

by 1960?[17] And why, by contrast, did a cheerful kind of anarchy come
about in British children's books. Was it perhaps as a reaction against
the authority and controls of the years of World War II? Was it related
to the relative prosperity of the 1960s and the social relaxations of
the so-called 'permissive society'?[18] (This was the era of the Beatles,
the miniskirt and the liberal reforms of the Labour Home Secretary
Roy Jenkins, we remember.) Whatever the reasons, an emphasis on
didacticism in modern American fiction and a revival in the vitality of
the anarchic tradition of British children's writing seem to have been
two quite clearly defined features of children's books in the 1970s.

During the 1980s and 1990s, however, the character of children's
fiction in Britain began to show remarkable changes, almost as if
it was trying to catch up with what had already happened in North
America. Books dealing with adolescent sex and abortion, crime,
divorce, drugs, homelessness and violence began to appear, often
winning important literary prizes for their outstanding qualities.

Not only was the new kind of writing unusual in its contents,
however, but the narrative thrust of these tales often seemed to be
based upon didactic purposes, for these novels often depicted the
problems teenagers face in a quasi-instructive mode. Thus the critic
Kimberley Reynolds observed in 1994 that

> the current emphasis on writing which helps young people
> deal with the world in which they live (both psycholog-
> ically and practically) can legitimately be compared to the
> didacticism which underlay much of the early writing for
> children [in the nineteenth century and earlier].[19]

Brian Alderson has even likened it to the tract-like literature of children's books by such authors as Hesba Stretton and said that 'Future
historians of children's literature will surely point to this widespread
publishing and honouring of books in the New Evangelical vein as
one of the distinguishing characteristics of the late twentieth century's
productions.'[20]

One reason for this remarkable change in the character of British
books, that of following what had already proved not only successful
but also artistically liberating, has already been suggested. The works
of Betsy Byars and Judy Blume had shown what was possible, even
in the supposedly Puritan climate of North America. Another reason
might be a reaction to the anarchical books of the 1970s, a part of that
cyclical alternation between periods when books were designed for
entertainment and periods which produced more instructive books,
as described by Frank Eyre and discussed in the introduction.

As has been seen, however, there are certain links between child-ren's literature and society that appear to transcend periods. Barbara Hofland's domestic tales relate to the development of Great Britain during the Industrial Revolution, and the adventure stories of G.A. Henty are connected with the nineteenth-century expansion of the British Empire. On this evidence, it is not difficult to perceive a connection between the changes in British children's books of the 1990s and the changing nature of British society. The Conservative governments of Mrs Thatcher from 1979-1990, and of John Major from 1990-1997 saw the introduction of widespread economic reforms in Britain, involving not only the privatisation of public utilities such as electricity, gas and the railways, but also the sale of council houses. Although this era brought prosperity to many, it was also accompanied by mass unemployment, a year-long miners' strike and violent demonstrations against a proposed Poll Tax. There were clear signs of a divided and alienated society.

Even a brief summary of the bare statistics gives some idea of what was going on at this time with unemployment peaking at 3.6 million in 1983 (about 13% of the population compared with 2.6% in 1970). The number of divorces rose from 63 per thousand of the population in 1970 to 168 in 1990, and illegitimate birth-rates for teenagers rose from 14.6 % of the population in 1971 to 19.7 % in 1985. During this same period, abortions rose from 75.4 to 141.1 per thousand of the population, 38 per thousand under the age of nineteen. Although it is difficult to obtain precise figures for the number of people made homeless or 'sleeping rough' in these years, there seems general agreement that there was a large increase in the 1980s, including not only the unemployed but also runaway children and teenagers. We do know that the figures for those deemed Statuary Homeless rose from 60,000 in 1980 to 140,000 in 1990. The figures for crime also accelerated dramatically in this period, the number of recorded burglaries, for example, rising from about 46,000 in 1960 to over 294,000 in 1980. Most alarmingly, the number of drug offences rose from 12,685 in 1970 to nearly 45,000 by 1990.[21]

At the same time the multi-racial nature of British society, which had continued to develop from the arrival of West Indians in the 1950s, increased strikingly in the 1990s, when, it has been calculated, the number of immigrants (from the European Union as well as Africa and Asia) rose to more than 100,000 per annum.[22] Children's literature reflected some of the problems borne of this increasing racial and cultural diversity, such as intolerance and bullying. Farrukh Dhondy (b. 1944) had produced fiction about these issues earlier in *East End*

At Your Feet (1976) and Bernard Ashley's *The Trouble with Donavon Croft* (1974) has already been noted. From the 1990s, however, the dramatic quality of the writing intensified. Beverley Naidoo (b. 1943) won the Carnegie Medal for *The Other Side of Truth* (2000), which vividly depicted the problems of two refugee children from Nigeria settling in London and having to cope with racism and bullying. More recently Bali Rai's *(un)arranged marriage* (2001) and *The Last Taboo* (2006) have depicted the difficulties that can arise when young people from different cultures fall in love. The ignorance and prejudice here culminates in hatred and a murderous violence, which is a far cry from the humorous anarchy of the 1970s.

Not surprisingly, many children's books reflect the problems of single-parent families, and show the difficulties children experience when their parents' marriages collapse and they find new partners. Although often amusing in tone, with a good deal of comedy and happy endings, work by Anne Fine (b. 1947) and Jacqueline Wilson (b. 1945) frequently focus on these difficult areas. In the former's *Goggle-eyes* (1989), Kitty bitterly resents her mother's attachment to the rather dull and steady Gerald, but gradually becomes reconciled to the situation when she recognises his common sense and protective qualities. A similar situation occurs in Wilson's *The Lottie Project* of 1997, when Charley, Jo's teenage daughter, becomes unhappy because of her mother's developing relationship with one of her employers, the divorced Mark. Eventually their problems are worked out and everyone is happily reconciled. Wilson's novel also depicts the economic problems of single parentage, as Jo struggles to earn a living by taking on two cleaning jobs at the same time.

In *Tracy Beaker* of 1991, Jacqueline Wilson shows us an even more dysfunctional situation, as ten year-old Tracy is in care, abandoned by her mother after her new boyfriend has beaten her up. Lively and intelligent, Tracy is also anti-social and disruptive, as she desperately longs for her mother's return. The badly damaged young girl undergoes many distressing experiences – violence, neglect, bad luck, frequent disappointments – but reaches some kind of haven at the end when it is suggested, rather improbably, that an investigative journalist, who happened to be visiting her care home, may agree to foster her.

The didacticism in these books is muted, far from the explicit morals preached by some nineteenth-century writers. It tends to work in three ways. First, by their depiction of the grim problems of modern living, these authors offer their readers a warning, deliberately setting out to alert young readers to contemporary temptations and dangers.

Secondly, they proffer solace through empathy, with the suggestion that if these *fictitious* characters can survive the harsh realities of modern life, then there is hope for similarly distressed readers. And finally these books extend to their readers the values and comfort of literature itself. Anne Fine spells this out at the end of *Goggle-eyes* where Kitty quotes her schoolteacher:

> Living your life is a long and doggy business, says Miss Lupey. And stories and books help. Some help you with the living itself. Some help you just take a break. The best do both at the same time.[23]

Teenage sex is another topic increasingly dealt with in these novels. Berlie Doherty's *Dear Nobody* of 1991 is about the love-affair between two A-level students and what happens when Helen discovers that she is pregnant. In the end she decides to have the baby but not to marry Chris, who, she realises, is not yet ready for marriage. There is no explicit criticism of the sixth-formers in the novel but instead a sensitive portrayal of the emotional and practical consequences of their behaviour. In the end the novel seems to underline – and thus warn its readers of – the precarious nature of all relationships, whether between young boys and girls, children and parents, or husbands and wives. Melvin Burgess's *Doing It* of 2003 is an even more explicit, if less searching, account of sexual relationships between teenagers, and aroused considerable controversy when it was first published. Anne Fine, in the *Guardian* newspaper, said that 'All of the publishers who have touched this novel should be ashamed of themselves'.[24] There are certainly detailed descriptions of Ben's activities with his schoolteacher Miss Young, and of Jonathan's physical encounters with his plump girlfriend Deborah. Even here, however, although it might be claimed that the writing is naturalistic, one senses the faint outline of a moral agenda, as when, for example, Ben is depicted gradually coming to realise that his schoolteacher-lover is actually sick and needs adult help, or when Jonathan comes to recognise Deborah's genuine attractions despite his friends' crude criticism of her.

Melvin Burgess's *Junk* of 1996 is one of the strongest accounts of dysfunctional families. The main story concerns two fourteen year olds, Tar and Gemma, who both run away from home – Tar because he is being abused by his alcoholic father – and live rough in a squat. They gradually get caught up in a world of drink, crime, drugs and prostitution. It is all bleakly moral – *Behave badly and this is what will happen to you!* – until Gemma finding herself pregnant decides to return home, and Tar, having reached some kind of understanding with his father, struggles to reform himself.

Along with *Junk*, Robert Swindell's *Stone Cold* of 1993 might be regarded as another archetypal book of the 1990s. (Both incidentally were Carnegie Medal winners.) *Stone Cold* is about the experiences of a young boy – he calls himself Link – who leaves his home in Bradford after his mother takes up with a new and unpleasant boy-friend. Swindell gives his readers a graphic picture of the hundred of dossers living rough on the streets of London, and Link learns to survive the cold, the hunger and the violence by begging. But parallel with Link's story, we learn of a psychopathic ex-soldier called Shelter who has resolved to remove the human garbage from the streets by murder. Link becomes another of Shelter's intended victims – he has already killed seven – when the police arrive just in time to save him. This is yet another bleak story among many of the 1990s. The problems are pointed out but no solutions suggested, except what Link himself says at the end – 'People will only start to make things better if they know what's going on. There has to be an end to this some day.'[25]

The books of the 1970s were, as we have seen, anarchical, cheerful and optimistic, but the world depicted in these novels of the 1990s is a broken one, rife with poverty and homelessness, and virtually devoid of love or hope. Relationships, whether between adults or adolescents, are fragile or fractured, and it is made clear that no real satisfaction is to be found in crude sex or drugs or crime. Although the writers of the 1990s depict and deplore the situation, their didacticism is a subtle one, vividly pointing out the problems young people face and urging the need for understanding and tolerance, but only quietly showing the way – if they do so at all. The friendship between Link and Ginger in *Stone Cold* and the tentative reform of Tar in *Junk* show only glimmers of hope in a dark world. In this way these books are reflecting the consequences of the age's political ideology:

> I think we've been through a period when too many people have been given to understand that if they have a problem, it's the government's job to cope with it. 'I have a problem, I'll get a grant.' 'I'm homeless, the government must house me.' They're casting their problems on society. And, you know, there is no such thing as society. There are individual men and women, and there are families. And no government can do anything except through people, and people must look to themselves first.
>
> (Mrs Thatcher, 1987)[26]

Chapter Twelve
The Historical Novels of Philip Pullman

We can't avoid displaying an ideology of some sort,
whether veiled or naked, so the best we can do is to be
intelligent about it.

(Philip Pullman)[1]

As we have seen in earlier chapters, the British boys' adventure
story came into existence in the nineteenth century, in response to
various literary and ideological pressures – the rapid expansion of the
British Empire, the development of education in Victorian England,
and the literary influence of such novelists as Daniel Defoe and Sir
Walter Scott. But by the end of the twentieth century, however, as
these pressures and influences changed, so too did the nature of the
adventure story, as we shall see if we examine the historical tales of
Philip Pullman.

Philip Pullman (b. 1946) is best known for his enormously successful trilogy of fantasy novels: *Northern Lights* (1995), *The Subtle
Knife* (1997) and *The Amber Spyglass* (2000), collectively known as
His Dark Materials. But prior to this work, Pullman had produced
a powerful series of historical novels set in the nineteenth century,
featuring the young heroine Sally Lockhart: *The Ruby in the Smoke*
(1985), *The Shadow in the North* (1987), *The Tiger in the Well* (1992)
and *The Tin Princess* (1994). A consideration of these novels in contrast to earlier historical fiction provides a clear demonstration of
how literature changes.

Although Sir Walter Scott was the key British figure in establishing the historical novel, Harriet Martineau's tale of eighteenth-
century pirates *Feats on the Fiord* (1841) and Captain Marryat's *The
Children of the New Forest* pointed the way forward for children.

But, although R.M. Ballantyne, H. Rider Haggard and R.L. Stevenson all produced notable works for young readers in the second half of the nineteenth century, the most prolific and perhaps most representative of all Victorian writers of historical tales for children was G.A. Henty. He wrote over eighty historical stories, ranging in setting from Ancient Egypt in *The Cat of Bubastes* (1889) to the contemporary history of the Boer War in *With Roberts to Pretoria* in 1902. Most of Henty's tales, as we have seen, follow the romance-structure typical of many nineteenth-century adventure stories, although with occasional formal problems as discussed in Chapter Four. Henty's narrative formula was to depict a youthful hero, usually a normal teenage boy, who, as the result of a domestic crisis leaves home to seek his fortune elsewhere.

Henty's historical tales are not value-free, of course, but reflect the ideology of a late-Victorian imperialist, for he was writing at a time when Britain was rapidly expanding her Empire, and he endorsed the values of British hegemony. Although he was not a religious writer, Henty took his moral duties seriously, and tried to guide his readers towards the social and political values of imperialism and empire-building, usually by advocating such virtues as courage ('pluck'), loyalty and honesty within the framework of Victorian *laissez-faire* capitalism and a hierarchical view of society.

His novel *With Clive in India: Or, the Beginnings of Empire* (1884) is a typical example. Using the characteristic romance-structure, it tells the story of sixteen-year-old Charlie Marryat who leaves home after the death of his father to obtain employment as a civilian writer for the East India Company in Madras. On the journey out, he distinguishes himself in action against privateers and then, on reaching India, volunteers for military service against the French with Captain Clive, the authentic historical figure. Acquiring a comic Irishman, Tim Kelly, as his servant and faithful companion, Charlie performs with great distinction over the next ten years, seeing action in such battles as Arcot (1751), Plassey (1757) and Pondicherry (1761). He rises from the rank of ensign to that of a colonel, and returns home to England to become a country gentleman and Member of Parliament.

There is little doubt that the main emphasis of Henty's tale is on Britain's imperial history, as the preface makes clear. The preface also gives the reader the sources Henty has drawn on for his story and the orthography of Indian place-names. A map of India precedes the first chapter, and there are five battle-plans to show military operations accurately. Although Charlie and his companions experience personal and fictitious adventures, the style of the book is essentially documentary, not least at the beginning of the story when a senior Indian resident devotes much of chapters 5 and 6 to a detailed exposition for Charlie and the reader's benefit of the early history of British rule. The accounts of battles are similarly detailed. All this is meant to demonstrate not just the reality but the superiority of British rule. Yet Henty was not an uncritical imperialist. While praising Clive's military genius, for example, he is not afraid to attack him for want of principles or for taking bribes.[2] But such critique is always within the context of general approval, as if by demonstrating fair-mindedness over minor matters, Henty's objectivity can be trusted over the larger question of imperialism in general.

The action of *With Clive in India* is completely dominated by men. Although Charlie's widowed mother and his sisters appear at the beginning and end of the tale, they are shadowy figures. The other female in the story is Ada, a merchant's young daughter, a passive figure whom Charlie rescues from the 'Black Hole of Calcutta', after which she returns home to England to wait for Charlie to marry her at the end of the book. Although many girls may have read *With Clive in India*, the female roles within it are peripheral and traditional.

So entrenched were the values and structure of this kind of traditional adventure story, that writers continued to copy them until well into the twentieth century. Herbert Strang, Percy F. Westerman and Captain F.S. Brereton (1872-1957), to mention only a few names, produced similar tales, while the newer genre of Flying Stories, such as those written by W.E. Johns, showed many of the same characteristics, as we have seen. There was some disquiet, however, and Geoffrey Trease, in his pioneering critical survey of children's fiction *Tales Out of School*, first published in 1948, raised serious questions about the nationalist bias of the traditional adventure story, challenged its attitude towards foreigners and foreign countries, and drew attention to the cult of the hero and the problem of violence.[3]

The events of the First and Second World Wars did eventually begin to affect the character of historical adventure stories, however. Not only did they introduce aspects of the new technology, such as wireless, aviation and tanks, but the massive loss of life eclipsing anything experienced in the nineteenth century clearly affected society's attitudes towards wars in general. (One thinks of the enduring influence of Wilfred Owen's poems, Eric Remarque's *All Quiet on the Western Front* and Robert Graves's *Goodbye to All That*.) After the shocks of the Somme, Dunkirk and Singapore – 'the worst single military defeat the British Empire ever suffered'[4] – many found it difficult to continue to believe in the unwavering superiority of British might. Under the influence of the new sciences of psychology and psychoanalysis the nature of heroism and leadership came under scrutiny, so that even admired figures such as Gordon of Khartoum and Lawrence of Arabia came to be seen as problematical. The establishment of international bodies such as the United Nations in 1945, and television's revelation of the world as a global village, together with the steady dismantling of the British Empire, beginning with India's independence in 1947, followed by Burma (1948), Ghana (1957), Nigeria (1960), and then Tanganyika, Uganda, Kenya, and the Caribbean Federation, removed the imperial basis of many enterprises. The rise of the Welfare State as signalled by the foundation of the National Health Service in 1947, the continued rise of feminism from suffrage to the right to initiate divorce proceedings, and the entry of numerous immigrants from Asia, Africa and the West Indies, with the Race Relations Act of 1968 making acts based solely on grounds of race and colour illegal, all changed the nature of British society. The ideology of an expanding and self-confident British Empire, which had underpinned many traditional adventure stories, such as *With Clive in India*, gradually eroded, and a new generation of historical novelists, such as Hester Burton, Leon Garfield, Cynthia Harnett, Robert Leeson, Jan Needle and Rosemary Sutcliff, grew up from the 1950s onwards, inspired by a more troubled, multi-racial and democratic humanism.[5]

As Western society moved into that stage of capitalism variously defined as the post-industrial or consumer society, adult literature moved from modernism to post-modernism. The production of novels sometimes defined as 'metafiction', has, in recent decades, begun to affect children's literature and the character of some historical tales.[6] Metafiction, according to one of its interpreters, Elizabeth Dipple, 'takes the reader's sophistication and complete absorption of genres from the past for granted, so that as a mode it builds ironically on top of the experienced literature of the past'. As well as using parody or even pastiche as playful elements, metafiction is also likely to be full of overt references to other literature, and to be witty and sometimes anti-representational.[7]

The recent historical novels of Philip Pullman reveal many of the characteristics of metafiction. Pullman was born in Norwich, the son of an RAF fighter-pilot who was killed in Kenya when he was very young, and he was brought up for a time by his grandparents in a Norfolk Rectory while his widowed mother worked in London. When his mother remarried they moved to Australia, where he enjoyed playing imaginative games with his younger brother and first began to make up stories. When the family returned to Britain, they settled in North

Wales, where Pullman was taught by a particularly inspiring teacher. He won a Scholarship to Exeter College, Oxford, where he decided to become a writer. Although his first novel was published in 1978, he had various jobs before becoming a teacher for thirteen years in various schools in Oxford. Eventually he became a Senior Lecturer at Westminster College, Oxford, where he helped train prospective teachers by running a course on storytelling. The success of the books Pullman wrote while teaching part-time helped him to become a full-time author, and the phenomenal popularity of the *Dark Materials* trilogy – *Northern Lights* won the Carnegie Medal in 1995 – which has been brilliantly staged at the National Theatre and the subject of a 2007 film released under the title of *The Golden Compass* (the American name for *Northern Lights*) has given him an international reputation. Although he seems to write with remarkable ease and fluency, it is clear that he brings to his work formidable intelligence.

Philip Pullman's four historical novels are all set in the second half of the nineteenth century, and focus on a teenage heroine, Sally Lockhart. In *The Ruby in the Smoke*, set in the back-streets of the London Docks in 1872, Sally discovers that her dead father was mixed up in a mysterious trade in the Far East involving a Chinese triad. Accompanied by some new friends, Frederick Garland, a photographer, Rosa, his sister, and an office boy, Jim Taylor, Sally manages to defeat the criminals, including a Chinaman named Ah Ling and the vicious Mrs Holland, who are all trying to regain a priceless ruby. In *The Shadow in the North*, set in 1878, Sally works as a financial adviser, investigating the activities of Axel Bellman, a Swedish businessman and arms manufacturer, and discovers that he is working to produce a frighteningly destructive Steam Gun. By now Sally has fallen in love with Frederick, but in the struggle to defeat their adversary Frederick himself is killed before Sally shoots Bellman and blow up the Steam Gun. *The Tiger in the Well* begins with Sally, who is unmarried but now the mother of Harriet, her daughter by Frederick, receiving a letter from a complete stranger suing her for divorce. Since the novel is set in 1881 (before Gladstone passed the 'Married Women's Property Act of 1882'), this means that her child and everything Sally owns actually belong to her alleged husband. Almost every step Sally takes seems to confirm that she is indeed married to this stranger. When she is forced to go into hiding, Sally encounters real poverty for the first time, and she learns from the socialist Daniel Goldberg of the need to change society. The labyrinthine plot takes many twists and turns – even the Chinese villain Ah Ling reappears determined to ruin Sally's life – before the mystery is solved and Sally finds happiness with Daniel. Finally, *The*

Tin Princess focuses upon a friend of Sally's, Becky Winter, who is a language teacher. Adelaide, Mrs Holland's servant in *The Ruby in the Smoke*, is now married to the Crown Prince of Raskavia, a small state sandwiched between Germany and the Austro-Hungarian Empire, and when Adelaide goes to Raskavia with her husband to help resist the threats of Prussia, Becky goes with them. All sorts of intrigues and assassination attempts follow. The old King is murdered, and the Crown Prince follows soon after. The new Queen Adelaide tries to save her small kingdom, but, despite the help of her friends, Becky and Jim Taylor, she fails, and Becky returns home to tell Sally about her adventures.

It is clear from even these brief summaries that remnants of the traditional adventure plot survive with the use of a teenage hero(ine), journeys and homecomings, and, though based upon more imaginary events than those of Henty, Pullman's historical stories also contain detailed and accurate descriptions of aspects of Victorian life. They do, however, concentrate far more on social rather than military history. He offers us fascinating glimpses of the early history of photography, which became popular from the middle of the nineteenth century, for example. The situation of married women's property rights, or rather the lack of them, is exposed, and the evils of Britain's involvement in the opium trade are revealed, as well as the cynicism behind the manufacture and sale of destructive weapons. Above all, however, Philip Pullman reminds us of the conditions of the poor in Victorian England, and describes the mass-immigration, the anti-semitism and the violence it bred.

The narrative techniques used in these tales are post-modernist, employing elements of metafiction which emerged in the second half of the twentieth century. Typical of this literature is the occasional and playful avoidance of the documentary realism found in Henty's novels. Pullman's stories are, for instance, deeply influenced by such authors as Charles Dickens and Wilkie Collins. Although it is going too far to call *The Ruby in the Smoke* a parody, its plot of Chinese triads, opium-smoking and murder will remind many readers of Collins's *The Moonstone* (1868) and Dickens's last novel, *The Mystery of Edwin Drood* (1870), while the influence of Dickens's great sociological detective story *Bleak House* (1851) lies not far below the surface of the melodramatic mystery of Philip Pullman's *The Shadow in the North*.

Like most post-modernists, Philip Pullman often gently reminds his readers that they are reading a story, not simply looking at a mirror of the world. He does this by drawing attention to the artificiality of his ingenious and multi-plotted structures, when he switches from one thread of his narrative to another, with such expressions as 'At the same time … ' or 'Mr Parish, by contrast, had just been having a highly satisfactory meeting with his lawyer'.[8] Authorial comments also remind us that we are still reading fiction when, for example, the narrator breaks off from describing the plight of thousands of immigrants to note that 'each of them had a story to tell; but we're concerned with the story of Sally Lockhart'. He even comments, when a character speaks with an unfamiliar accent: 'If it belonged anywhere, it belonged to the future; a hundred years from then, voices like Mr Brown's would be common, though Mr Windlesham could hardly be expected to know that.'[9] (In this way Philip Pullman reminds us that historiographic metafiction poses, as the Australian academic Robyn McCallum says, 'questions about the relationship between fiction, history and reality'.[10]) Finally, Pullman plays games with intertextuality, referring us by name in his story about financial corruption in the nineteenth century to Anthony Trollope's great Victorian novel about corruption, *The Way We Live Now* (1875): 'An amusing book about a financial speculator', says one of his characters.[11] Equally suggestive and witty is the way the heroine's innocent daughter, Harriet, swears at the end of *The Tiger in the Well* in a surely deliberate 'anticipatory' echo of Shaw's Eliza Dolittle in *Pygmalion* (1912): 'Not bloody likely.'[12]

Although Philip Pullman does not expect us to mistake his fiction for real life, he does want us to take it seriously. As he said in an article about some of his early books,

> We can't avoid displaying an ideology of some sort, whether veiled or naked, so the best we can do is be intelligent about it. What I write is art of a sort, I hope; it has to work in terms of a story and pattern, but nothing is unmixed, thank God; everything is confused and impure, and there's a sense in which I would have chosen to write about the late nineteenth century even if the other considerations hadn't brought me to it. Because I've got another purpose in mind as well. That was a time when the seeds of the present day were germinating. Feminism, to take an obvious example. I didn't set out to write a trilogy with a female protagonist and give her exciting and interesting things to do: the story chose me. But I was glad to find a medium in which I could show how feminism, for example, didn't spring fully armed from the head of Germain Greer, but was being discussed, and was influencing people, a hundred or

more years ago. The drug trade has a past as well; it didn't
begin with *Miami Vice*; it's intimately entwined with our
economic history. Terrorism – the modern sense of that
very word first appeared then, and one of the characters in
The Tiger in the Well learns it.

And finally, in the same book, I wanted to talk about
socialism. It's had a bad press in the past few years;
it's been depicted as the dreary source of every kind of
repression, misery, and failure. I wanted to show that it
has a better history than that, that there was a time when it
was the best response of the best people to the conditions
around them....[13]

Thus, in his racy but elaborately-plotted historical tales Pullman offers an extraordinary mixture of almost light-hearted entertainment,
combined with powerful subtexts of anger and sadness and admiration. Moreover, with heroines like Sally Lockhart, these stories
are addressed to girls as well as boys.

The Tin Princess is perhaps the best example. Telling the story of
sixteen-year-old Becky Winter's adventures when she accompanies
Adelaide and her husband to the tiny – but invented – European
kingdom of Raskavia, it contains many features similar to Henty's
historical tales. Set in 1882, it presents a teenage hero(ine), a faithful
companion, and a long journey to foreign parts. The Penguin edition
of *The Tin Princess* also contains a Henty-like map of Raskavia and
its royal capital Eschtenburg. But its account of intrigues and castles
and plots to regain a throne are almost a deliberate pastiche of such
Ruritanian romances as Anthony Hope's *The Prisoner of Zenda*
(1894) and John Buchan's *The House of the Four Winds* (1935). And
in the end, whereas Henty's heroes are always triumphant, Pullman's
romantic adventurers are foiled: Adelaide's husband, King Rudolph,
is assassinated; Raskavia is annexed by the German Empire; the hero
and her lover are defeated.[14]

What the story ultimately reveals, in other words, is almost the
opposite of Henty's triumphant romances. Jim Taylor almost dies
helping Becky defend the Raskavian flag:

Poor Becky seemed to have fainted again, because there
was nothing but silence from the heavy blanket. Jim noted
it grimly. No doubt it was dangerous to carry her like that;
no doubt she ran the risk of having a lung punctured by a
broken rib. It was a little picture of the whole muddle. He
was practically certain that they were going to die, here

in this forgotten little corner of Europe, for a struggle that was pointless anyway. Dan Goldberg was right: Germany would inevitably crush Raskavia, or Austria would.

And if you could trace cause and effect accurately enough, he thought, you might be able to follow the thread of it all back to the starting-point, and it might be a thousand miles away and many years ago, in the bank-books of a financier or the childhood of a frustrated princeling; but more probably there were a million such threads, and if any one of them snapped or twisted differently the outcome would have been utterly different, too. There was no pattern in things, Jim saw, no sense; everything was random and chaotic.[15]

Using the stuff of the traditional tale, young heroes, travel, intrigues and battles, *The Tin Princess* shows the grim *realpolitik* of Bismarck, shot through with commercial interests and betrayal. Raskavia is not annexed for its romantic castles but for its nickel mines. 'You and Adelaide and Jim gave it the best chance it could have had,' says Becky at the end of the story. 'You did everything that courage and wit and imagination could, but force wins. Enough force always does.'[16]

Most of the literature discussed in this book depicts British society realistically. Mrs Hofland's moral tales spring from her life in the early nineteenth century, as Amy Le Feuvre's religious and romantic stories reflect existence in the late-Victorian age. Even when she is using devices such as time travel, E. Nesbit deals with contemporary – in her case Edwardian – society. Pullman's work, however, is more distanced, and he reveals changes in twentieth century life largely through the critical sensibility he brings to his stories (rather like John Fowles' *The French Lieutenant's Woman* of 1969), although he uses the form of the historical novel like his great predecessor G.A. Henty.

Henty often depicted corruption and defeat in the course of his historical novels, though it is always within the context of the ideology of a triumphant British imperialism. But the events of the twentieth and twenty-first centuries have seen the end of such one-sided optimism. Whatever era he wrote about, Henty's historical tales – self-confident, imperialistic, male-oriented and hierarchical – reflect the nature and condition of Victorian Britain, and, paradoxically, they do so by a kind of historical realism. By contrast, Philip Pullman's tales of nineteenth-century Britain display a version of post-modernist metafiction in their literary techniques, while, in their values and ideology, they reflect the gains, uncertainties, ambiguities and ironies of European society in the contemporary world.

Notes

Introduction

1. Deborah Cogan Thacker and Jean Webb, *Introducing Children's Literature: From Romanticism to Postmodernism*, London: Routledge, 2002, p.2 (This thoughtful work, while acknowledging the importance of history, concentrates almost exclusively on the importance of *literary* movements.)
2. Mitzi Myers, 'Missed Opportunities and Critical Malpractice: New Historicism and Children's Literature', *Children's Literature Association Quarterly*, Vol. 13, No. 1 Spring 1985, p.42.
3. Frank Eyre, *British Children's Books in the Twentieth Century*, London: Longman, revised and enlarged edition, 1971, pp.17-19.
4. For details of education and literacy, see S.J. Curtis, *History of Education in Great Britain*, London: University Tutorial Press, fifth edition, 1963, pp.110-420; and Kenneth Levine, *The Social Context of Literacy*, London: Routledge and Kegan Paul, 1986, pp.77, 216.
5. For further information, see especially Marjorie Plant, *The English Book Trade*, London: George Allen and Unwin, second edition, 1965, pp.283, 289, 307-309, 316, 331 etc; and Julia Eccleshare, 'Most Popular Ever', 'The Launching of Harry Potter', and Stacy Gillis, 'The Brand, the Intertext and the Reader: Reading Desires in the 'Harry Potter' Series', in *Popular Children's Literature In Britain*, edited by Julia Briggs, Dennis Butts, and Matthew Grenby, Aldershot: Ashgate, 2008, pp.287-315.
6. D.H. Lawrence, *Studies in Classic American Literature* [1924], London: Heinemann, 1971, p.2.

Chapter One
Barbara Hofland: The Moral Tale and the Industrial Revolution

1. *The Evangelical Magazine*, May 1804, quoted by E.R. Norman, *Church and Society England 1770-1970*, Oxford: Clarendon Press, 1976, p.33.
2. For further details of Mrs Hofland's dealings with her publishers, see Dennis Butts, *Mistress of Our Tears: A Literary and Bibliographical Study of Barbara Hofland*, Aldershot: Scolar Press, 1992, pp.38-42.

3. *The Son of a Genius*, London: J. Harris, 1812, pp.iv-v.

4. Mary Mitford to Mrs Hofland, April 17th 1819; see Henry Chorley, *Letters of Mary Russell Mitford*, second series, two Vols. London: R. Bentley & Son, 1872, Vol. 1, p.69.

5. *The Son of a Genius, op.cit.*, p.21.

6. *Ibid.*, p.28.

7. *Ibid.*, p.33.

8. *Ibid.*, p.47.

9. *Ibid.*, p.51.

10. *Ibid.*, p.58.

11. *Ibid.*, p.79.

12. *Ibid.*, p.107.

13. *Ibid.*, p.108.

14. *Ibid.*, p.119.

15. *Ibid.*, p.151.

16. *Ibid.*, pp.172-3.

17. *Ibid.*, p.191.

18. *Ibid.*, p.222.

19. *Ibid.*, pp.232-249.

20. *Ibid.*, pp.61-62.

21. *Ibid.*, p.250.

22. Stephen C. Behrendt argues that these three books use the vehicle of popular fiction to present an alternative view of the familiar dilemma of indigent widowhood. 'The Officer's widow is portrayed as virtually helpless (especially at first) in dealing with her situation, the clergyman's widow copes much better, while the merchant's widow proves to be the most resilient of all.' Stephen C. Behrendt, 'Women without Men; Barbara Hofland and the Economics of Widowhood', *Eighteenth-Century Fiction*, Hamilton, Ontario: McMaster University, April 2005, Vol. 17, No. 3, p.491.

23. Gillian Avery, *Childhood's Pattern: A study of the heroes and heroines of children's fiction 1770-1950*, London: Hodder and Stoughton, 1975, p.24.

24. Quoted by Max Weber, *The Protestant Ethic and the Spirit of Capitalism*, translated by Talcott Parsons. London: Allen and Unwin, second edition, 1976, p.162.

25. R.H. Tawney, *Religion and the Rise of Capitalism*, Harmondsworth: Penguin, 1964, p.251.

26. E.M. Forster, *Marianne Thornton 1797-1887*, London: Edward Arnold, 1956, p.23.

27. E.R. Norman, *op.cit.*

28. Ian Watt, *The Rise of the Novel*, Harmondsworth: Peregrine, 1964, pp.62-96.

29. Barbara Hardy, *The Appropriate Form*, London: Athlone Press, 1964, p.56.

30. *The Son of a Genius, op.cit.*, p.129.

31. Aristotle, *On the Art of Poetry*, translated by Ingram Bywater. Oxford: Clarendon Press, 1947, pp.45-6.

Chapter Two
How Children's Literature Changed in the 1840s

1. Thomas Carlyle, 'Signs of the Times,' [1829] in *Critical and Miscellaneous Essays*, London: Chapman & Hall, 1899, 5 Vols., Vol. 2, p.59.

2. Edgar Taylor, quoted in Introduction, *Victorian Fairy Tales: The Revolt of the Fairies and Elves*, ed. Jack Zipes. New York: Methuen, 1987, p.xvii.

3. F.J. Harvey Darton, *Children's Books in England: Five Centuries of Social Change*, third edition, revised and corrected by Brian Alderson. London and New Castle, DE: The British Library and Oak Knoll Press, 1999, pp.221-228.

4. Thomas Carlyle, *op.cit.*, Vol. 2, p.59.

5. *Ibid.*, pp.62-63.

6. Catherine Sinclair, *Holiday House* [1839], London: Blackie, n.d., p.6.

7. F.J. Harvey Darton, *op. cit.*, p.240.

8. McLean, Ruari, *Joseph Cundall: A Victorian Publisher: Notes on His Life and a Check-List of His Books*, Pinner: The Private Libraries Association, 1976, pp.4-12.

9. Georg Lukács, *Studies in European Realism*, London: Merlin Press, 1992.

10. Anne Scott MacLeod, *American Childhood: Essays in Children's Literature of the Nineteenth and Twentieth Centuries*, Athens: University of Georgia Press, 1994, pp.87-113.

11. David Vincent, *Literacy and Popular Culture: England 1750-1914*, Cambridge: Cambridge University Press, 1993, pp.53-54.

12. Raymond Williams, *The Long Revolution*, Harmondsworth: Pelican, 1970, p.80.

13. *The Poetical Works of Elizabeth Barrett Browning*, London: Smith, Elder, n.d., p.247.

14. Raymond Williams, *op.cit.*, pp.64-65.

15. Benjamin Disraeli, *Sybil or the Two Nations* [1845], Harmondsworth: Penguin, 1954, p.73.

16. Captain Marryat, *The Children of the New Forest* [1847], edited with an Introduction by Dennis Butts. Oxford; Oxford University Press, 1991, pp.196-197.

17. Brian Alderson, *Hans Christian Andersen and his Eventyr in England: Some Notes and Observations*, Wormley: Five Owls Press, 1982, pp.22-24.

Chapter Three
Muscular Christianity and the Adventure Story

1. Charles Kingsley was Rector of Eversley, Regius Professor of History at Cambridge and Canon of Westminster Abbey. Charles Kingsley, *Brave Words for Brave Soldiers and Sailors* (1855), quoted in Margaret Farrand Thorp, *Charles Kingsley 1819-1875*, Princeton: Princeton University Press, 1937, pp.118-119.

2. M. Fisher, *The Bright Face of Danger*, London: Hodder and Stoughton,

1976; M. Green, *Dreams of Adventure, Deeds of Empire*, London: Routledge and Kegan Paul, 1976; J. Bristow, *Empire Boys: Adventure in a Man's World*, London: Harper Collins, 1991. See also Dennis Butts, 'Shaping Boyhood; Empire Builders and Adventurers', in Peter Hunt (ed.), *International Companion Encyclopedia of Children's Literature*, Second Edition. London: Routledge, 2 Vols., 2004, Vol. 1, pp.340-351.

3. *The Compact Edition of the Oxford English Dictionary*, London: Book Club Associates, 2 Vols.,1979, Vol.1, p.1880.

4. Elspeth Huxley, *The Kingsleys*, London: Allen and Unwin, 1973, p.61.

5. *Westward Ho!* [1855], London: T. Nelson and Sons, n.d., p.271.

6. *Charles Kingsley: His Letters and Memories of his Life*, edited by his wife. London: C. Kegan Paul, 2 Vols., eleventh edition, 1878, Vol. 1, p.433.

7. *Hereward the Wake* [1866], London: Blackie and Son, n.d., p.184.

8. See Graham Dawson, *Soldier Heroes: British Adventure, empire and the imagining of masculinities*, London: Routledge, 1994, pp.79-155. See also Richard Collier, *The Indian Mutiny*, London: Collins, 1966, pp.120-153, pp.286-87. Herbert Tingsten, *Victoria and the Victorians*, London: Allen & Unwin, 1972, pp.457-470.

9. A.C. Wilson, quoted by J.A. Mangan, *Athleticism in the Victorian and Edwardian Public School: The Emergence and Consolidation of an Educational Ideology*, Cambridge: Cambridge University Press, 1981, p.41.

10. Thomas Hughes, *Tom Brown's Schooldays*, By an Old Boy, fourth edition, London: Macmillan, 1857, pp.312-313.

11. R.M. Ballantyne, *The Coral Island: A Tale of the Pacific Ocean* [1858], edited with an introduction and notes by J.S. Bratton. Oxford: The World's Classics, O.U.P., 1991, p.262.

12. W.H.G. Kingston, *Peter the Whaler: His Early Life and adventures in the Arctic Regions* [1851], London: Blackie, n.d., p.252.

13. *Kingston's Magazine for Boys* [1859], quoted by J.S. Bratton, *The Impact of Victorian Children's Fiction*, London: Croom Helm, 1981, p.125.

14. J.S. Bratton, 'Evangelical into Imperialist: W.H.G. Kingston's Books for Boys', pp.115-133, in *The Impact of Victorian Fiction, op. cit.*

15. Quoted by J.A. Mangan, *op.cit.*, p.145.

16. Quoted by J.A. Mangan, *op.cit.*, J.G. Cotton Minchin, *Our Public Schools: their influence on English history*, London: 1901, pp.137-138.

17. See Peter Newbolt, *G.A. Henty: 1832-1902: A Bibliographical Study of his British Editions with short accounts of his publishers, illustrators and designers, and notes on production methods of his books*, Second Edition with Addenda and Corrigenda by Peter Newbolt and Stuart Wilson. Philadelphia: Polyglot Press, 2005, pp.659-660. Guy Arnold, *Held Fast for England: G.A. Henty: Imperialist Boys' Writer*, London: Hamish Hamilton, 1980, pp.17-28, pp.175-179.

18. G.A. Henty, *With Clive in India; or, The Beginnings of Empire* [1884], London: Blackie, n.d., p.11.

19. Jack Cox, *Take a Cold Tub, Sir! The Story of the Boy's Own Paper*, Guildford: Lutterworth Press, 1982, p.76.

20. Morton N. Cohen, *Lewis Carroll: A Biography*, London: Macmillan, 1995, p.134.
21. Henry Newbolt, *The Island Race*, London: Elkin Matthews, 1898, p.77.
22. *Ibid.*, pp.81-82.
23. J.A.Mangan, *op.cit.*, p.145.

Chapter Four
Conflicting Loyalties: Ideology and Form in the Tales of G.A. Henty

1. G. Manville Fenn, *George Alfred Henty: The Story of an Active Life,* London: Blackie, 1907, p.320.
2. Peter Newbolt, *G.A. Henty 1832-1902: A Bibliographical Study of his British Editions with short accounts of his publishers, illustrators and Designers, and notes on production methods used for his books, op.cit.*, p.587.
3. Peter Newbolt, 'G.A. Henty: The Earlier Books for Boys, 1871-1885', *Antiquarian Book Monthly Review*, 4, (1977), pp.438-447.
4. Kathryn Castle, *Britannia's Children: Reading Colonialism through Children's Books and Magazines*, Manchester: Manchester University Press, 1996, p.55. Mawuena Kossi Logan, *Narrating Africa: George Henty and the Fiction of Empire*, New York: Garland, 1999, p.80.
5. Henty's own accounts of his writing methods are quoted by Peter Newbolt, *op. cit.*, pp.556-557. See also *Six Dusty Diamonds: Unpublished Short Stories by G.A. Henty*, edited by Dennis Butts. Winchester: The Henty Society, 2006, pp.1-7.
6. Robert L. Dartt, *G.A. Henty: A Bibliography*, New Jersey: Dar-Web Inc., 1971, p.155.
7. Guy Arnold, *Held Fast for England: G.A. Henty Imperialist Boys' Writer*, *op. cit*, pp.91-92.
8. G.A. Henty, *St. George for England: A Tale of Cressy and Poitiers* [1885], London: Blackie, n.d., p.iii.
9. G.A. Henty, *With Roberts to Pretoria: A Tale of the South African War*, London: Blackie, 1902, pp.15-16.
10. Peter Newbolt, 'G.A. Henty: Some Notes on the Blackie First Editions', *Antiquarian Monthly Review*, (4), 1977, pp.83-92; and *G.A. Henty 1832-1902, op.cit.*, pp.586-590.
11. Mawuena Logan, 'History and the Ashantis', *Children's Literature Association Quarterly*, Summer 1991, Vol. 16, No. 2, p.82.
12. Quoted in George Bennett (ed.), *The Concept of Empire; Burke to Attlee 1774-1947*, London; A. & C. Black, 1953, p.65 and pp.367-368.
13. G.A. Henty, *With Lee in Virginia: a story of the American Civil War* [1890], New York: Blackie-Scribner, n.d., p.v.
14. *Ibid.*, p.11.
15. *Ibid.*, p.14.
16. *Ibid.*, p.12.

17. *Ibid.*, p.11.

18. *Ibid.*, p.14.

19. Among many studies of slavery, see especially Eugene Genovese, *Roll, Jordan, Roll: the World the Slaves Made*, New York: Vintage Books, 1976, particularly 'The Moment of Truth', pp.97-112.

20. David Thomson, *England in the Nineteenth Century (1815-1914)*, Harmondsworth: Penguin, 1955, p.158.

21. E. Halévy, *A History of the English People in the Nineteenth Century, Victorian Years 1841-1895*, incorporating 'The age of Peel and Cobden', trans. by E.I. Watkin. New York: Barnes and Noble, 1961, p.430.

Chapter Five
Rider Haggard and the Pattern of Defeat

1. Graham Greene, 'Rider Haggard's Secret', *Collected Essays*, London: The Bodley Head, 1969, p.213.

2. See Lilias Rider Haggard, *The Cloak that I Left: A Biography of Henry Rider Haggard K.B.E.*, London: Hodder and Stoughton, 1951, pp.121-123; and D.S. Higgins, *Rider Haggard: The Great Storyteller*, London: Cassell, 1981, pp.70-71.

3. See Morton Cohen, *Rider Haggard: His Life and Works*, London: Hutchinson, 1960, pp.94-95; and Higgins, *op. cit.*, p.85.

4. Although Cetewayo was the form Haggard regularly used, the more correct rendering of the Zulu chief's name is Cetshwayo. For much information about the history of the Zulu nation, see Donald R. Morris, *The Washing of the Spears: A History of the Zulu Nation under Shaka and its Fall in the Zulu War of 1879*, London: Cape, 1966.

5. V. Propp, *Morphology of the Folktale*, first edition translated by Laurence Scott with an Introduction by S. Pirkova-Jacobson; second edition revised and edited with a Preface by Louis A. Wagner/New Introduction by Alan Dundes. Austin: University of Texas, 1975.

6. H. Rider Haggard, *The Days of My Life*, London: Longman, Green, 2 Vols., 1926, Vol. 2, p.90.

7. See H. Rider Haggard, *The Days of My Life*, ibid., Vol. 2, p.92.

8. H. Rider Haggard, *ibid.*, Vol. 2, pp.92-93.

9. R.L. Stevenson, 'A Gossip on Romance', *Memories and Portraits: Memoirs of Himself: Selections from his Notebooks*, London: Heinemann, Tusitala Edition, 1923-1927, 35 Vols., Vol. xxix, p.123.

10. Lilias Rider Haggard, *op. cit.*, pp.92-93.

11. Lord Ernle, *English Farming: Past and Present*, London: Heinemann and Frank Cass, New (Sixth) Edition, 1961, p.386. R.D. Lobban, *Farming* London: Batsford, 1973, pp.57-58.

12. H. Rider Haggard, *Allan Quatermain* [1887], Oxford: Oxford University Press, edited with an introduction by Dennis Butts, 1995, p.28.

13. *Allan Quatermain*, *op. cit.*, p.282.

14. Leslie A. Fiedler, *Love and Death in the American Novel* London: Paladin, 1970, pp.242-313.
15. Sandra M. Gilbert and Susan Gubar, *No Man's Land: The Place of the Woman Writer in the Twentieth Century*, New Haven, Conn: Yale University Press, 2 Vols., 1989, Vol. 2, Sexchanges, pp.3-82.
16. Graham Greene, 'Rider Haggard's Secret', *op. cit.*, p.213.
17. Wendy Katz, *Rider Haggard and the Fiction of Empire; A Critical Study of British Imperial Fiction*, Cambridge: Cambridge University Press, 1987.
18. H. Rider Haggard, *Nada the Lily*, London: Longmans, Green, 1892, p.172.
19. Andrew Lang, quoted in Higgins, *op. cit.*, p.140.
20. H. Rider Haggard, *Child of Storm*, London: Cassell, 1913, pp.89-90 and pp.vi-vii.
21. H. Rider Haggard, *King Solomon's Mines* [1885], Oxford: Oxford University Press, edited with an introduction by Dennis Butts, 1989, p.62.
22. *Ibid.*, pp.217-218.

Chapter Six
Some Questions about Kidnapped: Stevenson and the Act of Union

1. *Vailima Letters being correspondence addressed by Robert Louis Stevenson to Sidney Colvin, November 1890-October 1894*, London: Methuen, 1912, p.83.
2. Robert Louis Stevenson, *The Wrong Box*, London: Longmans, Green, 1889, p.126.
3. Among many biographies, see especially: J.C. Furnas, *Voyage to Windward: The Life of Robert Louis Stevenson*, London: Faber & Faber, 1952; and Frank McLynn, *Robert Louis Stevenson: A Biography*, London: Pimlico, 1995.
4. Patricia Beer, 'Kidnapped', *Children's Literature in Education*, New York: Agathon Press, Vol. 14, Number 1, Spring 1983, p.61.
5. Henry James, 'From Robert Louis Stevenson', *Century Magazine*, April 1888, quoted in *Robert Louis Stevenson: The Critical Heritage*, edited by Paul Maixner. London: Routledge & Kegan Paul, 1981, p.311.
6. R.L. Stevenson, *Kidnapped being Memoirs of the Adventures of David Balfour in the Year 1751*, London: Cassell, 1886, p.305.
7. R.L. Stevenson, 'Victor Hugo's Romances' [1874], *Familiar Stories of Men and Books*, London: Chatto & Windus 'sixth edition', 1901, pp.32-33.
8. *Kidnapped, op. cit.*, p.107.
9. Ann C. Colley, *Robert Louis Stevenson and the Colonial Imagination*, Aldershot: Ashgate: 2004, p.5.
10. Georg Lukács, *The Historical Novel*, translated by Hannah and Stanley Mitchell. Harmondsworth: Penguin, 1969, p.69.
11. Ian Bell, *Robert Louis Stevenson: Dreams of Exile: A Biography*, London: Headline, 1993, p.194.
12. Robert Louis Stevenson, *Kidnapped and Catriona*, edited by Emma Tetley with an Introduction. Oxford: World's Classics, 1986, pp.xvii-xxv.

13. Frank McLynn, *op.cit.*, pp.266-267.

14. Christopher Hardie, 'The Politics of Stevenson', in *Stevenson and Victorian Scotland*, edited by Jenni Calder. Edinburgh: Edinburgh University Press, 1981, pp.107-125.

15. Kidnapped, op. cit., p.248.

16. J.R. Hammond, *A Robert Louis Stevenson Companion: A guide to the novels, essays and short stories*, London: Macmillan, 1984, p.131.

17. See Note 1.

Chapter Seven
The Railway Children and the Strange Death of Liberal England

1. E. Nesbit, 'Inasmuch as ye did not … '*Ballads and Lyrics of Socialism 1883-1908*, London: The Fabian Society, 1908, p.77.

2. Julia Briggs, *A Woman of Passion: The Life of E. Nesbit*, London: Hutchinson, 1987, pp.31-34, 182-184, 242-245, etc.

3. John Rowe Townsend, *Written for Children: An Outline of English-Language Children's Literature*, Harmondsworth, Kestrel, Pelican, second revised edition, 1983, p.106.

4. See Michael Freeman and Derek Aldcroft, *The Atlas of British Railway History*, London: Croom Helm, 1985; and Philip Unwin, *Travelling by Train in the Edwardian Age*, London: Allen & Unwin, 1979.

5. Julia Briggs, *op.cit.*, p.xi.

6. E. Nesbit, *Wings and the Child, or the Building of Magic Cities*, London: Hodder and Stoughton, 1913, p.20.

7. E. Nesbit, *The Railway Children*, edited with an introduction by Dennis Butts. Oxford: Oxford University Press, 1991, p.30.

8. *Ibid.*, p.149.

9. Noel Streatfeild, *Magic and the Magicians: E. Nesbit and her Children's Books*, London: Ernest Benn, 1958, p.122.

10. Julia Briggs, *op.cit.*, p.27.

11. *The Railway Children, op.cit.*, p.85.

12. *Ibid.*, p.182.

13. *Ibid.*, p.19.

14. Fred Inglis, *The Promise of Happiness: Value and Meaning in Children's Fiction*, Cambridge: Cambridge University Press, 1981, pp.113-117.

15. *The Railway Children, op. cit.*, p.121.

16. George Dangerfield, *The Strange Death of Liberal England*, London: Constable, 1936.

17. Roy Hattersley, *The Edwardians*, London: Abacus, 2006, p.73.

18. Alan O' Day (ed,), *The Edwardian Age: Conflict and Stability 1900-1914*, London: Macmillan, 1979, pp.(1)-12; and especially T.R. Gourvish, 'The Standard of Living, 1890-1914', pp.13-34.

19. E. Nesbit, *The Story of the Amulet*, London: T. Fisher Unwin, 1906, pp.195-196.

20. E. Nesbit, *The House of Arden* [1908], London: Ernest Benn, 1947, pp.319-320.
21. E. Nesbit, *Harding's Luck* [1910], London: Ernest Benn, 1961, pp.1-2.
22. See Nigel Hand, 'The Other Nesbit', *The Use of English*, Winter, 1974, pp.108-116.
23. See Julia Briggs, *op.cit.*, pp.346-356.

Chapter Eight

From Evangelism to Feminism: The Works of Amy Le Feuvre

1. Amy Le Feuvre, *'Probable Sons'*, London: The Religious Tract Society (RTS), (1894), p.34; Amy Le Feuvre, *Jock's Inheritance*, London: Ward, Lock, 1927, p.247.
2. See *From the Dairyman's Daughter to Worrals of the WAAF: The Religious Tract Society, Lutterworth Press and Children's Literature*, edited by Dennis Butts and Pat Garrett. Cambridge: Lutterworth Press, 2006. Mrs Walton's books are published by Grace and Truth, Sand Springs, Oklahoma.
3. Mathew Arnold, 'Dover Beach', *Matthew Arnold: a Selection*, by Kenneth Allott. Harmondsworth: Penguin, 1954, pp.191-192.
4. Stephen Neil, *Anglicanism* Harmondsworth, Penguin, 1958, p.262; and figures supplied by the Archbishop's Council, Research and Statistics, c-of-e.org.uk.
5. For much of this information, apart from National Census Records, see *The Times* (May 3rd 1929); *The Okehampton Post* (May 11th 1929); and 'In Memoriam: Amy Le Feuvre', by Mary E. Tongue, *The Girl's Own Paper Annual*, Vol. 50, pp.748-749. Some details of Amy's literary earnings have been supplied privately by the Lutterworth Press. See also the Hodder and Stoughton Archives in the Guildhall Library, London; and the RTS Archives in the School of Oriental and African Studies (SOAS) at London University.
6. Judith Rowbotham, *Good Girls Make Good Wives: Guidance for Girls in Victorian Fiction*, Oxford: Basil Blackwell, 1989, p.74.
7. Amy Le Feuvre, *Us, and Our Empire* [1911], London: RTS, n.d., p.250.
8. Amy Le Feuvre, *'Us, and Our Charge'* [1916], London: RTS, n.d., p.188.
9. *'Us, and Our Charge'*, *op.cit.*, p.209.
10. Amy Le Feuvre, *On the Edge of a Moor*, [1897] London: RTS, n.d., p.84.
11. Amy Le Feuvre, *Jock's Inheritance*, London: Ward, Lock, 1927, p.247.

Chapter Nine

Imperialists of the Air: Flying Stories 1900-1950

1. W.B. Yeats, 'An Irish Airman Foresees his Death', *The Collected Poems of W.B. Yeats*, London: Macmillan, 1952, p.152. Viscount Templewood, *Empire of the Air: The Advent of the Air Age*, London: Collins, 1957, p.90.
2. David Lloyd George, *The Great Crusade: Extracts from Speeches Delivered*

During the War, quoted by Laurence Goldstein, *The Flying Machine and Modern Literature*, London: Macmillan, 1986, p.87.

3. Viscount Templewood, *op.cit.*, p.181.

4. For further information on the history of British aviation, see C.H. Gibbs-Smith, *Aviation: an Historical Survey from the Origins to the end of World War II*, London: H.M.S.O., 1970; Robert Higham, *Britain's Imperial Air Routes 1918-1939*, London: Foulis, 1960; John Stroud, *Annals of British and Commonwealth Air transport 1919-1960*, London: Putnam, 1962; and for a popular account, see W.E. Johns, *Some Milestones in Aviation*, London: John Hamilton, 1935.

5. Thomas Pynchon, *Gravity's Rainbow*, London: Picador, 1975, p.159.

6. W.E. Johns began his science fiction with *Kings of Space* (London: Hodder & Stoughton) in 1954, the same year as Rosemary Sutcliff published the first of her distinguished trilogy of adventures set in Roman Britain, *The Eagle of the Ninth* (London: O.U.P., 1954).

7. Harry Collingwood, *The Log of the 'Flying Fish': a story of aerial and submarine peril and adventure* London: Blackie, 1887.

8. Herbert Strang, *King of the Air; or, To Morocco on an Airship*, London: Hodder & Stoughton, 1908.

9. Percy F. Westerman, *A Lad of Grit*, London: Blackie, 1908; *The Flying Submarine*, London: Nisbet, 1912; *The Secret Battleplane*, London: Blackie, 1916; *Winning His Wings*, London: Blackie, 1919; *The Amir's Ruby*, London: Blackie, 1932; *The Westow Talisman*, London: Blackie, 1934; *Standish of the Air Police*, London: Blackie, 1935; *Ringed by Fire*, London: Blackie, 1936; *Standish Gets His Man*, London: Blackie, 1938; *Standish Loses His Man* London: Blackie, 1939; *Standish Pulls It Off*, London: Blackie, 1940. For further details, see Dennis Butts, 'Percy F. Westerman', *Book Collecting & Library Monthly*, London: October, 1968.

10. Quoted by Peter Berresford Ellis and Jennifer Schofield in *Biggles! The Life Story Of Capt. W.E. Johns: Creator of Biggles, Worrals, Gimlet and Steeley.* Godmanstone, Dorset: Veloce, 1993, pp.132-133.

11. W.E. Johns, 'The White Fokker', *Popular Flying*, Vol. 1, no. 1, London, 1932; *The Camels are Coming*, London: John Hamilton, 1932; *Biggles of the Camel Squadron*, London: John Hamilton, 1934; *Biggles Learns to Fly*, London: The Boys' Friend Library, 1935; *The Black Peril*, London: John Hamilton, 1935; *Biggles – Air Commodore*, London: O.U.P., 1937; *Biggles Flies South*, London: O.U.P., 1938; *Biggles Flies North*, London: O.U.P., 1939; *Biggles Defies the Swastika*, London: O.U.P., 1941; *Worrals of the W.A.A.F.*, London: Lutterworth, 1941; *Sergeant Bigglesworth C.I.D.*, London: Hodder & Stoughton, 1946; *Biggles Gets his Men*, London: Hodder & Stoughton, 1950. The works of W.E. Johns have been much discussed, notably by Geoffrey Trease, *Tales Out of School*, 2nd edn., London: Heinemann, 1964, pp.77-94; D.R. Barnes, 'Captain Johns and the Adult World', *Young Writers, Young Readers*, ed. Boris Ford, rev.ed., London: Hutchinson, 1963, pp.115-122; and by Bob Dixon, *Catching Them Young 2:Political Ideas in Children's Fiction*, London: Pluto Press, 1977, pp.74-119. More sympathetic

accounts are given by A.E. Day, 'Biggles: anatomy of a hero', *Children's Literature in Education*, Vol. 5, No. 4, New York, 1974, pp.19-28; by John Gough, 'Intrepid birdmen of the Great War; genre stories of war in the air,' *English in Education*, Vol. 18, No.2, Sheffield: 1984; and by Dennis Butts, 'Biggles – Hero of the Air', *A Necessary Fantasy: The Heroic Figure in Children's Popular Culture*, ed. Dudley Jones and Tony Watkins, New York and London: Garland, 2000, pp.137-152. There is an excellent bibliography of Johns in the revised biography by Peter Berresford Ellis and Jennifer Schofield, *Biggles! The Life Story of Capt. W.E. Johns, op.cit.*, and a useful comparison of Johns and G.A. Henty by Margery Fisher in *The Bright Face of Danger*, London: Hodder & Stoughton, 1986, pp.349-363.

12. Peter Berresford Ellis and Jennifer Schofield, *op.cit.*, pp.124-130, 181, etc.

13. Willing's Press Guide gives much of this information about periodicals in its annual volumes. See also Philip Warner, *The Best of British Pluck: the Boy's Own Paper Revisited*, London: Macdonald and Jane's, 1976. The information about books, though necessarily incomplete, is based upon material in the author's collection, the British Museum's *General Catalogue of Printed Books to 1955*, Compact Edition, 27 Vols., New York, Readex, 1967; and www.copac.ac.uk. See also W.O.G. Lofts and D.J. Adley, *The Men Behind Boys' Fiction*, London: Howard Baker, 1970

14. See Mary Cadogan, *Women with Wings: Female Flyers in Fact and Fiction*, London: Macmillan, 1992, pp.117-119, 130-135, 154.

15. J.F.C. Westerman, *Menace from the Air*, London: O.U.P., 1938.

16. C.E. Montague, *Disenchantment* [1922], London: McGibbon & Kee, 1968, pp.29-106. See also Goldstein, *op.cit.*, chapter 5.

17. Percy F. Westerman, *Winning his Wings, op. cit.*, p.11.

18. Jan Penhay, *The Secret Flight Squad*, London: Juvenile Productions, 1937; L.E.O. Charlton, *The Bush Aerodrome*, London: O.U.P., 1937.

19. Lucien Goldman, *Towards a Sociology of the Novel*, translated from the French by Alan Sheridan. London: Tavistock, 1975, pp.136-139.

20. The space-fiction series by W.E. Johns, featuring Professor Brane and the spaceship *Tavona* began with *Kings of Space* in 1954, and contained ten different adventures, the last, *The Man who Vanished into Space* appearing in 1963. All were published by Hodder & Stoughton, London.

21. J.F.C. Westerman, *The Air Record Breakers*, London: Ward, Lock, 1937, p.12.

22. George E. Rochester, *The Scarlet Squadron* [1938], London: Ace publishing, n.d., pp.175-176.

23. E. Keble Chatterton, *Scouts of the Sky: a story of High Adventure by Sea and Air*, London: Warne, 1948, p.243; Major J.T. Gorman, *Gorilla Gold* [1937], London: Blackie, n.d., p.37; Michael Poole, *Couriers of the Air* [1936], London: Sampson, Low, n.d., p.219; W.E. Johns, *Biggles Defies the Swastika, op.cit.*, p.94.

24. Cecil Lewis, *Sagittarius Rising* [1936], London: Corgi, 1969; Antoine de Sainte-Exupéry, *Wind, Sand and Stars* [1940], London: Heinemann, 1955. P.F. Westerman, *Winning his Wings, op.cit.*, p.25.

25. G. Trease, *Tales Out of School, op.cit.*, p.80; George E. Rochester, *The Flying Beetle*, [1935] London: John Hamilton, n.d., p.182.

26. Bernard Porter, *The Lion's Share: a Short History of British Imperialism 1850-1970*, London: Longman, 1975; C.L. Mowat, *London between the Wars 1918-1940*, London: Methuen, 1964. The work of the Empire Marketing Board is well discussed by Stephen Constantine in 'Bringing the Empire Alive: The Empire Marketing Board and imperial propaganda, 1926-1933' in *Imperialism and Popular Culture*, ed. John Mackenzie. Manchester: Manchester University Press, 1986, pp.192-231. See also Lord Beaverbrook, *The Resources of the British Empire*, London: Lane, 1934.

27. Bob Dixon, *Catching Them Young, op.cit.*, p.76.

28. W.E. Johns, *Biggles Flies Again* [1934], London: Thames, n.d., pp.158-159.

29. Jack Heming, *The Air Spies*, London: A. & C. Black, 1936, p.2.

30. Eric Wood, *Wings Over India* [1938], London: Ace Publishing, n.d., p.8.

31. Jack Heming, *The Air Spies, op. cit.*, pp.37, 238.

32. J. Railton Holden, *Wings of Revolution*, London: John Hamilton, 1934; Rowland Walker, *Captain McBlaid of the Air Police*, London: Partridge, 1932; J. F. C. Westerman, *Menace from the Air, op. cit.*, p.175.

33. George E. Rochester, *The Flying Beetle op. cit.*, pp.12, 182; *The Scarlet Squadron* [1938], London: Ace Publishing, n.d., p.97.

34. Raymond Williams, *Keywords: A Vocabulary of Culture and Society*, London: Fontana, 1976, p.132.

Chapter Ten
The Retreatism of the 1930s: A Few Dissenters

1. Stanley Baldwin, 'England', *On England* [1926], London: Hodder and Stoughton, 4th edition, 1938, pp.20-21. George Orwell, *The Road to Wigan Pier*, London: Gollancz, 1937, p.5.

2. Kenneth O. Morgan, *The Oxford Illustrated History of Britain*, Oxford: O.U.P., 1986, p.537. See also John Stevenson and Chris Cooke, *Britain in the Depression: Society and Politics, 1928-1939*, London: Longman, 2nd Ed, 1994. Andrew Thorpe, *Britain in the 1930s: The Deceptive Decade*, London: Blackwell, 1992.

3. Kenneth O. Morgan, *op. cit.*, p.542.

4. Peter Hunt, *Children's Literature: An Illustrated History*, edited by Peter Hunt. Oxford: O.U.P., 1995, pp.193-195.

5. Referred to in the BBC programme 'The Invention of Childhood' broadcast on Radio 4 on December 24th-29th 2006.

6. Andrew Thorpe, *op.cit.*, pp.92-94.

7. Edith Whettam, *The Agrarian History of England and Wales*, Cambridge: C.U.P. 1978, Vol. VIII, 1914-1939, pp.213, 236, 236. See also Andrew Thorpe, *op.cit*, pp.67-68.

8. One has to note, however, that the circulation of the Magnet, had fallen to 41,000 in 1940 (compared with 120,000 in 1930) and that, though many

Working-class readers paid tribute to its qualities, they only made up 16.13 % of its total readership. The majority of working-class readers preferred D.C. Thomson's publications. For a good account of Frank Richards and his much-debated debated books, including George Orwell's famous essay on 'Boys' Weeklies,' see Jeffrey Richards, *Happiest days: The public schools in English fiction*, Manchester: Manchester University Press, 1988, pp.266-297.

9. Brian Doyle, *The Who's Who of Children's Literature*, London: Hugh Evelyn, 1968, pp.117-118. Stuart Hannabuss, 'Starting Points: research triggers in historical children's literature,' *Library Review*, Vol. 48, No. 5, 1999, pp.251-259.

10. Eleanor Grahame, *The Children who Lived in a Barn* [1938], Harmondsworth, Puffin, 1963, p.128.

11. Eleanor Grahame to her publisher, May 22ᵗʰ 1938, Reading University Archives RK 91/7.

12. Eleanor Grahame, *The Children who Lived in a Barn*, London: Persephone Books, with a *Preface* by Jacqueline Wilson, 2003.

13. Terrence Molloy, *Eve Garnett: Artist, Illustrator, Author: A Memoir*, Lewes: The Book Guild, 2002, p.48.

14. Eve Garnett, *Is It Well with the Child?* London: Muller, 1938, Note No. 9.

15. Eve Garnett, 'The How and Why of the Ruggles', quoted in Terrence Molloy, *op.cit.*, p.5.

16. John Rowe Townsend, *Written for Children: An Outline of English-language Children's Literature*, *op. cit.*, p.187.

17. Christopher Hopkins, 'One End Street? Eve Garnett and Proletarian Pastoral for children, 1937-1962', *The Journal of Children's Literature Studies*, Lichfield: Vol. 1, Issue No. 3, November 2004, pp.1-16.

18. Eve Garnett, *The Family from One End Street* [1937], Harmondsworth: Puffin, 1987, p.85.

19. *Ibid.*, p.138.

20. *Ibid.*, p.129.

21. Geoffrey Trease, *A Whiff of Burnt Boats*, London: Macmillan, 1971, pp.144-145.

22. Geoffrey Trease, *Bows Against the Barons*, London: Martin Lawrence, 1934, p.152.

23. *Ibid.*, pp.73-74.

24. Geoffey Trease, *A Whiff of Burnt Boats*, *op.cit.*, pp.145-146. Margaret Meek, *Geoffrey Trease: A Bodley Head Monograph*, London; The Bodley Head, 1960, pp.22-23.

25. Geoffrey Trease, *A Whiff of Burnt Boats*, *op. cit.*, p.149.

26. Geoffrey Trease, *Comrades for the Charter* [1934], Leicester: Brockhampton Press, 'revised edition', 1972, p.128.

27. Friedrich Engels, 'Letter to Margaret Harkness' April 1888. Quoted in *Marxists on Literature: An Anthology*, edited by David Craig. Harmondsworth, Penguin, 1975, pp.270-271.

28. L.A.G. Strong, *The Fifth of November* London: J.M. Dent, 1937, p.9.

29. L.A.G. Strong, *King Richard's Land: A Story for Boys* [1933], London: J.M. Dent, 1938, p.56.

30. Peter Kingford, *The Hunger Marches in Britain 1920-1939*, London: Lawrence and Wishart, 1982, pp.33-222.

31. L.A.G. Strong, *King Richard's Land*, *op.cit.*, p.157.

32. 'Hunger Marches' from *Coalfield Web Materials*, www.ager.org.uk/cwm/themes/events/hunger

33. The Research Centre, University of Worcester.

34. W.E. Johns, *Popular Flying*, March 1939. Quoted by Peter Berresford Ellis and Jennifer Schofield, *Biggles! The Life Story of Captain W.E. Johns: Creator of Biggles, Worrals, Gimlet and Steeley*, *op. cit.*, p.157.

35. W.E. Johns, *Biggles in Spain* [1939], London: May Fair Books, 1963, pp.103-104.

36. W.E. Johns, *Biggles in the Baltic* [1940], London: Armada Books, 1963, p.5.

Chapter Eleven
Anarchy, Didacticism and Politics: The 1970s and the 1990s

1. Samuel T. Coleridge, *Table Talk*, in *Coleridge: The Clark Lectures 1951-1952*, by Arthur Humphrey House, London: Hart-Davis, 1969, p.90.

2. Ernest Hemingway, *For Whom the Bell Tolls* New York: Scribner's, 1940; and *The Sun Also Rises*, New York: Scribner's, 1926.

3. The statistics for single-parent families can be found at www.bookrags.com/researchtopics/singleparentfamilies/02.html. For crime statistics see disastercenter.com/crime/uscrime.htm. For the treatment of lesbian relationships, see, for example, *Ruby* by Rosa Guy. New York: Viking, 1976.

4. Betsy Byars, *The Pinballs*, London: Puffin, 1980, p18.

5. Betsy Byars, *ibid.*, p.93.

6. Patricia Craig, *Twentieth Century Children's Writers*, ed. D.L. Kirkpatrick. New York, Macmillan, 1983, p.94.

7. Henry James, *The Ambassadors*, [1903] London: Dent, 1950, p.129.

8. Mark Twain, *The Adventures of Huckleberry Finn*, [1884] London: Nelson, n.d., p.i.

9. Juliet Dusinberre, *Alice to the Lighthouse: Children's Books and Radical Experiments in Art*, Basingstoke: Macmillan, 1987, p.1.

10. Richmal Crompton, *Just William*, London: Newnes, 1922. The series ran till the appropriately named *William the Lawless*, (London: Newnes) in 1970.

11. Raymond Briggs, *Father Christmas*, London: Hamish Hamilton, 1973; *Fungus The Bogeyman*. London: Hamish Hamilton, 1977.

12. Gene Kemp, *Gowie Corbie Plays Chicken*, London: Faber, 1981, p.43.

13. Jan Mark, *Thunder and Lightnings*, London: Puffin, 1987, p.150.

14. Leo Baxendale, *A Very Funny Business*, London: Duckworth, 1978, p.136. To see examples of Leo Baxendale's work, it is probably most convenient to find annual publications of *The Beano Book* published by Thomson of

Dundee and London, from 1953 onwards.

15. Robert Cormier, *The Chocolate War*, New York: Pantheon, 1974; Robert Cormier, *Beyond the Chocolate War*, New York, Knopf, 1985.

16. Bernard Ashley, *The Trouble with Donovan Croft*, London: Oxford University Press, 1974; Jan Mark, *The Ennead*, London: Kestrel, 1978.

17. See Arthur S. Link and William B. Catton, *American Epoch: A History of the United States since 1900, Volume III, The End of the Cold War 1946-1973*, New York: Alfred A. Knopf, 4th edition, 1974, pp.83-84. Alexis de Tocqueville, *Democracy in America* edited by J.P.Mayer, a new translation by George Lawrence. New York: Anchor Books, Doubleday, 1969, p.456.

18. See, for example, *The Oxford Illustrated History of Britain*, edited by Kenneth O. Morgan. Oxford: Oxford University Press, 1986, pp.576-577.

19. Kimberley Reynolds, *Children's Literature in the 1890s and the 1990s*, Plymouth: Northcote House, 1994, p.44.

20. Brian Alderson, 'Postlude: The Universality of Tracts', in *From the Dairymaid's to Worrals of the WAAF: The Religious Tract Society, Lutterworth Press and Children's Literature*, edited by Dennis Butts and Pat Garrett. Cambridge: The Lutterworth Press, 2006, pp.205-210.

21. The figures for abortion, crime, illegitimacy and unemployment are taken from *British Social Trends since 1900*, ed. A.H. Halsey. Basingstoke: Macmillan, rev. ed., 1988, pp. 60, 64, 174, 637. The figures for divorce are taken from www.ukstats.html. Homeless figures were supplied by Tara Guinnessy at tara.guinnessy&communities.gov.uk and the drug statistics were compiled by Dr Russell Newcombe in the *Lifeline Project*, October 22nd 2008, and are available at www.lifeline.org.uk.

22. T.J Hatton, 'Explaining Trends in UK Immigration', *Journal of Population Economics*, Vol. 18 (4), 2005. pp.719-740.

23. Anne Fine, *Goggle-Eyes*, London: Penguin Books, Puffin, [1989],1990, p.139.

24. Anne Fine, *The Guardian*, March 29th 2003.

25. Robert Swindells, *Stone Cold*, London: Penguin Books, Puffin [1993], 1995, p.131.

26. Margaret Thatcher, *Women's Own Magazine*, October 31st 1987.

Chapter Twelve
The Historical Novels of Philip Pullman

1. Philip Pullman, '*Daddy,* or Serendpity', *Children's Literature in Education*, Vol. 23, No. 3, September 1992, p.164.

2. G.A. Henty, *With Clive in India; Or, The Beginnings of Empire* [1884], London: Blackie, n.d., pp.273, 280.

3. Geoffrey Trease, *Tales Out of School, op. cit.*, pp.77-94.

4. Colin Cross, *The Fall of the British Empire*, London: Paladin, 1970, p.240.

5. Hester Burton, *Time of Trial*, London: Oxford University Press, 1963; Leon Garfield, *Black Jack*, London: Longman, 1968; Cynthia Harnett,

The Load of Unicorn, London: Methuen, 1959; Robert Leeson, *Maroon Boy*, London: Collins, 1974; Jan Needle, *A Fine Boy for Killing*, London: André Deutsch, 1979; Rosemary Sutcliff, *The Eagle of the Ninth*, London: Oxford University Press, 1954.

6. See Frederic Jameson, 'The politics of theory; ideological positions in the postmodernism debate', and Terry Eagleton, 'Capitalism, modernism and postmodernism', both quoted in David Lodge, ed., *Modern Criticism and Theory: A Reader*, London: Longman, 1988, pp.385-398.

7. Elizabeth Dipple, *The Unresolvable plot; reading contemporary fiction*, London: Routledge, 1988, p.9.

8. Philip Pullman, *The Shadow in the North*, Harmondsworth: Penguin-Puffin, 1973, p.74; *The Tiger in the Well*, Harmondsworth, Penguin, 1992, p.81.

9. Philip Pullman, *The Tiger in the Well*, *ibid.*, p.19; *The Shadow in the North*, *op.cit.*, p.155.

10. Robyn McCallum, 'Metafictions and experimental work', in Peter Hunt (ed.), *International Companion Encyclopedia of Children's Literature*, London: Routledge, 2 Vols., 2004, Vol. 1, p.596.

11. Philip Pullman, *The Shadow in the North*, *op.cit.*, p.155.

12. Philip Pullman, *The Tiger in the Well*, *op. cit.*, p.392.

13. Philip Pullman, '*Daddy,* or Serendipity', *op.cit.*, pp.164-165.

14. Nicholas Tucker, in his otherwise admirable introduction to Philip Pullman's work, seems to miss the point of this, criticising *The Tin Princess* as 'almost pure romance'. This is what Pullman is satirising. See Nicholas Tucker, *Darkness Visible: Inside the World of Philip Pullman*, Cambridge: Wizard Books, 2003, pp.45-49.

15. Philip Pullman, *The Tin Princess*, London: Puffin, 1994, pp.258-259.

16. Philip Pullman, *The Tin Princess*, *ibid.*, p.285.

Bibliography

Introduction

The standard history of British children's literature is by F.J. Harvey Darton in his magisterial *Children's Books in England: Five Centuries of Social Life*, Third Edition, revised and corrected by Brian Alderson. (London and New Castle, DE: The British Library and Oak Knoll Press, 1999). Peter Hunt edited *Children's Literature: An Illustrated History* (London: Oxford University Press, 1995), and John Rowe Townsend *Written for Children: An Outline of English-Language Children's Literature* (Harmondsworth: Kestrel, Pelican, second revised edition, 1987). Humphrey Carpenter deliberately covers a shorter period in his *Secret Gardens: A Study of the Golden Age of Children's Literature* (London: Allen and Unwin, 1985) and Gillian Avery also covers a limited period of American children's literature in *Behold the Dream: American Children and their Books 1621-1922* (London: The Bodley Head, 1994). Joyce Irene Whalley and Tessa Rose Chester have co-authored *A History of Children's Books Illustration* (London: John Murray with the Victoria and Albert Museum, 1988).

The history of publishing and the book trade in Britain generally is discussed by, among others, Marjorie Plant in *The English Book Trade* (London: Allen and Unwin, 1965) and by James Raven in *The Business of Books: Booksellers and the English Book Trade 1450-1850* (New Haven, CT: Yale University Press, 2007). The history of the publishing of children's books has been covered in a much more fragmentary way. *Be Merry and Wise: Origins of Children's Book Publishing in England, 1650-1850* by Brian Alderson and Felix de Marez Oyans (London: British Library, 2006), although originally the catalogue of an exhibition, contains much important historical information. There are also accounts of individual publishers such as

Marjorie Moon's *John Harris's Books for Youth, 1801-1843: being a checklist of books for children and young people published for their amusement and instruction by John Harris and his son, successors to Elizabeth Newbery; including a list of games and toys: with the supplement, published in 1983* (Winchester: St. Paul's Bibliographies, 1987): Asa Briggs, *A History of Longmans and Their Books 1724-1990: Longevity in Publishing* (London: The British Library, 2008); and Elizabeth James (ed.), *Macmillan: A Publishing Tradition* (Basingstoke: Palgrave, 2002). Kimberley Reynolds has discussed modern publishing in *Children's Book Publishing in Britain since 1945* (London: Scolar Press, 1998).

The critical approaches followed here derive from many different sources, some not always associated with the discussion of children's literature, such as Terry Eagleton's *Marxism and Literary Criticism* (London: Methuen, 1976) and his *Myths of Power: a Marxist Study of the Brontës* (London: Macmillan, 1975); Lucien Goldman's *The Hidden God: A Study of the Tragic Vision in the Pensées of Pascal and the Tragedies of Racine*, translated by Philip Thody (London: Routledge and Kegan Paul, 1976) and *Towards a Sociology of the Novel* translated by Alan Sheridan (London: Tavistock, 1976); Fred Inglis's *The Promise of Happiness: Value and Meaning in Children's Fiction* (Cambridge: Cambridge University Press, 1981); and Raymond Williams's *The Long Revolution* (Harmondsworth: Pelican, 1971) and *The English Novel from Dickens to Lawrence* (London: Chatto and Windus, 1970). Two essays have been particularly useful: Mitzi Myers's, 'Missed Opportunities and Critical Malpractice: New Historicism and Children's Literature' (*Children's Literature Association Quarterly*, Vol. 13, No. 1, Spring 1985, pp.41-43) and Tony Watkins's 'History and Culture' in the *International Companion Encyclopaedia of Children's Literature*, edited by Peter Hunt (London: second edition, Routledge, 2 Vols, Vol. 1, 2004, pp.76-98).

Chapter 1
Barbara Hofland: The Moral Tale and the Industrial Revolution

The tradition of evangelical and moral tales from which Mrs Hofland's works emerged is well discussed in Harvey Darton's, *Children's Books in England*, *op. cit.*, chapters IX, X and XI. *Childhood's Pattern: A study of the heroes and heroines of children's fiction 1770-1950* (London: Hodder & Stoughton, 1975) and *Nineteenth Century Children: Heroes and Heroines in English Children's Stories*

1780-1900 (London: Hodder & Stoughton, 1965), both by Gillian Avery, have interesting observations on early nineteenth-century children's books, and Nancy Cutt's *Ministering Angels: A Study of Nineteenth-century Evangelical Writing for Children* (Wormley: Five Owls Press, 1979) is one of the key-works on this genre. Works on individual writers include Marilyn Butler's *Maria Edgeworth: A Literary Biography* (Oxford: Oxford University Press, 1972), Dennis Butts on *Mistress of Our Tears: A Literary and Bibliographical Study of Barbara Hofland* (Aldershot: Scolar Press, 1992) and Nancy Cutt on *Mrs Sherwood and her Books for Children* (London: Oxford University Press, 1974).

Discussion of the relationship between economics, industry and religion is found in two classic works *The Protestant Religion and the Rise of Capitalism* by Max Weber [1904] (translated by Talcott Parsons). (London: Hodder & Stoughton, second edition, 1976) and *Religion and the Rise of Capitalism* by R.H. Tawny [1926] (Harmondsworth: Penguin, 1964).

Chapter 2
How Children's Literature Changed in the 1840s

Discussions of the historical changes in Britain and Europe in the middle of the nineteenth century are found in *The Age of Improvement 1783-1867* by Asa Briggs (London: Longman, 1963) and by E.J. Hobsbawn in *The Age of Revolution 1789-1848* (New York: Mentor, 1964.) Thomas Carlyle's 'Signs of the Times' can be found in his *Critical Essays* (London: Chapman and Hall, 1899). Other important studies of the period include *The Condition of the Working Classes in England* by Frederick Engels ([1845] London: Panther Books, 1969) and *The Bleak Age* by J.L. and Barbara Hammond ([1934] West Drayton: Penguin Books, 1947).

Accounts of the literary changes that were beginning to take place include *Studies in European Realism* by Georg Lukàcs (London: Merlin Press, 1992) and *The Long Revolution* by Raymond Williams, *op.cit.*, More specific discussion of the changes in children's books can be found in F.J. Harvery Darton's *Children's Books in England*, *op. cit.*, chapters XII-XIV, and in chapter 4 of *Children's Literature: An Illustrated History*, edited by Peter Hunt, *op. cit.*. Changes in book illustration are discussed in chapter IV of *A History of Children's Book Illustration* by Joyce Irene Whalley and Tessa Rose Chester, *op. cit.*, and there is an account of the important work of Henry Cole and *The Home Treasury* in *Joseph Cundall: A Victorian Publisher* by Ruari McLean (Pinner: Private Libraries Association, 1976). Other important works on the literature of the period include *Hans Christian Anderson and his Eventyr in England* by Brian Alderson (Wormley: Five Owls Press, 1982) and *Victorian Fairy Tales; the Revolt of the Fairies and Elves*, edited by Jack Zipes (London: Methuen, 1987).

Many biographies of writers of this period include *Edward Lear* by Vivien Noakes (London: revised edition, Fontana, 1979), *Captain Marryat: Seaman, Writer and Adventurer* by Tom Pocock (London: Chatham Publishing, 2000) and *Hans Christian Andersen: The Life of a Storyteller* by Jackie Wullschlager (London: Allen Lane, 2000).

Chapter 3
Muscular Christianity and the Adventure Story

Discussion of the evolution of the adventure story can be found in 'Shaping boyhood: British empire-builders and adventurers' by Dennis Butts in the *International Companion Encyclopaedia of Children's Literature*, edited by Peter Hunt, *op. cit.*, Vol. 1, pp.340-351). There are important studies of the adventure story by J.S. Bratton in *The Impact of Victorian Children's Fiction* (London: Croom Helm, 1981): Joseph Bristow, *Empire Boys: Adventures in a Man's World* (London: Harper Collins, 1991); Margery Fisher, *The Bright Face of Danger* (London: Hodder & Stoughton, 1976); and Martin Green, *Dreams of Adventure, Deeds of Empire* (London: Routledge and Kegan Paul, 1976). There are valuable contributions to cultural history by Graham Dawson in *Soldier Heroes: British Adventure, empire and the imagining of masculinities* (London: Routledge, 1994) and by J.A. Mangan in *Athleticism in the Victorian and Edwardian Public School: The Emergence and Consolidation of an Educational Ideology* (Cambridge: Cambridge University Press, 1981).

Charles Kingsley's *Letters and Memories of his Life* was edited by his widow in two volumes (London: Henry S. King, 1877), and there have been modern biographies by Susan Chitty, *The Beast and the Monk; a Life of Charles Kingsley* (London: Hodder & Stoughton, 1974) and Brenda Colloms, *Charles Kingsley: The Lion of Eversley* (London: Constable, 1975).

Chapter 4
Conflicting Loyalties: Ideology and Form in the Tales of G.A. Henty

G.M. Fenn's biography *George Alfred Henty: The Story of an Active Life* (London: Blackie, 1907) is limited but indispensable. Guy Arnold's *Held Fast for England: G.A. Henty: Imperialist Boys' Writer* (London: Hamish Hamilton, 1980) contains some more up-to-date information, though largely descriptive in its critical approach. Peter Newbolt's *G.A. Henty 1832-1902: A Bibliographical Study of his British Editions* (Philadelphia, PA: Polyglot Press, second edition, 2005) is far more than bibliographical because of its helpful appendices.

   Discussion of the relationship between Henty's adventure stories and the nature of British society and imperialism in the nineteenth century has proliferated in recent years with such books as Patrick Howarth's *Play Up and Play the Game: The Heroes of Popular Fiction* (London: Eyre Methuen, 1973); 'With Henty to Africa' by Jeffrey Richards in *Imperialism and Juvenile Literature*, edited by Jeffrey Richards (Manchester: Manchester University Press, 1989; *Britannia's Children: Reading Colonialism through Children's Books and Magazine* by Kathryn Castle (Manchester: Manchester University Press, 1996; and Mowuena Kossi Logan's *Narrating Africa: George Henty and the Fiction of Empire* (New York: Garland, 1999).

Chapter 5
Rider Haggard and the Pattern of Defeat

Britain's relations with Southern Africa in the latter half of the nineteenth century are discussed by, among others, Thomas Pakenham, *The Boer War* (London: Weidenfeld and Nicolson, 1979) and Donald R. Morris, *The Washing of the Spears: A History of the Rise of the Zulu Nation under Shaka and its Fall in the Zulu War of 1879* (London: Cape, 1966). Studies which relate literature to Anglo-African history include *Rider Haggard and the Fiction of Empire: A Critical Study of British Imperial Fiction* (Cambridge: Cambridge University Press, 1987) and *The Wheel of Empire: A Study of the Imperial Idea in Some Late Nineteenth and Early Twentieth Century Writers* by Alan Sandison (London: Macmillan, 1967).

   Rider Haggard's autobiography *The Days of My Life*, was edited by C.J. Longman (London: Longman, Green, 2 Vols., 1926). *The Private Diaries of Sir H. Rider Haggard 1914-1925* were edited by D.S. Higgins (London: Cassell, 1980). Haggard's daughter Lilias

Haggard also wrote a biography of her father *The Cloak That I Left; A Biography of the Author Henry Rider Haggard K.B.E.* (London: Hodder & Stoughton, 1951). Among modern biographies the best is *Rider Haggard: The Great Storyteller* by D S Higgins (London: Cassell, 1981). Victoria Manthorpe has shown how most of the Haggard family also had imperial interests in her *Children of the Empire: the Victorian Haggards* (London: Gollancz, 1996).

Chapter 6

Some Questions about *Kidnapped:* Stevenson and the Act of Union

Robert Louis Stevenson has been the subject of biographies, by, among many others, J.C. Furnace, *Voyage to Windward: The Life of Robert Louis Stevenson* (London: Faber & Faber, 1952); Ian Bell, *Robert Louis Stevenson: Dreams of Exile* (London: Headline, 1993) and Frank McLynn, *Robert Louis Stevenson: a Biography* (London: Pimlico, 1995.) Stevenson's work has been regularly and highly praised, notably by Henry James in the *Century Magazine* of 1888 (included in *Robert Louis Stevenson: the Critical Heritage* edited by Paul Maixier, London: Routledge and Kegan Paul, 1981).

Stevenson's treatment of history, imperialism and Scotland has also come under scrutiny, notably in *Robert Louis Stevenson and the Scottish Highlands* by David B. Morris (Stirling: Eneas Mackay, 1929), *Stevenson and Victorian Scotland*, edited by Jenni Calder (Edinburgh: Edinburgh University Press, 1981) and Anne C. Colley in *Robert Louis Stevenson and the Colonial Imagination* (Aldershot: Ashgate, 2004).

Chapter 7

The Railway Children and the Strange Death of Liberal England

The history and politics of the Edwardian Age has received a good deal of attention, notably by George Dangerfield in *The Strange Death of Liberal England* (London: Constable, 1936), and more recently in *The Edwardian Age: Conflict and Stability* edited by Alan O'Day (London: Macmillan, 1979), and Roy Hattersley's *The Edwardians* (London: Little, Brown, 2004.) Philip Unwin discusses the railway history of the period in *Travelling by Train in the Edwardian Age* (London: Allen and Unwin, 1979).

There are numerous studies of E. Nesbit, for example, by Noel Streatfeild in *Magic and the Magicians: E. Nesbit and her*

Children's Books (London: Putnam, 1962), but the standard work is Julia Briggs's *A Woman of Passion: The Life of E. Nesbit 1858-1924* (London: Hutchinson, 1987). E. Nesbit's reminiscences of her childhood, first published as magazine articles in the 1890s, have been reprinted as *Long Ago When I Was Young* (London: Whiting and Wheaton, 1966).

Chapter 8
From Evangelism to Feminism: The works of Amy Le Feuvre

Apart from brief references in the studies of Gillian Avery and M. Nancy Cutt already cited, most material given in this chapter comes from the National Census, the archives of the Lutterworth Press and the publishers Hodder & Stoughton. The Library of the School of Oriental and African Studies at London University (SOAS) also holds some information about Amy Le Feuvre and the Religious Tract Society.

Wendy Forrester illustrates the nature of many girls' reading in *Great Grandmamma's Weekly: A Celebration of the Girls' Own Paper 1880-1901* (Guildford: the Lutterworth Press, 1980). Kimberley Reynolds discusses the emergence of different reading for boys and girls in the late nineteenth century in *Girls Only? Gender and Popular Children's Fiction in Britain, 1880-1910* (Hemel Hempstead: Harvester, 1990); and Judith Rowbotham has explored the way girls' literature produced in the second half of the nineteenth century began to challenge contemporary ideas of femininity in *Good Girls Make Good Wives: Guidance for Girls in Victorian Fiction* (Oxford: Blackwell, 1989). The connections between the evangelical movement and children's books is discussed in *From the Dairyman's Daughter to Worrals of the WAAF: The Religious Tract Society, Lutterworth Press and Children's Literature* edited by Dennis Butts and Pat Garrett (Cambridge: Lutterworth, 2006).

Chapter 9
Imperialism of the Air: Flying Stories 1900-1950

The history of British aviation is discussed by C.H. Gibbs-Smith in *Aviation: An Historical Survey from the Origins to the end of World War II* (London: H.M.S.O., 1970): Robert Higham, *Britain's*

Imperial Air Routes 1918-1939 (London: Foulis, 1960); and John Stroud, *Annals of British and Commonwealth Air Transport 1919-1960* (London: Putnam, 1962). The politician Viscount Templewood shows the clear connection between the development of British aviation and imperialism in his *Empire of the Air: The Advent of the Air Age* (London: Collins, 1957).

Discussion of the treatment of flying in literature can be found in Laurence Goldstein's *The Flying Machine and Modern Literature* (London: Macmillan, 1986) and Mary Cadogan's *Women with Wings: Female Flyers in Fact and Fiction* (London: Macmillan, 1992). Amongst much writing on W.E. Johns, the standard work is *Biggles! The Life Story of Capt. W.E. Johns: Creator of Biggles, Worrals, Gimlet and Steeley*, by Peter Berresford Ellis and Jennifer Schofield (Godmanstone, Dorset: Veloce Publishing, 1993).

Chapter 10
The Retreatism of the 1930s: a Few Honest Doubters

The history of Britain during the 1930s is still being debated by, among others, C.L. Mowat, *London Between the Wars 1918-1940* (London: Methuen, 1964); John Stevenson and Chris Cooke, *Britain in the Depression: Society and Politics, 1929-1939* (London: Longman, second edition, 1994); and Andrew Thorpe, *Britain in the 1930s: The Deceptive Decade* (London: Blackwell, 1992). Peter Kingford discusses some of the social protests of the time in *The Hunger Marches in Britain 1920-1939* (London: Lawrence and Wishart, 1982).

Discussion of children's books in the period can be found in chapter 8 of *Children's Literature: An Illustrated History* edited by Peter Hunt, *op. cit.*, and in chapter 13 of John Rowe Townsend's *Written for Children: An Outline of English-Language Children's Literature*, *op. cit.* Terence Molloy has produced a memoir of his aunt *Eve Garnett: Artist, Illustrator, Author* (Lewes: The Book Guild, 2002). Geoffrey Trease produced his autobiography in two volumes: *A Whiff of Burnt Boats* (London: Macmillan, 1971) and *Laughter at the Door: A Continued Autobiography* (London: Macmillan, 1974). There is also a brief critical study of him by Margaret Meek *Geoffrey Trease: A Bodley Head Monograph* (London: The Bodley Head, 1960).

Chapter 11
Anarchy, Didacticism and Politics: The 1970s and the 1990s

The history of modern Britain has been much discussed by many writers, including David Childs on *Britain Since 1939: Progress and Decline* (Basingstoke: Macmillan, 1995); Alan Skeld and Chris Cook, *Post-War Britain: A Political History* (Harmondsworth: Penguin, fourth edition, 1993): A.H. Halsey (ed.), *British Social Trends since 1900* (Basingstoke: Macmillan, revised edition, 1988); Arthur Marwick, *British Society Since 1945* (Harmondsworth: Penguin, third edition, 1996); and Anthony Seldon and Daniel Collings in *Britain Under Thatcher* (Harlow: Longman, 2000).Recent American history has been interpreted by, among others, James T. Patterson in *The Restless Giant: The United States from Watergate to Bush v. Gore* (Oxford: Oxford University Press).

Although recent writers tend to have been discussed in such periodicals as *Children's Literature in Education*, the American *Children's Literature Association Quarterly*, and *Signal*, there are useful chapters on many American and British authors of the period under discussion in *The Marble in the Water* by David Rees (Boston, MA: The Horn Book, 1980) and by Michael Rosen in *Treasure Islands 2: An Adult Guide to Children's Writers and Illustrators* (London: BBC, 1993).

Chapter 12
The Historical Novels of Philip Pullman

The history of post-war Britain, with particular reference to its colonial policies, are discussed by Colin Cross in *The Fall of the British Empire* (London: Hodder & Stoughton, 1968) and Piers Brendan in *The Decline and Fall of the British Empire* (London: Cape, 2007).

Accounts of experiments in children's literature, and the effects of Modernism and Post-Modernism, can be found in Juliet Dusinberre's *Alice to the Lighthouse: Children's Books and Experiments in Art* (Basingstoke: Macmillan, 1987) and in Kimberley Reynolds's *Radical Children's Literature: Future Visions and Aesthetic Transformations in Children's Fiction* (Basingstoke: Macmillan, 2007). Most criticism of Philip Pullman's work tends to focus upon the trilogy *His Dark Materials*, but there is some discussion of the historical novels by Nicholas Tucker in *Darkness Visible: Inside the World of Philip Pullman* (Cambridge: Wizard Books, 2003).

Index

DH

809.
892
82
BUT

9 780718 892081